D1058347

THE GOOD-NATURED MAN

ALSO BY LEONARD WIBBERLEY

FICTION

Mrs. Searwood's Secret Weapon
Stranger at Killnock
The Quest of Excalibur
Take Me to Your President
McGillicuddy McGotham
Beware of the Mouse
The Mouse That Roared
The Mouse on the Moon
The Mouse on Wall Street
A Feast of Freedom
The Island of the Angels
The Hands of Cormac Joyce
The Road from Toomi
Adventures of an Elephant Boy
The Centurion
Meeting with a Great Beast
The Testament of Theophilus
The Last Stand of Father Felix
1776—And All That
One in Four
Homeward to Ithaka

NONFICTION

The Shannon Sailors
Voyage by Bus
Ah Julian!
Yesterday's Land
Towards a Distant Land
No Garlic in the Soup
The Land That Isn't There

THE GOOD-NATURED MAN

A PORTRAIT OF OLIVER GOLDSMITH

by **LEONARD WIBBERLEY**

WILLIAM MORROW AND COMPANY, INC.
NEW YORK 1979

Library of Congress Catalog Card Number 79-89683
ISBN 0-688-03522-1

Printed in the United States of America.

First Edition

1 2 3 4 5 6 7 8 9 10

FOREWORD

I WROTE THIS BOOK ABOUT OLIVER GOLDSMITH BECAUSE I love the man. I love his writing, I love his mind, I love his laughter, tears, poverty, pride, and his unrestrained display.

One thinks of novelists as writing fiction, as producing works of the imagination which may have some grounding in observation, but have none at all in fact.

That view, however, limits too harshly the scope of the novelist. Sometimes he wants to relate the actual story of a man's life, a man with whom he finds some deep affinity. In doing so, of course, he has no license to interfere with the facts. But he has a license to interpret those facts, to give them meaning and emotion, to put them in human perspective and by sifting through all the details to bring out gradually the shape of the subject of his biography.

This is what I have attempted to do with Oliver Goldsmith, drawing my factual material entirely from the works of various scholars who have meticulously documented his life. Nowhere have I consciously misstated these facts, and nowhere have I consciously misconstrued them. But I have made deductions about Goldsmith that are denied the scholar who, remaining within his own limits, must stick to whatever is documented.

To give an example, no scholar will flatly state that Goldsmith in his later years fell deeply in love with Mary Horneck, a girl of seventeen when they met. Reynolds introduced him to the family and thereafter Goldsmith was constantly in their company. But it was in Mary that he took the greatest delight, it was to her that he read his unpublished novel, and it was she who cut a lock of his hair, which she kept for the rest of her life, when he lay dead in his coffin. It was to defend Mary that he got into a brawl with a newspaper editor, and she herself had no lover until Goldsmith had been dead for a year. She did not marry until three years after he had died, and in her old age her face brightened up whenever Goldsmith's name was mentioned.

Given these circumstances, the only conclusion I could come to was that there was a deep but unspoken love between the two. I think the conclusion warrantable.

Conversations are not necessarily reported chronologically, and there may have been times when I have put several conversations together. This is not carelessly done, but is designed to give a shape to Goldsmith's views and feelings, rather than leave them scattered throughout the manuscript for the sake of mere dates. As many dates, however, as I feel necessary to locate the reader in time have been inserted.

As I said, I wrote the book because I love the man. When you have read it, I hope you will love him too.

CHAPTER

I

Oliver Goldsmith was an Irishman. He wrote like an Irishman, spoke like an Irishman, thought like an Irishman. He wept, laughed, spent money, exulted and was thrown down, dreamed, and loved (he was incapable of hate) all in a thoroughly Irish manner.

He was as innocent and as sensitive as a child and he lived on dreams and fancies.

It is essential in any account of Goldsmith's life to stress his Irishness, for otherwise his behavior and the way he felt cannot be understood. His contemporaries knew he was Irish and so they understood him very well and they loved him too. Had they thought he was English or Finnish or German they might have quickly clapped him in Bedlam, for no Englishman, Finn, or German would, in polite company, have thrown his wig up to the ceiling out of sheer joy, danced a jig or hornpipe, or set out on a tour of Europe on foot, with a flute and poverty as his only companions, and expected that the whole world would receive him with smiles.

It was after Goldsmith's death that he subtly became English in the popular regard, and that on the strength of his poem *The Deserted Village*.

Goldsmith invented a dream village inhabited by dream people, and presented it for the enjoyment of non-dreamers. He lived the whole of his life in a dream and made the most desperate poverty and hardship tolerable by dreaming of riches and plenty ahead. (It is a fact ignored by historians that the whole history of Ireland is a dream and will continue to be to the end of time. The nation is populated by dreamers; Goldsmith was the greatest dreamer of them all and thus truly representative of his countrymen.)

Goldsmith was born on November 10, 1728, though the marble plaque in his memory in Westminster Abbey gives the date as 29th November, 1731. The wording on the plaque (in Latin) was supplied by Sam Johnson, who in this instance misstated a fact, which was unusual for him. But maybe he got the information from Goldsmith, who had little use for facts.

The place of Goldsmith's birth is not known for certain. Some hold he was born in a lonely and, at the time, almost unreachable Irish village called Pallas or Pallasmore on the banks of the River Inny, in County Longford; others that he was born at Smith-Hill house, Elphin, Roscommon, which was the residence of his mother's father, the Reverend Oliver Jones, after whom he was named. Goldsmith's father was the Reverend Charles Goldsmith and came of a family which had been long enough in Ireland to be reduced to genteel poverty.

Four children had been born into the family when Oliver arrived as a new burden for his impoverished father, who made so little as a clergyman that he had to farm a few acres to keep his family fed. They were Margaret (who died in infancy), Catherine, Henry, and Jane. In the next ten years after Oliver arrived, three more boys were born to the Goldsmiths—Maurice, Charles, and John. Catherine married a wealthy husband and Jane a poor one. Henry entered the ministry, married young, and lived and died poor but respected. Maurice became a cabinet-maker who lived from hand to mouth in Charlestown, Roscommon; Charles migrated to Jamaica, and John died in childhood of a fall from a horse.

Oliver, an unexpected baby, was born seven years after Jane and Henry, who were twins. Two years after Oliver's birth, his mother's uncle, the Reverend Mr. Green (the first name is uncertain), died. The Reverend Charles Goldsmith succeeded to his substantial living in the barony of Kilkenny West, and his income went from forty pounds a year to nearly two hundred pounds a year. The family moved into Mr. Green's fine house in the village of Lissoy, Westmeath, and would have had no more money problems but for the fact that Charles Goldsmith, like his son, was also an Irishman and so could no more be trusted with money than a child can with a loaded pistol.

Goldsmith's early schooling, as a matter of happenstance, was excellent for a boy of his nature. A young woman, Elizabeth Dewlap, who was a distant relative, started to teach Oliver to read and write when he was perhaps four years of age. She found him dull and "impenetrably stupid" and this provided her with a topic of conversation until she was ninety and Goldsmith dead thirteen years.

But his family didn't find him dull and stupid at all. His mother quickly recognized that this was the brightest of her children and so did his father and all his adoring adult relatives. His wit was quick. So was his temper. He was expected to produce funny remarks on every occasion and the things he said were repeated by the admiring adults. Without a doubt, young Oliver was spoiled as a child by all this admiration. As a result, at times he would be lively and gay and at other times, whatever the company, he would sulk.

He didn't like work, which was probably the reason his first teacher called him impenetrably stupid. She had the task of teaching him the alphabet and the sounds of the letters, the difference between vowels and consonants, and all the spelling rules of the day. He resisted this training. But he took to playing with words, finding those with similar sounds but different meanings—rhyming, in short. He became very good at this game so that all the writing he did, when he could write, was in rhyme.

When the bleak Irish rain battered on the roof and made the windows stream with water, and the scouring wind flattened the meadow grass to silver, he sat for hours alone turning out rhyme after rhyme on any scrap of paper that offered, and then burning each one.

Goldsmith could produce rhymes readily when he was seven years of age or thereabouts. He took to thinking in rhymes, playing with words as other children played with hoops, balls, and ropes, until he could produce, at any moment, not merely a rhyme but one that made apt sense, word and meaning fitting as neatly as a hand in a good glove.

There is a story of this rhyming told by his sister Catherine after his death. It goes as follows. There was a considerable company for tea one day at the Goldsmiths' house and a small boy was asked to pass the kettle full of hot water. The handle being hot, he took the skirt of his coat to lift the kettle up. There was a big rent in the boy's breeches. Everybody started laughing, particularly the ladies. Goldsmith laughed and said to his father that he could write a humorous verse on the incident. The Reverend Charles Goldsmith promised him a reward of a slice of gingerbread if he could. Here is what Goldsmith came up with:

Theseus did see as poets say
All Hell and its abysses
But had not half as sharp an eye
As our young charming misses
For they could through boy's breeches peep
And view what e'r he had there
It seemed to blush and they all laughed
Because the face was all bare.
They laughed at that
Which sometimes else
Might give them greatest pleasure.
How quickly they could see the thing
Which was their darling treasure.

Plainly, the Reverend Charles Goldsmith was not so prim as he has been painted, nor Goldsmith either.

Oliver was a very ugly child. He had a small receding chin, a bulging forehead, a long upper lip and loose mouth, and a small but bulky figure so that he seemed to shamble rather than walk. He was from the first very sensitive about his appearance, and he never got over this sensitivity. Once at a dance in the house of his Uncle John, who was very fond of him, a guest twitted Oliver on his appearance.

"Why, Noll," he said, "you have become a fright. When do you mean to get handsome again?"

Goldsmith ignored the remark but the man, who was noted for his drinking, gambling, and womanizing, repeated the question. Oliver turned on him and said, with everybody waiting for his reply, "I mean to get better, sir, when *you* get better."

Score another for Oliver. It was always dangerous to bait him. Undoubtedly, people teased him to sample his wit and in doing so they both hurt him and spoiled him. Years later, when he attempted to shine in adult company, without the advantages of being a quick-minded child, he couldn't, and often made a fool of himself. But he was always trying to recapture the applause he had received in Irish country houses before he had reached his teens.

There is one more tale told by his sister of this rhyming wit of his which made everybody who knew him say what a bright boy Oliver was. For all his clumsiness he was a pretty good dancer. One evening there was a large company gathered together at Uncle John's house (Uncle John was a great entertainer). A young man who thought himself a greater wit than Goldsmith was playing the fiddle, and the company began begging Oliver to dance a hornpipe, a sailor's dance of many movements and a lively thing to watch if well done. Oliver was nine years of age and more ugly than usual for he had recently had smallpox and his face was covered with bright red marks. Eventually, Uncle John pretty well ordered Goldsmith to do the dance, so he got up and began. Thereupon, the fiddler, seeing his chance, cried out, "Aesop! Isn't he the very figure of Aesop now, by God!"

Aesop of the fables was noted for his ugliness and everybody joined in teasing Oliver, who was still dancing around, crying out, "Aesop! Aesop! He's the spitting image of him," and so on. When they'd all had their fun and the fiddler was smirking at having proved himself wittier than Goldsmith, Oliver stopped and, pointing to him, said:

Heralds! Proclaim aloud! All saying
See Aesop dancing—and his monkey playing.

The laugh was on the fiddler now and Goldsmith returned happily to his chair, to be embraced by Uncle John and given a reward of sweets.

His second teacher was the best he ever had. He was sent, having learned to read and write at the age of six, to a school run by a Mr. Thomas Byrne, who had been a quartermaster in Lord Galway's regiment under Marlborough in the Spanish wars, and who was a strict disciplinarian (which Oliver needed). He also had the enormous advantage from Goldsmith's point of view of having a huge fund of fairy stories, heroic myths, tales of highwaymen, pirates, outlaws, and outright lies, which was just the stuff that Goldsmith needed to feed the dreamer in him.

Tale after tale Byrne poured out to his fascinated pupils—stories, perhaps, of sea monsters, of cities stormed, of enchanted stones that sang in the moonlight, shipwrecks, battles, accursed jewels and castles that disappeared and then appeared in another place—in short, every tale he could imagine himself or had heard from others and embroidered with his own active mind. Goldsmith swallowed them all delightedly. When it came to music, Quartermaster Byrne taught his pupils ballads: "The Cruelty of Barbara Allen," "The Bailiff's Daughter of Islington," "The Derby Ram," and Goldsmith loved this too, for he had an ear for music and a good singing voice.

About this time, Goldsmith is supposed to have heard the blind Irish harper, Turlough O'Carolan, play. There is no certainty that the meeting took place but it isn't unlikely. O'Carolan, riding a horse with a boy to guide him, was a famous itinerant harper. He made the rounds of the better houses in County Longford, and the Goldsmith house was reckoned one of these. O'Carolan had been blinded by smallpox; and the blind in Ireland often learned to play the harp so they could make a living for themselves in their darkness.

The roaming life of a traveling musician was just the sort to appeal to Goldsmith. No dull hours to be kept, no stern desk to sit at, but all the world to travel in, free as the wind, and every door thrown open with smiles by the magic of music. O'Carolan made a good living and to have him visit a house was counted a great honor. Many a purse of sovereigns was slipped into his hand and many a quart of whiskey put beside him as he played. He was accorded love, admiration, and honor, and those were the things young Oliver craved.

The meeting is important because it was while he was still at Quartermaster Byrne's school that Goldsmith himself caught smallpox. It was the common disease of the day, and to have had smallpox and so be over with it was an advantage in applying for work. Goldsmith caught the same variety as had blinded O'Carolan—the confluent pox with the pustules so close together they ran into each other, making deep craters and pits in the skin if the patient survived.

Goldsmith wasn't blinded. But, as noted, he became even uglier, and perhaps with O'Carolan in mind he learned to play the flute and maybe dreamed of the doors opening to the wandering musician, and the smiles and welcomes and honor that would be poured on him in house after house.

Goldsmith's father was a good, generous, and utterly impractical man. He loved his children and was loved by them. He never turned a beggar away from his door. Goldsmith said of him that he taught his children to give away thousands of pounds before he taught them how to earn a farthing. He liked to entertain—an excellent story teller, he could set the whole room laughing with his jokes—but he had the abandoned Irish sense of hospitality so that he would spend his last penny on company, smiling cheerfully when his wife told him there was no money left and assuring her that God would provide.

God quite often didn't but, ignoring the realities, the Reverend Charles Goldsmith held all his life that it is better to give than receive, and Goldsmith learned from him to spend every penny he made and many pennies that had not yet come in. His mother had to do all the worrying in the family, torn between balancing the budget and trusting in God.

Oliver loved his brother Henry, who taught him to make tops and bait a line for fishing, row a boat, kick a ball, and hunt for birds' nests. They spent a great deal of time together but were at last separated, for Charles Goldsmith sent Henry off to Trinity College, Dublin, as a paying student to get his degree in Divinity, and Oliver was left solitary, having little to do with his two sisters.

He spent his free time roaming the lush meadows of Longford; peering into hedges for birds' nests; watching the slyness of foxes and the sleek play of otters hunting fish in the river; collecting the white mottled eggs of thrushes and the sky-blue eggs of blackbirds; noting how skylarks, when they landed, always walked away from their nests as a means of protecting their young; listening to the stillness of the center of a copse though the wind was brisk enough outside; and hiding himself in a clump of furze and dreaming that he was a robber about to attack some passerby, or perhaps an outlaw, with a bounty on his head, hiding from his pursuers.

He especially loved birds—finches, wagtails, sparrows, wrens, robins, larks, lapwings, teal, mallard, swan, and bittern. He knew them all by sight and by sound and delighted in them as living, singing jewels. These were the creatures he felt closest to so that he was never lonely in walking along the banks of the Inny, or wading over to one of the islets in its center, or lying in a meadow deep in ox-eye daisies and dreaming of paradise. Here he didn't have to compensate for his ugliness with his quick wit.

Goldsmith went to three other schools to finish his primary education while his brother Henry was off at Trinity. When he was perhaps eight he went to stay with his admiring Uncle John at Ballyoughter, so he could attend the school of the Reverend Mr. Griffin, at Elphin, Roscommon. It was a school with a good local reputation and he learned enough Latin to translate passages from Ovid and Horace. He loved both poets because they too had delighted in rivers and trees and birds. He liked Horace's story of how the woodpigeons had covered him with leaves when he fell asleep on a hillside as a child. He made few friends at Dr. Griffin's school because his classmates teased him for his ugly face, and his biting wit turned them against him. But though he didn't like studying, he was a bright pupil, quick to learn.

From Dr. Griffin's school he went to stay with a Reverend Mr. Campbell at Athlone to be taught more Latin and elementary theology.

His father had now decided that Oliver as well as his brother Henry should enter the church. He endured the theology and accepted the Latin for two years and then, the Reverend Campbell becoming ill, he went to the school at Edgeworthstown kept by the Reverend Patrick Hughes.

More Latin, more theology.

To Ovid and Horace were added Cicero (whom he hated for Cicero was no storyteller and no lover of nature), Livy, and Tacitus. But he also played handball and fives, and at Edgeworthstown he learned how to make friends.

His temper was still quick, but he was eager to forgive as well, and he was no longer as spoiled as he had been. He became popular at Edgeworthstown. He raided orchards and overturned carts, in these escapades often being the ringleader. The Reverend Hughes, a friend of his father, liked him. Oliver began to get some self-confidence and feel a little worth in himself. But he was still, beneath it all, a dreamer, vain, childlike, and moody.

In Oliver's last year at Edgeworthstown, after the summer holidays spent at Lissoy, his father gave him a borrowed horse to ride to school and a guinea to go with it. Mounted on the horse, and with the guinea in his pocket, Goldsmith dreamed himself rich and handsome—a gentleman of independent means and unquestionable taste. So instead of heading directly to Edgeworthstown, he took the road to Ardagh a few miles away, which he reached by nightfall.

He'd never stayed at an inn, though he knew great gentlemen did so when traveling about. He decided to stay at one and asked the first person he met to direct him to the best house in town. It was his bad luck that the man he asked was the local wag, a fencing master called Cornelius Kelly.

"The best house in the town?" said Kelly. "I'll take you there myself, young sir." And so he did, taking Oliver to the ample home of Squire Featherstone, one of the richest men in Ardagh.

Goldsmith rode up to the door and called for the hostler. When he arrived, Goldsmith told him to rub down, water, and stable his horse. He pushed in through the front door and found himself in a handsome parlor with a man, whom he took to be the landlord, seated before a good fire.

"Good evening, young sir," said the squire, not a bit surprised. "A little cold for the time of the year, I think."

"It is indeed," said Goldsmith, warming his hands before the fire. "I think a bottle of wine would be no bad thing on a cold night like this, and since I've been fasting all day, my dear sir, I would be glad of a good dinner to go with it."

The squire went along with the joke. He rushed out and told his wife to get dinner ready, and a waiter soon appeared with a bottle and two glasses. Oliver and his host sat by the fire with their bottle, and the squire inquired about Oliver's father and where he lived and his family and so on. At the table were the squire and his wife and his two daughters, whom Oliver bade welcome. He ordered two more bottles of wine to show what a generous patron he was. He was shown to a very good room but before going to bed he asked for an early breakfast, ordering a hotcake to go with it.

He got his hotcake for breakfast. Only when he came to pay his bill did the squire tell him that he was not at an inn at all but at a private house, and he owed nothing for he was delighted to have entertained the son of a friend and neighbor.

Years later, Goldsmith used the incident as the plot for his play *She Stoops to Conquer*.

CHAPTER

THE GLORIOUS PROSPECT THAT NOW LAY AHEAD OF GOLDSMITH was to go to Trinity as his brother Henry had done. He'd be a paying student with money in his pocket, an undergraduate in a university with a greater reputation for learning than either Oxford or Cambridge. His friends envied him and his teachers prophesied that he would be a brilliant student.

Then his sister, Catherine, married a wealthy young man, Daniel Hodson. It was a great blow to Goldsmith. The marriage cost him the money which would have been spent on his college education, and his golden dream was shattered.

His father did not agree to the match. Catherine was marrying above her station and without his consent. But married Catherine was and her father-in-law immediately got in touch with the Reverend Charles Goldsmith and told him that custom provided that he give to the groom not only a virgin but also a subtantial marriage portion—the one was as important as the other.

This touched the pride of Charles Goldsmith. Without a thought for Oliver, he hurried down to Dublin and made out a deed by which he was bound to pay four hundred pounds to his son-in-law, lest his daughter have to hang her head every time money was mentioned in the family.

Four hundred pounds was two years' income for the Reverend Goldsmith, and since he gave away money to every beggar and friend in need, he had no savings. With the marriage settlement the family was poor again and there wasn't a penny to send Oliver to Trinity.

The effect was shattering. Spoiled, sensitive, and proud, he'd boasted of going to Trinity, and he was now ashamed before all his friends. He'd been put aside for his sister without any thought and he became despondent, moody, and afraid to face those to whom he had bragged.

His father and mother did not understand how heavy was the blow. They proposed that Oliver should still go to college but as a sizar—a student-servant who, in return for tuition, swept the courtyards, put out the garbage, carried the meals to the dining room, cleared off the dishes, and so on.

Oliver would have nothing to do with such a plan. The come-down was terrible. He had suffered enough as a schoolboy without having to suffer more as a college servant. He said he'd rather get a job in some kind of trade than graduate from Trinity on such terms. But the idea of entering a trade was horrendous in the Goldsmith family, whose men were all clergymen—and very good ones too though the clergy of the day were a branch, as it were, of the civil service, preaching Christianity in a form approved by the government and paid out of taxes.

There was in the Goldsmith clan, however, a certain Reverend Thomas Contarine, who had married Charles Goldsmith's sister. (She died at about this time, leaving him with one unmarried daughter, who played the harpsichord and was a close friend of Oliver.) Oliver liked Uncle Contarine, who tried to help the boy in his predicament where his mother and father had failed. He had several conversations with Oliver about going to college and pointed out gently that he himself had been a sizar at Trinity, had obtained his degree in Divinity, and now had an excellent living.

"The sizars are often the best students, respected by their tutors," he said. "It is not whether you have a broom in your hand that matters, but whether you have culture and learning in your mind. Many of our most eminent men today were formerly Trinity sizars. What holds you back from joining their company? You will not suffer so very much, I assure you."

Oliver was at last persuaded, went to Dublin, passed the necessary Latin examinations, and entered Trinity June 11, 1745, at the age of sixteen.

Nothing Uncle Contarine had said about suffering proved true. He was given the usual miserable garret, which he shared with another sizar, a long smock of coarse black material with the sleeves cut off short, and a red cap to put on his head. This was the uniform of the sizar—a uniform derided by other students—and Goldsmith hated it. Already he felt a need for presentable clothing to make up for his appearance.

Worse still, the tutor to whom he was assigned, Dr. Theaker Wilder, though a brilliant mathematician, was a savage bully who loved to inflict mental and physical punishments. He took an immediate dislike to Goldsmith with his weak chin, bulging forehead, pocked face, and shambling figure and made him suffer accordingly.

Wilder had an ungovernable temper and lashed out with his fists whenever he became angry. Thumping a student's head against the wall was one of his favorite methods of instilling knowledge. Once, when a coachman's whip accidentally flicked him in the street, Dr. Wilder dragged the coachman off his box and beat him insensible. (He was himself beaten to death in a brawl later on.) Yet at times he could be almost charming. Meeting a pretty girl face to face on the only dry strip in a muddy street in Dublin, he kissed her and said, "Take that for being so handsome" and stepped into the mud to let her pass.

Trinity in Goldsmith's day was a democratic institution. The sons of peers mixed with the sons of brewers, shoemakers, candlemakers, butchers, and clergymen. Goldsmith, however, cut so poor a figure and was so quick to resent the slightest personal remark that he made no friends among his new acquaintances. None of his fellow students, after Oliver became famous, could remember a single anecdote about him. At Trinity he did not exist except as a contemptible underling.

The few friends he had were those he had known at home —a boy named Beatty, who had been to school with him at Edgeworthstown, and Robert Bryanton, whom he had known at Ballymahon. Also a relative of Goldsmith, he subsequently became an alcoholic. Beatty and Bryanton were sizars too and shared some of Oliver's misery. But neither was as poor as he, nor as ill-made. The result was that the little self-confidence Goldsmith had achieved at Edgeworthstown was soon torn to shreds under the savagery and mockery of Theaker Wilder and the brutal loneliness of Trinity College.

Mathematics was a subject Goldsmith loathed. He became the butt of the class, the source of all the sycophantic laughter. But once at least he was able to turn the tables on his tormentor with the same wit he had used on the fiddler who had called him Aesop. Wilder asked Goldsmith to explain what was meant by the center of gravity and Goldsmith could not. Wilder sarcastically supplied the definition and then, turning on Goldsmith, said, "Now, sir. You have listened to the definition. Pray tell me where is my center of gravity."

"Why, sir," said Goldsmith, "according to the principles which you have so carefully laid down, I would say that it was in your behind." The laughter made him a hero for the while and Wilder could not at the moment retaliate. But in the end Goldsmith avoided the mathematics lectures and roamed about the courtyards of the college, solitary and brooding, or sat in the garret room playing the flute. At night he would roam the streets talking to beggars more miserable than himself.

Dublin at the time, though one of the most elegant cities in Europe, swarmed with half-naked, sore-infested, starving beggars who slept in doorways and in gutters and ditches.

Homeless, hungry, and hopeless people were common, of course, to all the cities of Europe. But they were perhaps more evident in Dublin because of the fierce laws against

Catholicism. Dispossessed Catholic peasants, their tiny hovels pulled down, thronged into the city looking for work in such numbers that Swift had proposed their children be fattened, slaughtered, butchered, and sold as meat to the landlords who had dispossessed them, the money going to support their mothers.

The greater number of beggars were women and children. The men to relieve their misery entered the Army or went to England as sedan-chair men or laborers if they had any physique at all. Some were impressed into the Navy. The majority of the sedan-chair men in London at this time were Irish. Many of the women turned to or drifted into prostitution, and when that source of income was gone, wheedled what living they could from passersby, with a brood of sickly children clinging to their ragged dresses.

The workhouses established in England since the days of Elizabeth had no counterpart in Ireland. There the poor were permitted to starve slowly or die of exposure. Death by starvation was a common entry in the mortality lists. Babies were often abandoned and when at last a founding hospital was organized, such was the savagery and neglect of the nurses that of some twenty-five thousand babies admitted between 1784 and 1796, seventeen thousand died.

To offset this neglect there was a touch of official charity toward the widows of men who had been executed. A woman whose husband had been beheaded was given his body minus the head on a bale of straw. This she was allowed to display in the street to raise what she could while her children wailed around her. It is not clear whether this privilege was extended to the wives of men who had been hanged.

At the other end of the social scale was another group of the uprooted—the younger sons of middle-class and wealthy English families who migrated in large numbers to Dublin where there were no social family restraints upon them. "Half-mounted gentlemen" they were called, and they duelled, drank, gambled, went whoring, and headed gangs of toughs who would attack anyone their masters told them to.

They had no religion but hedonism, which at times turned into Satanism. Many belonged to the Hellfire Club (founded in Dublin by the first Earl of Rosse) which had a meeting place in the center of the city where they held black masses, sexual orgies, and drinking bouts. They also supported an abduction club, whose object was to kidnap the daughters of wealthy families and rape them. Having lost their virginity, the girls were compelled to marry their kidnappers, whose only interest in them was the fortune belonging to the reluctant brides.

Buck English, one of this sort, becoming annoyed with a waiter, shot him and coolly suggested that the matter be settled by putting the price of the waiter on the dinner bill at fifty pounds. Another of the half-mounted gentlemen, though not of the English immigrants, had his young nephew shanghaied and sent to America, where he was sold as a slave, so that the uncle could inherit his estates. The nephew escaped after many years and returned to Ireland. He shot a man accidentally while hunting. The uncle, overjoyed, insisted that his nephew be charged with murder and went to London to demand that he be found guilty and hanged.

The nephew was acquitted, but he never succeeded to his estates though the courts ruled in his favor.

The Bucks, Bullies, Pinkindindies, and Sweaters—these were the clubs they belonged to. The Pinkindindies cut off the ends of their sword scabbards and, prowling the streets at night, stabbed or slashed lone men or women to recover their losses at the gambling tables. Two infamous brothers were known as Kilkelly and Kilcoachy—the one because he had shot a man called Kelly and the other because in a fit of temper he had shot his coachman.

It must be remembered, however, that Dublin was a prosperous and growing city, and no city could prosper and grow given over to ruffians. Decent, law-abiding families abounded and it is a mark of the loneliness of Goldsmith that whatever his father's connections in Dublin, he seems never to have been invited to any of their homes.

The Four Courts, Dublin. Eighteenth century, though somewhat later than Goldsmith's time. BETTMANN ARCHIVE.

Religious warfare broke out often in the Dublin streets as it still does in some parts of Ireland. The butchers of the Ormonde market, for instance, were all Catholics and their great enemies were the Liberty Boys, a band of militant Protestants. The two groups fought each other savagely. The butchers, when they captured any of the Liberty Boys, cut the tendons in their legs. The Liberty Boys retaliated by hanging the butchers by their jaws on their own meat hooks. The warfare between the two went on through the whole of the eighteenth century in Dublin.

Wandering among Dublin's beggars, Goldsmith did what he could to help them. He'd bring them bread or meat stolen from the college kitchen, or give them in a moment of compassion his coat or shirt or waistcoat or whatever he thought he could do without. Sometimes he pawned his books and gave the money to the poor, with no plan at all as to how he was to redeem them. Once, finding a woman and her children shivering in a doorway, he went back to his room and returned with the thin blankets off his bed to give them. Back in his garret he shivered for an hour and then slit open his mattress and spent the rest of the night sleeping in the stuffing.

Some of the street people were ballad singers and Goldsmith loved to listen to them. Since he'd been making rhymes from the time he was seven years of age, he tried writing ballads. He found an occasional market for them at five shillings apiece and gloried to hear his work sung at times in cracked voices in the Dublin streets.

His father died when Goldsmith had been eighteen months at Trinity. That ended the remittances of a few shillings a month. Uncle Contarine sent him a guinea or two now and then. He wrote more ballads, pawned more books, borrowed tiny sums from Bryanton, Beatty, or Edward Mills (another relative of his at Trinity), and soon looked almost as poor as the beggars he tried to help. The sizar cloak and cap were needed now to cover his raggedness.

He was a good classical student, though, and did well at his examination in Latin and Greek. And he took some French, a language which was to be of the greatest use to him in later life.

After a couple of years at Trinity, with a ballad or two sold, and now almost inured to the insults of Wilder, Goldsmith became bolder. In the summer of 1747 a bailiff arrested one of the undergraduates and carried him off to jail. Goldsmith decided to join a dozen or more students headed by one "Gallows" Walsh in seeking revenge. Out they went into the city and searched every bailiff's den in Dublin until they found the man who had made the arrest. They stripped the bailiff naked, dragged him to the college pump, and ducked him. Theaker Wilder happened to pass by and called out, "Gentlemen! Gentlemen! Do not be so cruel as to nail his ears to the pump." The students took the hint and the bailiff, screaming with pain, was left nailed to the pump by his ear.

Next the gang decided to go to the Newgate Jail (called The Black Dog) and liberate their comrade. They were met by fire from the one small cannon that defended the place. Several bystanders were killed by the shot and the undergraduates were arrested. Five were expelled and the rest, Goldsmith among them, publicly admonished before the faculty and student body.

Goldsmith decided to restore himself to good grace by attempting to win a classical scholarship. He didn't, but did well enough to be given a prize worth thirty shillings. This was something to be celebrated, so he called his few friends together, brought in some young ladies, including a few whores, and held a party in his garret. Wilder was informed, appeared in the midst of the party, and floored Goldsmith with a blow of his fist in front of his guests. The disgrace was more than Oliver could endure. He sold what books he had left, borrowed a shilling or two from his friends, and left Trinity.

He haunted the streets of Dublin, sleeping where he could, until he was down to his last shilling. Then he decided that there was no hope for him in Ireland and he ought to go to America. He walked to Cork, lived for three days on his shilling, pawned his coat, shoes, and hat, and decided to try to stow away on an America-bound ship, or find one that would let him work his passage. He couldn't get aboard a ship to stow away and nobody wanted any hands.

Penniless, coatless, and barefoot, he decided to go back home to Lissoy. On the way he was given a handful of cold peas, gray with age, by a woman at a wake. He'd had nothing to eat for twenty-four hours and often said later that the peas were the most delicious meal he ever had in his life.

His mother was horrified by the exploit and could not understand what had happened to her talented son who was supposed to be studying so hard at Trinity. She particularly could not understand such behavior now that his father was dead. She was deeply disappointed in him.

Henry understood. He'd been through Trinity as a paying student, but he knew something of the life of a sizar. He listened sympathetically to the whole story, talked Oliver into returning to college, and effected a reconciliation of sorts with Wilder.

Somehow Goldsmith struggled through the remaining months, until at last he was given his diploma as a bachelor of arts. His name was the lowest on the list. The date was February 27, 1749, and Goldsmith was just over twenty years of age.

CHAPTER

His mother looked forward hopefully to Oliver's return from Dublin. She was sure he would go to work and help support the family, for her husband was dead, the two hundred pounds a year was gone, and the Lord, whom the Reverend Charles Goldsmith was always sure would provide, seemed at the time to be absent-minded.

Mrs. Goldsmith was living with her two younger children in a tiny rented cottage on the outskirts of Ballymahon, her youngest child, John, being dead of a fall from a horse as earlier noted. Henry, now a minister in the Established Church, was married and had a living of only forty pounds a year and with it a small elementary school to run. That forty pounds had to support himself, his wife, his mother, and the young children. Oliver was the great hope. He had a Trinity degree and could surely find a position as a tutor or secretary in some wealthy family.

Oliver disappointed them all. He had been through a purgatory in Dublin, resulting from being put aside for his sister. He was not ready to help his mother. He disappointed her again by just lazing around and recovering from his own sufferings. They owed him something. He could not see that he owed them anything. In any case after the hardships of Dublin life—the skimpy meals, the ragged clothes, the pinching winter cold, and the miserable Trinity garret—the tiny cottage in Ballymahon into which he moved with his mother, sharing a bed with his little brothers, was pure luxury.

The few shillings a week, donated by Henry on which all had to live, seemed to him ample for everybody's needs. After all, there were potatoes from the garden, there was milk from the cow, there was bread, home baked, there were peas, beans, carrots, and onions, all garden raised, there was a little meat now and again, and an occasional dish of tea. There was a good thatched roof over their heads, stout walls to keep out the wind, and a fire on the hearth, fed by turf, on which to cook and which kept the cottage snug in winter. What more was needed?

Nothing, Oliver decided, and settled down to enjoy himself. Despite his mother's pleas he let day after day go by. Instead of working, Oliver caught a salmon or a trout for the table now and then, or brought home a couple of rabbits or a hatful of plover's eggs (the flavor is delicate) to add to the larder. He played with his little brothers and the other children of the village, whom he sometimes taught in Henry's school, for he was one who would love children all his life.

Trying to heal himself he lounged about the blacksmith's forge, hour after hour, watching the horses being shod, watching the strips of black iron being heated in the glowing forge, a piece cut off with one blow on the anvil and then fashioned into a horseshoe. He watched the blacksmith pare the horses' hooves with his knife, pull out the old nails, file each hoof smooth, and then clap the hot shoe into place and nail it there without a quiver from the horse. He liked to work the bellows, hold the white-hot iron on the anvil with pincers while the smith showed him how to beat it into shape. He made wagers with the smith as to how far he could throw a six-pound sledgehammer. The smith always won for there is a knack to throwing one. When Oliver had learned it, he won a prize at hammer throwing at the local fair, and came home very pleased with himself to give the money to his mother. She took it, but with no great thanks. Had he earned a Trinity degree to win a prize throwing a sledgehammer? Her disappointment in the child of whom she had thought so highly grew. She could not understand him.

Goldsmith knew every poacher and every gamekeeper too. He knew enough about wildlife to be of assistance to all. He caught a young otter and tried to train it to catch fish for him, and he laid out rabbit traps which he visited every morning and evening. He knew the nesting places of swans, moorhens, finches, and wrens. He spent hours sitting in a snug corner of a hedge or under a tree just looking at things —at clouds and waving branches of trees and the sparkle of sunshine on leaves and the jewelled frogs leaping through the long, wet grass and striped caterpillars crawling up the stems of marigolds. He was never bored, for everything in Nature delighted him, and Nature lay all around.

There was a Catholic priest living nearby—a man avoided by all above the level of the peasantry. Goldsmith became his friend, and the priest continued his education in French, in which he was soon proficient. He started reading all the French literature that came to hand.

He also made friends with George Conway, who owned the local pub, and organized a club, which included Bob Bryanton, to meet there, sing songs, tell stories, play cards, and drink a few tankards of beer or ale. Goldsmith was an excellent tenor, and a passable flute player. He knew a great number of ballads, a favorite being "Johnny Armstrong's Last Good Night," which had been taught him by Peggy Golden, a milkmaid who had served as his nurse.

He made up ballads of his own, to everybody's delight, for he was incapable of writing anything, even a ballad, that was poor or dull. His had a good tavern swing to them, and the devil-may-care tavern wit.

He spent many evenings also at his Uncle Contarine's house. There he played flute while Jane, his uncle's daughter, played harpsichord. Uncle Contarine believed that Oliver might one day amount to something; that hidden somewhere in that hulking figure and irresponsible mind there was real worth.

Everybody still wanted young Goldsmith to follow the family profession of clergyman. His mother and his brother talked to him about it over and over again until he hated the subject. He did not want to be a clergyman. His father had been poor all his life as a churchman and his brother Henry was in a fair way to following in the cold shadow of his father's poverty. He was not an ordinary Goldsmith and nobody could understand that. He liked cards. He liked an evening of drinking and singing in taverns. He was attracted to women though his experiences were limited to the shilling prostitutes of the Dublin alleys. He liked to be free and he would have to give up his freedom to enter the church. He hated the idea; hated even the thought of having to dress in sober black clothing for the rest of his life, cut off by his very office from his fellowmen. No scarlets, blues, greens, and golds—no cockade stuck jauntily in his three-cornered hat. Just blacks, browns, and decorous living. He hated the idea.

But Uncle Contarine thought Oliver should take Holy Orders. "Not a bad life," he said, peering thoughtfully at him over the top of his glasses. "Look at me. Master of over two hundred pounds a year. Fine house. Good farm. Not too much parish work to do. I still have my glass of wine, my musical evenings, my game of cards." The church wasn't a prison by any means. There was plenty of time for reading and writing and a quiet mind to enjoy both pleasures.

To oblige Uncle Contarine, who quietly returned time and again to the subject, and rid himself of his mother's constant harping on it, Oliver at last consented to apply to the Bishop for Holy Orders when he was twenty-three—which gave him two more years to himself, during which time anything could happen.

In the meantime he was supposed to study theology, the sound arguments against the damnable Catholic doctrine of Transubstantiation, the writings of the learned doctors on the significance of the Nothing out of which God made the world, and the reason why the King and not the Pope should be head of the church.

Instead he studied hammer throwing, French, ballad making, and wildlife. He had, the story goes, a very simple plan worked out to insure that his interview with the Bishop of Elphin would be a failure. On the day of the interview, it is said, he presented himself to His Grace in a pair of outrageous scarlet breeches, his eyes swollen from spending the previous night in a tavern. The bishop took one look at him and barred him from the church forever. Oliver came happily home, triumphant in his failure. He looked forward to more happy days poaching and rambling around, but Uncle Contarine found him a post as a tutor to the family of a certain Mr. Flinn (the Christian name is unknown), a gentleman of the county.

The position required that Oliver not only teach the children Latin and Greek, but also take a hand at cards for reasonable stakes of an evening. He had learned to gamble at Trinity, where the stakes were halfpennies, and a few shillings in the pot were a fortune. But he wasn't a good card player. He played not out of card sense, but out of fancy, daring, risking, out of hunches and excitement. So he lost far more often than he won, though when he did win, the pot (because of his style of playing) was often huge.

In any case he stayed with the Flinn family for a year, teaching the classics and playing whist and loo. Then he suspected that he was being cheated at cards and said so. He probably wasn't being cheated, but was losing hand after hand because of his reckless method of playing. A quarrel arose and he left the Flinns to return to Ballymahon. But he had thirty pounds in his pocket, had lived well for a year, and was the owner of a good riding horse.

He settled down in his mother's cottage again. Though he bought a few things including toys for the children, it didn't occur to him to turn any big portion of his savings over to his mother, or to offer to pay her rent for a few years. Instead he kept his money and his horse, on which he rode about the village, feeling himself a fine figure of a gentleman.

His anxious mother tearfully asked Oliver what he proposed to do with his life. He replied that he was planning to go to America. He'd ride to Cork on his horse and pay his passage with the money he had earned at the Flinns'.

America fascinated him—the dark forests, full of boding silences, the savage Mohawks, the thundering fall of Niagara, the rich tobacco plantations in Virginia, the free land on the frontier, there for the taking, the bears and tigers (he thought there were tigers in America) and the deadly snakes, the terrible snows, the howling winds that scoured a continent, the fish-filled seas, the mighty buffalo and moose. These were things to dream about. Certainly America, uninhibited, unfettered, and scarcely touched by human habitation, was the place for any man of imagination to go, away from his anxious family and their predictable lives.

He sang a final song at George Conway's, had the horse fresh shod at the blacksmith's, said goodbye to the priest who had taught him French, and talked wisely to the yokels about the Hudson and the Mississippi and the Ohio, and the horrors of Indian warfare.

He was back penniless in a few weeks on a skeleton of a horse which he called Fiddleback, and his mother was in tears and so angry she would not have him in the house. He stayed with Henry or Uncle Contarine and wrote his mother a letter to explain the whole thing. The letter read as follows:

> *My dear Mother:*
>
> If you will sit down and calmly listen to what I have to say, you shall be fully resolved in every one of those many questions you have asked me. I went to Cork and converted my horse, which you prize so much higher than Fiddleback, into cash, took a passage in a ship bound for America and, at the same time, paid the captain for my freight and all the other expenses of my voyage. But it so happened that the wind did not answer for three weeks; and you know, mother, that I could not command the elements. My misfortune was that when the wind served I happened to be with a party in the country, and my friend the captain never inquired after me, but set sail with as much indifference as if I had been on board. The re-

mainder of my time I employed in the city and its environs, viewing everything curious, and you know no one can starve while he has money in his pocket.

Reduced, however, to my last two guineas, I began to think of my dear mother and friends whom I had left behind me, and so bought that generous beast Fiddleback, and made adieu to Cork with only five shillings in my pocket. This, to be sure, was but a scanty allowance for man and horse towards a journey of above a hundred miles; but I did not despair for I knew I must find friends on the road.

I recollected particularly an old and faithful acquaintance I made at college, who had often and earnestly pressed me to spend a summer with him, and he lived but eight miles from Cork. This circumstance of vicinity he would expatiate on to me with peculiar emphasis. "We shall," says he, "enjoy the delights of both city and country and you shall command my stable and my purse."

However, upon the way I met a poor woman all in tears, who told me her husband had been arrested for a debt he was not able to pay, and that his eight children must now starve, bereaved as they were of his industry, which had been their only support. I thought myself at home, being not far from my good friend's house, and therefore parted with a moiety of all my store; and pray, mother, ought I not to have given her the other half-crown, for what she got would be of little use to her? However, I soon arrived at the mansion of my affectionate friend, guarded by the vigilance of a large mastiff, who flew at me and would have torn me to pieces but for the assistance of a woman whose countenance was not less grim than that of the dog; yet she with great humanity relieved me from the jaws of this Cerberus and was prevailed on to carry up my name to her master.

Without suffering me to wait long, my old friend, who was then recovering from a fit of sickness, came down in his night-cap, nightgown, and slippers, and embraced me with a most cordial welcome, showed me in, and, after giving me a history of his indisposition, assured me that he considered himself peculiarly fortunate in having under his roof the man he most loved on earth, and whose stay with him must, above all things, contribute to his perfect recovery.

I now repented sorely I had not given the poor woman the other half-crown, as I thought all my bills of humanity would be punctually answered by this worthy man. I revealed to him I had but one half-crown in my pocket; but that now, like a ship after weathering out the storm, I considered myself secure in a safe and hospitable harbor. He made no answer, but walked about the room, rubbing his hands as one in deep study. This I imputed to the sympathetic feelings of a tender heart, which increased my esteem for him, and, as that increased, I gave the most favorable interpretation to his silence. I construed it into delicacy of sentiment, as if he dreaded to wound my pride by expressing his commiseration in words, leaving his generous conduct to speak for itself.

It now approached six o'clock in the evening, and as I had eaten no breakfast, and as my spirits were raised, my appetite for dinner grew uncommonly keen. At length the old woman came into the room with two plates, one spoon, and a dirty cloth, which she laid upon the table. This appearance, without increasing my spirits, did not diminish my appetite. My protectress soon returned with a small bowl of sago, a small porringer of sour milk, a loaf of stale brown bread, and the heel of an old cheese all over crawling with mites. My friend apologized that his illness obliged him to live on slops, and that better fare was not in the house; observing, at the same time, that a milk diet was certainly the most healthful. At eight o'clock he again recommended a regular life, declaring that for his part he would lie down with the lamb and rise with the lark. My hunger was at this time so exceedingly sharp that I wished for another slice of the loaf, but was obliged to go to bed without even that refreshment.

This lenten entertainment I had received made me resolve to depart as soon as possible; accordingly next morning, when I spoke of going, he did not oppose my resolution; he rather commended my design, adding very sage counsel upon the occasion. "To be sure," said he, "the longer you stay away from your mother the more you will grieve her and your other friends; and possibly they are already afflicted at hearing of this foolish expedition you have made." Notwithstanding all this, and without any hope of softening such a sordid heart, I again renewed the tale of my distress and, asking how he thought I could travel above a hundred miles upon one half-crown, I begged to borrow a single guinea, which I assured him would be repaid with thanks. "And you know, sir," said I, "it is no more than I have often lent you." To which he firmly answered, "Why look you, Mr. Goldsmith, that is neither here nor there. I have paid you all you ever lent me and this sickness of mine has left me bare of cash. But I have bethought myself of a conveyance for you; sell your horse, and I will furnish you with a much better one to ride on."

I readily grasped at this proposal, and begged to see the nag, on which he led me to his bedchamber and from under the bed he pulled out a stout oak stick. "Here it is," said he, "take this in your hand, and it will carry you to your mother's with more safety than such a horse as you ride." I was in doubt, when I got it into my hand, whether I should not, in the first place, apply it to his pate; but a rap at the street door made the wretch fly to it, and when I returned to the parlor he introduced me, as if nothing of the kind had happened, to the gentleman who entered, as Mr. Goldsmith, his most ingenious and worthy friend, of whom he had so often heard him speak with rapture. I could scarcely compose myself; and must have betrayed indignation in my mien to the stranger, who was a counsellor at law in the neighborhood, a man of engaging aspect and polite address.

After spending an hour, he asked my friend and me to dine with him at his house. This I declined at first, as I wished to have no further communication with my hospitable friend; but at the solicitation of both I at last consented, determined as I was by two motives; one, that I was prejudiced in favor of the looks and manner of the counsellor; and the other that I stood in need of a comfortable dinner. And there indeed I found everything that I could wish, abundance without profusion and elegance without affectation.

In the evening, when my friend, who had eaten plentifully at his neighbor's table, but talked again of lying down with the lamb, made a motion to me for retiring, our generous host requested I should take a bed with him, upon which I plainly told my old friend that he might go home and take care of the horse he had given me, but that I should never re-enter his doors. He went away with a laugh, leaving me to add this to the other little things the counsellor already knew of his plausible neighbor.

And now, my dear mother, I found sufficient to reconcile me to all my follies; for here I spent three whole days. The counsellor had two sweet girls to his daughters, who played enchantingly on the harpsichord; and yet it was but a melancholy pleasure I felt the first time I heard them; for that being the first time also that either of them had touched the instrument since their mother's death, I saw the tears in silence trickle down their father's cheeks. I every day endeavored to go away, but every day was pressed and obliged to stay. On my going, the counsellor offered me his purse, with a horse and a servant to convey me home; but the latter I declined, and only took a guinea to bear my necessary expences on the road.

Oliver Goldsmith.

There is a mystery about this letter and indeed about the whole adventure. The original is not to be found, and the copy is thought to be a forgery. Nonetheless, Goldsmith's sister Catherine wrote that this was the detailed story he gave to his mother and brothers and sisters at a family conference and her account follows the letter almost word for word.

At the end of the family conference his mother asked whether he had written to thank the gentleman who had befriended him.

"No," said Goldsmith. "I have not."

"You are an ungrateful and savage monster," she exploded, "not to have sent your deepest thanks to so kind a man." His brothers and sisters agreed. Goldsmith received all this calmly and then said that he hadn't written to thank the man because the whole thing was fiction. Later, he reversed himself and told Catherine that it was all true.

What happened then between his disappearance on a fine fat horse with thirty pounds in his pocket and his return on a bony nag with hardly a penny is a mystery. He never gave any other explanation. Maybe he just spent the money on high living and gambling, getting away from the accusing presence of his mother and the restrictions of life in the little village with everybody constantly asking what he was going to do with himself. He returned only when he was penniless and had nowhere else to go. He had plenty of time on the way back to think up a plausible story to explain his absence.

Mrs. Goldsmith now would have nothing more to do with him and he moved into Henry's house. Her brilliant son had proved himself utterly irresponsible, with no care for her or his family, and an outrageous liar into the bargain. The love between them died at that time.

Uncle Contarine alone believed that Oliver would one day settle down. They had many conversations together and Goldsmith, who was susceptible to persuasion, finally agreed that since he certainly didn't want to be a clergyman he should become a lawyer. He loved reading. He liked arguing.

He was well versed in Latin and Greek. Sometimes he argued very well, and sometimes foolishly. But law would give him freedom and finally his uncle got together a purse of fifty pounds and sent him to Dublin to study law.

He was back again penniless in a few days. He had met a college friend, been enticed into a game of cards, and lost the whole of his money. He roamed the streets of Dublin for a while and then returned. He didn't even go to his mother; Henry took him in. But it wasn't long before even Henry could not stand his idleness, his irresponsibility, and his evenings in the tavern. He threw him out after a quarrel.

Uncle Contarine's door alone remained open and there he went. He was given a new suit of clothes and in return he played his flute, sang songs, told stories, and wrote verses for his uncle. These were the only things he had any real talent for. They talked about books—the classical writers and French writers, and particularly Voltaire, of whom Goldsmith was very fond. He had the gift of being the most agreeable company and the defect of being utterly aimless.

His uncle thought about the situation for several weeks. Another relative suggested that Oliver could study medicine. They were grasping at straws. A clergyman. A lawyer. A doctor. Any kind of profession but the Army. It might be possible to buy him a commission but even the Army could not endure an officer of such irresponsibility.

A nice thing about studying medicine was that Oliver would have to go abroad—to Edinburgh—which, if they could get him on a ship, would prevent his turning up in rags at Ballymahon a few weeks after setting out. Uncle Contarine agreed to the plan and again, with daring optimism, put up some of the money—the rest to be supplied by his brother-in-law, Daniel Hodson.

But this time Uncle Contarine didn't give Oliver a big sum. He paid his passage, put enough in his purse for immediate expenses, and told him he could have more when he needed it, but it would be in credit, not cash. In other words, he would establish a fund against which Oliver could draw, but he must report to his uncle what had been spent and for what purpose.

So Goldsmith left for the third time and took the coach to Dublin, determined to make something of himself. He never saw his mother or Uncle Contarine or his brother Henry again. He had been launched out of the safe harbor of Ireland and into the world.

CHAPTER IV

Oliver Goldsmith arrived in Edinburgh in the autumn of 1752 when he was not quite twenty-four years of age. The last rising of the Scots had been put down only six years before with the defeat of the Jacobite Army in the Battle of Culloden in 1746. The Duke of Cumberland, victor in the battle and uncle of George III, earned the title of Cumberland the Butcher for suppressing the rebellion. He strewed the Scottish Highlands with gallows from which dangled the bodies of rebels and those thought to have harbored rebels. He decorated London Bridge and Temple Bar with the heads of others. Estates were forfeited, clansmen and crofters turned off their lands to become beggars. Many of the Scottish nobility who escaped with their lives, being now landless, earned their livings as tradesmen in Edinburgh and Glasgow. Lord Kilcoubry, for instance, became a glover.

The day Goldsmith arrived in Edinburgh he nearly lost all his clothes. As soon as he was off the ship, he called a porter who took him to a lodging house where he paid a week's rent and left his chest of clothes in his room. Then he went off happily to explore one of the most picturesque cities of Europe, forgot both the name of the landlady and the address of his lodging, and was utterly lost. He found his way down to the docks and luckily ran into the same porter, who told him where he was lodged, and so was saved.

Edinburgh was one of the smallest capitals in Europe, but it was also one of the tallest. It was a walled city, and since it was not fashionable to live outside the walls, most of its population of perhaps fifty thousand lived within them.

This resulted in story upon story being added to buildings, so that there were whole blocks of tenements which were fourteen and fifteen stories high—eighteenth-century skyscrapers not to be found in any other city in the world.

All of these were without running water or inside toilets. The result was that the tenants had to carry what water they needed up cramped flights of stairs, the unlucky ones to the fourteenth or fifteenth floor. Garbage likewise had to be carried all the way down the stairs or flung out of the window, and the same was true of sewage. It was usual to put everything into a barrel and, after nine in the evening, open a window, shout "Gardeyloo"—a corruption of "Gardez-vous"—and dump everything into the street or wherever it landed in a high wind. Walking about Edinburgh after nine at night was a considerable hazard, for there was not a street on which the pedestrian was safe from a noisome deluge.

The congestion in Edinburgh caused by everybody's determination to live within the city walls resulted in coffeehouses, taverns, and clubs proliferating since there was no space for entertainment in the tiny rooms of the tenements. Even wealthy famiiles could afford only two or three rooms too small for entertainment and used taverns or coffeehouses for dinner parties. It was the custom for lawyers to consult with their clients in a coffeehouse. The result was a very friendly city and it was not possible to be there for a week or so without being invited to join one of Edinburgh's numerous clubs.

Clubs were often formed on a whim. The Pious Club, for example, was the outgrowth of a terrible pun—the members ate pies. The Spendthrifts undertook to spend no more than four pence halfpenny on their evening's entertainment. The Ten Tumbler Club, whose members were all judges, lawyers, and gentlemen of high degree, required that a man be able to drink ten tumblers of toddy without it affecting his walking, speech, or thinking. Heavy drinking was considered normal but that applied everywhere and a man who drank two bottles of claret in an evening was not thought to have over-indulged. There were other clubs whose emphasis was on sex and brutality—the Hellfire Club, the Sweaters, and the Dirty Club—counterparts of those that existed in Ireland and in England.

Goldsmith soon made friends among his fellow students at the university. He joined several clubs, selecting those that liked singing, literature, and card playing. He was no great drinker though he got drunk occasionally and was never ashamed of it. His fellow countryman, Burke, on getting drunk, spent several days of remorse as a penalty and tried to avoid mentioning the matter.

Goldsmith wrote to Bob Bryanton, who was now the squire of Ballymahon, that there were handsome women in Scotland and handsome men to keep them company and added, "An ugly and a poor man is society for himself; and such society the world lets me enjoy in great abundance." So he was lonely for feminine company.

In the beginning Goldsmith was delighted with Edinburgh—a new city, a new university, new friends. It was exciting and he felt important attending the lectures on chemistry and physics and anatomy and talking over those subjects with his fellow students. Anatomy was taught by Dr. Alexander Munro, who founded at Edinburgh one of the most famous departments of anatomy in Europe. The work was continued by his son, also named Alexander.

Goldsmith acquired a skeleton which was his sole companion in his room, but its presence didn't depress him. He liked the anatomy lectures, for a while at least, and wrote to his uncle in glowing terms about Dr. Munro. The man didn't stick to bones and muscles but went off into other fascinating fields. His lectures were crowded and his fame such that he attracted students from as far away as Russia. He had the gift of simplifying what was complicated, without distorting it, and making clear what was obscure.

Oliver studied the technique rather than the subject matter—the technique of concentrating on what was relevant and giving it shape, while throwing out all that was mere lumber, and at the same time not sounding pompous. He was learning the art of compiling rather than the art of anatomy.

He never was much good at anatomy anyway and probably used his skeleton to hang his clothes on. Later in life, for instance, he maintained that in eating it was the upper jaw that moved as well as the lower and was supplied with the needed muscles. This he said could be proved by holding the head immovable and opening and shutting the mouth over the edge of a table. The experiment would prove exactly the opposite, but Goldsmith seems never to have performed it properly. He is said to have informed an astonished audience at the University of Padua later, lecturing in Latin, that the human kidney was situated in the center of the lung. The story may be a complete fiction, for there are many such tales told about Goldsmith. But it is the kind of fiction that fitted the truth. Goldsmith, though determined to become a physician, a profession of dignity and respect, was handicapped in that he much preferred fancy to fact.

He plainly didn't like the other lecturers in the school of medicine. Andrew Plummer, lecturer on chemistry, knew his business, he said, but was dull. Charles Alston, professor of botany and materia medica, by which may have been meant drugs, was verbose and rarely made his point while the others said little that couldn't be found in books.

It wasn't long before Goldsmith was ducking his lectures and taking rambles in the countryside. This, however, was Scotland and not Ireland—or rather the very English-looking part of Ireland around Roscommon. The scenery lacked trees and woods and flowering lanes and quiet streams. It depressed him.

"Every part of the country presents the same dismal landscape," he wrote Bryanton on September 26, 1753. "No grove or brook lend their music to cheer the stranger or make the inhabitants forget their poverty."

Nonetheless, inspired by glowing accounts of the grandeur of the Scottish Highlands, he set out on a tour of them, starting on foot. He had a corn on his great toe when he started and in one day it was too painful for walking. So he hired a pony—not much bigger than a sheep, he said—and went away for a month, returning in his usual homecoming condition—ragged and penniless. He probably took enough money with him for a month's tour, but he also probably played a few hands of cards and lost it.

Soon he had become disenchanted with Scotland. Travel fever gripped him and the problem was to find some way of getting out of Edinburgh. Three years was the usual course of study for a medical degree. He couldn't think of spending three years in Edinburgh. He was hardly in the city six months before he was writing his uncle saying that he would stay there through the following winter benefitting from Dr. Munro, and then he would go to hear Albinus, "the great professor at Leyden."

His uncle didn't write telling him to stay where he was, but Oliver, with an escape prepared, settled down to spend the next few months through the grim winter as best he could.

Goldsmith's absence from the university on trips into the country or visits around the town was not remarkable in his day. His fellow students were perhaps absent as frequently as he. Edmund Burke, for example, studying law at Trinity earlier, was notorious for skipping lectures though he went on to become an outstanding lawyer, orator, and statesman. The difference was that Goldsmith got so very little out of the lectures he did attend. He was convinced he was gaining knowledge. Actually he learned almost nothing.

The social life of the town, outside of the cafe, club, and tavern life, was conducted with a formality that he found as depressing as the countryside. He was surprised, after the freedom of Ireland, to find that at dances in Scotland, the ladies gathered at one end of the room and the men at the other, and there was no more socializing between them than between two nations at war.

The proceedings would open with an elderly "directress" picking a gentleman and lady to perform a minuet, which was done at a walk "with a formality that approaches despondence," said Goldsmith. Five or six couples would go through this same ceremony and then all would get up for country dances. However lively these were, they were performed in strict silence. To talk to your partner at a dance seemed a social sin in Scotland. And Goldsmith was a man who couldn't help talking.

He was, in all, eighteen months in Edinburgh—half the time required to get his medical degree—and then in 1754 took off for Leyden and "the great Albinus." But first he splurged on a new wardrobe which included a sky-blue satin coat, lined with blue shalloon—a closeknit and expensive cloth—and breeches of claret-colored material, all topped off with a cocked hat trimmed with silver lacing. The suit was extravagant for the times and especially so for a medical student. But he needed the bright and expensive clothes to improve his self-image. He was introduced in his new suit to the Duke of Hamilton, whose wife, the former Miss Gunnings of County Roscommon (thought by some to be Goldsmith's natal county), was Irish. He hoped to cut a fine figure, talking of medicine, anatomy, poetry, literature, and so on. But he found the Duke was more interested in him as a kind of jester—a singer of songs and a source of laughter. He dropped the Duke and wrote his uncle that he disdained so servile an employment "unworthy my calling as a physician."

Thinking over his Leyden plans he decided to go to Paris first. He wrote his uncle, "After having spent two winters in Edinburgh I now prepare to go to France the 10th of next February [1754]. I have seen all this country can exhibit in the medical way, and therefore intend to visit Paris, where the great Farhein, Petit and du Hammel de Monceau instruct their pupils in all the branches of medicine. They speak French and consequently I shall have much the advantage of most of my countrymen, as I am perfectly acquainted with that language and few who leave Ireland are so."

Since he had been so frivolous in the past he needed to impress his uncle and himself with the idea that there had been a reformation in his character. He wrote a couple of sentences about the practice of medicine depicting an Oliver Goldsmith who didn't exist, but one he believed existed to the end of his life.

"A quack," he wrote, "unable to distinguish the particularities of each disease, prescribes at a venture: if he find such a disorder may be called by the general name of fever, for instance, he has a set of remedies which he applies to cure it, nor does he desist until his medicines are run out or his patient has lost his life. But the skillful physician distinguishes the symptoms; manures the sterility of nature or prunes her luxuriance; nor does he depend so much on the efficacy of medicines as on their proper allocation."

Off to France then, drawing on his uncle for a final twenty pounds. But first he was arrested and spent a miserable couple of days in debtor's prison. He didn't owe any money himself, but had gone bail for a fellow student who had run off without settling his bills. Two friends, Laughlan Maclean and a Dr. J. F. Sleigh, rescued him. He thanked them and set out cheerfully.

He booked passage on the *St. Andrew,* Captain John Wall commanding, bound for Bordeaux. There were, said the captain, six very agreeable young gentlemen on board who would make the best of company on the voyage.

But the *St. Andrew* was only two days at sea when it ran into such a violent storm that the ship had to put in at Newcastle on Tyne for shelter. Nothing to do about that but to go ashore, rest up from the voyage at a dockside inn, and have some fun with his six agreeable companions. They were all singing and drinking merrily together when a sergeant and twelve grenadiers burst into the room, bayonets screwed on the end of their muskets, and arrested the whole company in the name of the King.

It turned out that Goldsmith's companions were Scotsmen in the French service who had been in Scotland recruiting for the French Army, and it is probable that Captain Wall was the man who tipped the authorities off to this. Goldsmith was put in jail on a charge which carried the death penalty. He was two weeks in jail before he could prove his innocence, but luck was with him on this occasion. The ship sailed while he was in jail and was wrecked with the loss of all aboard off the mouth of the Gironde on the French coast.

Goldsmith now changed his travel plans for reasons he never explained, deciding to skip France and go to Holland. He took a ship bound for Rotterdam, and from there he walked to Leyden in southern Holland and enrolled at the university as a medical student. He put the whole account in a letter to his uncle, written from Leyden. The letter, a long one, is undated.[1]

Holland amazed and delighted him, he wrote. Arriving off the coast, he found he could look down on the land from the ship's deck, for the land lay below sea level and was protected by dykes. The men wore no coat but instead seven waistcoats and nine pairs of breeches so that their hips reached almost to their armpits. As for the women, for every pair of breeches the men wore, they put on two petticoats. The men smoked continuously, which Goldsmith thought gave them their ruddy complexions. The women, in their petticoats, walked as if they were straddling a go-cart. They also carried a pot of lighted coals about with them which they put under their petticoats when they sat down and dozed, comforted by the warmth. The pot of coals was often borrowed for a moment by husband or male companion for the lighting of a pipe. None of the Hollanders were poor, but all decently employed. As soon as the canals froze, the people practically lived on the ice, traveling in horse-drawn sleds or in ice boats driven by the wind and moving as fast as a mile and a half a minute. Everybody whizzed about on skates. On the horse-drawn barges the Dutch slept, the French chattered, and the English played cards.

So Goldsmith wrote his uncle in his first known letter

[1] Some suspect that the whole story is untrue and that he was in debtor's prison all the while. But this is a mere speculation so let us be charitable and assume that all occurred as Goldsmith reported.

Goldsmith. After the portrait by a pupil of Sir Joshua Reynolds. BETTMANN ARCHIVE.

from Leyden. Scholarly men have with ingenuity calculated that Goldsmith arrived in Holland in mid-March, so he could not have seen the ice scenes he described, for the canals at that time are beginning to thaw. Still, he had to tell his uncle something about Holland and it is not unknown for writers to present scenes from guide books as if they had personally experienced them.

At Leyden University, Goldsmith was no more interested in his medical studies than he had been at Edinburgh. He had not a word to say about the great Albinus, who was the pretext for going there, but he did make a friend of a Dr. Gaubius, who taught chemistry. He developed an interest in chemistry and learned how to mix drugs to satisfy the various prescriptions of the day. But this was the work of an apothecary or chemist rather than a doctor. He earned some kind of living as a tutor teaching the Hollanders to speak English. But since he didn't speak Dutch himself, his students were few, for he had to converse with them in Latin or French.

There was only one other Irishman in Leyden, a man named Ellis, whom Goldsmith had met at Edinburgh. Ellis later became clerk of the Irish House of Commons. He sometimes lent Goldsmith money, which Oliver as often as not spent at cards. On one occasion, however, his luck turned and after an evening of play his winnings were so huge he had money bursting from every pocket.

A friend begged him to play no more; to put the money aside and use it to complete his education.

"I will," said Oliver. "I will."

Predictably, he didn't, and a day later he had lost every penny.

Goldsmith stayed a year at Leyden so that in all he had two and a half years of medical studies to his credit. Six months more and he might have had clear title to a medical degree, but unfortunately, at the end of Oliver's first year, Baron Ludvig Holberg died. His name is scarcely known today outside Denmark, but Baron Holberg at the time was reckoned the greatest writer in Europe with the exception only of Voltaire. But what impressed Goldsmith was that Holberg had started life as an impoverished student, had traveled about Europe supporting himself by playing on the violin and the flute, and had gone on to write poetical satires, histories, biographies of great men, books of travel, and finally plays. Goldsmith felt an immediate identity with Holberg. He was fired with the ambition to follow in his footsteps and devised a madcap plan. He would take his flute and a few shillings, quit the dull lecture halls, and study mankind in the university of the world—or at least of Europe.

Without a doubt, he assured himself, he would soon be as famous as his idol and maybe a baron as well. The prospect was glorious and not to be resisted. Fame and Fortune he felt were calling him, and only a coward would hold back. If he needed further persuasion it was provided by his earlier meeting with O'Carolan, who made a fabulous living, though blind, with his harp.

No sooner decided than done. Oliver borrowed a little

money from Ellis, who was unable to dissuade him from his adventure, picked up his flute, rolled some clothes up in a blanket to carry on his back, and set out early in 1755—the month is unknown. By bad luck he passed a flower shop on the outskirts of Leyden, in which he found some tulip bulbs for which Uncle Contarine had been looking for years. He bought a parcel of the bulbs, which were very expensive, and shipped them off to his uncle, thus reducing his grubstake to a few shillings. That was but right, he reasoned, for it was with but a few shillings that his hero Holberg had started out on his journeys.

The first place he headed for was Louvain in Flanders (modern Belgium) and he stopped there long enough, he claimed afterward, to complete his medical studies and become a doctor of medicine. The University of Louvain dated from 1426 but fortunately (or perhaps unfortunately) for Goldsmith the records were burned and there is no way of establishing for certain that he was even registered as a student. He was always called Dr. Goldsmith in later life. Nobody challenged the title and there were enough people who did not like him to issue such a challenge if there had been sufficient grounds.

Of the year of travel through Europe which followed, perhaps the most fascinating year in his life, nothing is known for certain. All has to be reconstructed out of chance sayings, guess-work, and passages in his articles and books relating to incidents in Europe which, he told his friends later, described actual happenings.

Samuel Johnson complained that he never could get the story of Goldsmith's European tour straight. Neither could anyone else. He wrote letters to his friends in Ireland—to his rich brother-in-law Daniel Hodson, to his sister, to his cousin, the daughter of the trusting Uncle Contarine, who was now married to a certain Mr. Lawder, first name unknown. But they have all been lost. What follows then is what is generally accepted, though plainly far less than what actually happened.

In Flanders, Goldsmith found he could always get a bed and a meal by playing at a peasant's house—the poorer the better, for the poor were more generous than the wealthy. On then to Paris, where, since he could speak French, he seems to have been engaged for a while as a traveling companion to a young man out to see the curiosities of the city. The young gentleman proved, however, to be a miser. He would go to any museum that was free but invariably asserted that those that charged money were not worth seeing, and Goldsmith soon parted with him, according to the story. He went to the university, attended some lectures on chemistry in which he was now interested, noted the abundance of fat game in the approaches to the city while the peasants went hungry and in rags, and concluded from this that they lived under a tyranny which wouldn't last long.

In Paris, Goldsmith claimed to have met and talked with Voltaire, whom he adored. But Voltaire was at the time in Switzerland. This didn't stop Goldsmith from relating how Voltaire, hearing the English attacked by Fontenelle, had for three hours defended them brilliantly as a noble, generous, and freedom-loving race, silencing all opposition.

From France, after traveling for a time along the Loire, playing his flute for a living, he went into Germany and Switzerland, then down into Italy. All the time he was collecting material about customs and peoples which he would use later in his poem *The Traveller*.

In Italy he seemingly suffered more than in any other country. Everybody sang or played a musical instrument so that his flute was useless to him. But he found that there was a custom at the universities in different towns which permitted strangers to debate subjects of interest, and if they did well, they were given lodging for the night and meals for a day. So he debated before students and faculty in Florence and Verona, Mantua, Milan, and Padua. Where universities and places of learning failed him, he turned to monasteries whose friars gave him a meal or a place to sleep. His clothing was soon in tatters, his shoes worn out, his stockings filthy and full of holes. He went from house to house, still undaunted, begging for clothes as well as food. He froze in the Alps, flushed woodcock for a meal, trapped rabbits, brought down hares with stones, and remained convinced to the end that at the next town, or over the next mountain, his fortunes would change and all his hardships be forgotten.

While he was in Padua he learned that Uncle Contarine had become senile. He had often written witty and interesting letters to his uncle during the course of which he intimated that he could use some money.

He was now in a quandary. He wanted to write his cousin Jane (Mrs. Lawder) a letter of sympathy on her father's condition but he was afraid that any letter from him might be misread as an appeal for help. His pride was such that he did not write at all, and she and her husband were deeply hurt and became cold toward him. On their part they decided that as soon as her father had become mentally incompetent, Goldsmith had stopped writing, so he was no real friend but had merely used the family. Try as he might in later years, he could not repair that breach and lost for life the friendship of a woman who had been very close to him. Not even when he became famous would Jane or her husband unbend, despite all his efforts.

He remained in Padua for weeks, for he was expecting a remittance in the form of a letter of credit from his brother-in-law, Daniel Hodson. It never came. Hodson had collected some money and sent it, but this Goldsmith found out only many years later. To fill in time, he did some more medical studying at Padua, and used to claim that he had been issued a medical degree there also.

Had Hodson's remittance arrived, Goldsmith intended to return to Ireland and set up in practice. When it didn't, he decided to go to England instead and see what kind of living he could make for himself there. The non-arrival of the letter of credit was, therefore, a turning point in his life.

He did not want to turn up in Ireland penniless and in rags again. He could not bear being thought a failure once more. He'd chance his hand in England.

The second winter of his travels loomed and Goldsmith, hungry, destitute, and in tatters, headed for Calais and London. He traveled in sleet, snow, rain, frost, and wind across the Alps and across France and arrived in Calais with just enough to pay his fare as a deck passenger to Dover. There was talk in France of war with England and he arrived in Dover February 1, 1756, just as that war was breaking out.

He was, of course, penniless.

CHAPTER

ENGLAND WAS POSSIBLY THE WORST COUNTRY IN EUROPE for Goldsmith to visit in the mid-1750s. He could claim to be a doctor and practice medicine—at least by the standards of his day. But a ragged and penniless doctor would never attract any patients except among the very poor, who, of course, would not be able to pay anything. He had not a friend in the whole of England. There were no monasteries with hospitable friars who would give him a meal and a night's lodging. Englishmen did not patronize itinerant musicians, whom they regarded as mere beggars. On top of it all he spoke with a thick Irish accent, and the whole of England was anti-Irish, the Irish being disdained as Papists, beggars, and rebels. Each one of those charges was largely true.

So Oliver made the miserable rounds of all the apothecaries he could find in London, begging for work mixing plasters, pounding mortars, and delivering medicines. Most wouldn't even look at him in his rags with his unpopular accent, and how he survived the first few weeks in the city is a mystery. He later made one reference to this period at a fashionable dinner in the exquisite dining room of Sir Joshua Reynolds, mentioning that he had at one time lived among the beggars of Axe Lane. The company was shocked for Axe Lane was the Skid Row of eighteenth-century London.

At last a man called Jacob, who had a shop on the corner of Monument Yard and Fish Street, listened to him long enough to discover that Goldsmith really did know something about chemistry. He gave him a second-hand suit of clothes and a job as an assistant with a small salary. Goldsmith rented a room at three shillings a week, which was pure luxury after sleeping in doorways and abandoned, rat-filled cellars, and was able to get one lukewarm dinner a day, mostly of mouldy potatoes, from a local cookshop.

London was twenty times the size of Edinburgh or Dublin. At the turn of the century its population was put at 750,000 and by the 1750s it was nearly a million. It was overcrowded, prosperous, and growing. By the middle of the century a thousand new buildings a year were being erected—ugly things of brick and stone with flat roofs of slate tiles and mostly jerry-built. Many of the older buildings dated from the Great Fire of 1666, and there were thousands of houses in narrow alleys which were much older than that. These were crumbling into ruin. A ladder put up against a wall brought down a shower of plaster, mortar, and sometimes loose bricks. Walls were black with the soot that poured out of a hundred thousand chimneys, and over the city, even in midsummer, a pall of smoke obscured the sun at midday.

The chemical action of this sulphurous smoke, wetted by frequent rains, loosened the mortar. The heavy rumble of coaches and drays over the cobbled streets often sent bricks and tiles tumbling down. Sometimes a whole section of a wall fell, sometimes a building collapsed. But there were no building codes or building inspectors; no one to pull down structures which were unsafe though still occupied.

The street noise in the center of the city during the day was murderous. It was compounded of the thundering of iron-rimmed wheels over cobbles, the shouting of coachmen, porters, and chairmen, the incessant cracking of whips, the cries of hawkers, and the heavy clumping of horses' hooves. The stench was appalling. Downwind, London could be smelled from three miles away in the country. Gutters ran down the center of each street and into the gutters went all the filth of the town including (as usual) urine from chamberpots emptied out of windows. There was nothing remarkable about this—nothing with which to fault London particularly—for this was the general method of disposal in European cities. The difference lay in the fact that London was so big that there were hundreds of thousands of chamberpots. Swarms of flies buzzed everywhere in the summertime. The droppings of hordes of horses were daily ground into the cobbles, their piss streaming into the noisome central gutter in which, on quieter streets, little children played. There was no organized street cleaning.

There were no public toilets. The poor relieved themselves against any convenient wall, the women squatting in some corner. A hundred thousand outhouses served private residences, though the water closet, an English invention, dated from 1596. Dungmen, who were private contractors, cleaned the cesspits and buckets by night, emptying the contents onto a gleaming bank on the north shore of the Thames by Blackfriars. This mountain of excrement was collected in barges and ferried over to the south bank to manure the vegetable gardens there. (Almost every city in Europe had vegetable gardens in the suburbs fertilized from the same source. The vegetables were excellent.)

A serious sanitary problem lay in the fact that London got its water not only from the highly polluted Thames but also from hundreds of springs dug into the chalky subsoil. These springs were themselves polluted both from outhouses and graveyards. Wealthy Londoners bought water from street vendors who claimed to get their supplies from country sources. But often the water they sold was the same old polluted London water. Because of the pollution problem, water as a drink was distrusted. It was made safe by boiling it for tea or coffee but many drank wine to quench their thirst. This accounts in part for the heavy wine consumption at that time.

The Thames was both the city's only major sewer and its principal highway. Into it eventually flowed all the filth of the streets and houses. There were rows of tanneries on the south bank, which stained the water with dyes, and when hospitals were built they were put close to the river if possible for convenience in getting rid of amputated limbs. The river was mercifully scoured twice every twenty-four hours by the tide; otherwise it would have become the foulest waterway in all Europe.

It was crowded with boats and ships, some under sail, some anchored in midstream, some ferrying cargoes ashore to be lodged in warehouses or taken off in drays. The bodies of convicted pirates still swung, sundried, from the gallows at Deptford and the heads of traitors mouldered on pikes on London Bridge.

For all this the river was still a popular thoroughfare. Shooting the rapids between the arches of London Bridge was a popular sport. Ladies and gentlemen went on boating picnics, sometimes followed by another boat full of musicians. It was pleasanter to go from place to place by boat than through the crowded and noisy streets, where it was not uncommon to be pitched out of a sedan chair by angry Irish chairmen, or thrown out of a coach when a wheel broke suddenly.

Houses were not yet numbered but were recognized by signs hung outside. There were scores of Blue Boars, Red Lions, and Deer Heads, and Black Swans. More imaginative were such signs as the Dog and Gridiron, the Fox and Seven Stars, the Hog in Armor, and the Lamb and Dolphin. Taverns were identified not necessarily by a sign but by a bunch of ivy leaves hung over the door. Coffeehouses were known by the name of the owner—Will's, Black's, and so on. Admission was a penny and a cup of coffee cost twopence, which was also the price of a cup of tea. They were the meeting places of the town, where men could exchange news, play cards, and read the newspapers, collect their mail, or just be seen.

The city had its enchanting side too. There were innumerable "Gardens" such as Vauxhall and Rawleigh and Marylebone, with beautiful walks, pagodas, elegant public buildings in which to parade, orchestras, firework displays, restaurants, and so forth. A great number of squares were being laid out, architect-designed, by noblemen with an eye to making a fortune in real estate. Grosvenor Square, Russell Square, Bedford Square, Hanover Square, Berkeley Square—they were all high-priced real estate developments with a central garden of trees and grass and fashionable—indeed, beautiful—houses surrounding it. Inside the wealthier houses all (with the exception of the servants' quarters) was elegance which has perhaps never since been matched. Adams fireplaces, Chippendale furniture, Turkish and Wilton carpets, Chinese screens, mirrors and glass from Venice, pictures and statuary from Italy, and magnificently bound books—these were the furnishings.

The shops that bordered the fashionable streets were a delight. They were not our block-long plateglass-window emporiums, but each only the width of a somewhat narrow house, the fronts always newly painted and gilded, the steps scrubbed gleaming white and all the brasswork shining like gold. In the small windows were the treasures of the world—delicate china and crystal ware, silverware, gloves, lace, hats, and fabulous watches and clocks, snuffboxes, walking sticks, dress swords, silk hose, and gowns. Some specialized in candlesticks, some in saddles, some in riding boots, some in chinaware. Many days of delight could be spent in just window shopping though the crowded conditions of the streets—there were no sidewalks—made the pastime somewhat perilous. The tradesmen lived above their shops and were often as wealthy as their patrons. Some became rich enough to have country houses in which to spend a weekend, away from the London clamor.

The country was not far to reach. The city had expanded along the Thames so that by Goldsmith's time London from the Tower to Tyburn was about four miles long. However, a mile or a mile and a half walk north away from the river brought one into the open country, and enough of the country remained for farm girls to sell milk, cheeses, and eggs through

The new Tower Bridge across the Thames. BETTMANN ARCHIVE.

the streets. It was also possible to get a glass of milk straight from the cow in St. James's Park.

In this noisy, stinking, overcrowded and yet elegant city, Goldsmith ran about, delivering medicines, or rolling pills in the back of the apothecary's shop. Jacob (his first name is unknown) took a liking to him. When he had been some weeks in London, Goldsmith got lucky. On one of his trips delivering medicines, he discovered that a certain Dr. Sleigh was living in a nearby house.

Sleigh? That couldn't possibly be Dr. J. F. Sleigh, his old friend from Edinburgh who had rescued him from debtor's prison? It certainly was. On the following Sunday, when he didn't have to work, Goldsmith washed and dressed with special care, putting on all the least dirty and least patched items of second-hand clothing he had in his wardrobe. Satisfied that he would pass muster, he called on his college friend.

Sleigh opened the door and didn't recognize the ragged, haunted figure that stood smiling before him.

"I'm sorry, sir," he said, "but I do not recall having had the pleasure of your acquaintance."

"But my dear Dr. Sleigh," said Oliver, "I am your old friend Goldsmith."

"Good heavens," said Sleigh, "whatever has become of you?" He pulled him in and shut the door.

"Why, I am a citizen of the world now," said Goldsmith, "and I have, to cap it all, my doctor's degree. My present circumstances are, I admit, straitened, but it is all only temporary. I am working as an assistant to a noted apothecary—one of the best known in the city—as a preparation to setting up in the practice of medicine on my own. It is, of course, necessary to become acquainted with the town at first and gradually build up a prospective clientele."

Sleigh was not taken in. He was a Quaker and a fine example of that brotherhood whom Voltaire admired. He lent Goldsmith what money he could. With this and what he could squeeze out of his own wages, Oliver bought himself a much better second-hand suit of clothes, of trimmed black velvet. To be sure, the nap of the velvet had worn away in several places in the front and these were covered by a large patch which did not match the coat. With this suit went a hat, a cane, and a wig. The hat was most important. Goldsmith used it to hold over the patch in front of his coat in a pose which was both practical and elegant.

With his second-hand suit and a little spare cash he now started practicing as a doctor.

But he had no office.

The miserable room, rented for three shillings a week, was too small for anything but the pallet bed on which he slept. His clothes he hung on nails in the wall, for there was no cupboard. He therefore had to consult with his patients in the street or visit them in their own squalid homes. Few could pay him anything at all. In any case, he was so tender-hearted he couldn't ask them for anything. He knew they could scarcely afford the drugs he prescribed. Mostly they were suffering from starvation, exposure, and filth. He was largely a doctor to the dying, to those whom no other physician would attend. He did his best but his best was little more than sympathy and encouragement.

One day he was asked to call on a printer's workman who was complaining of stomach trouble. Goldsmith went to the man's miserable lodgings, took the patient's pulse, stared into his eyes, asked to see his tongue, all the while holding his hat over the front of his coat to cover the patch.

"Sir," said the workman, "would you not be more comfortable if you put down your hat?"

"Do not trouble yourself about it," said Goldsmith. "It is a mannerism of mine to hold it in this position."

The examination went on, the hat still held over the patch. At last the workman, who had been examining the worn velvet suit, guessed the purpose of Goldsmith's hat and said he did not wish to intrude but he knew of many clever and highly educated men who had been reduced to poverty in London. He worked for Mr. Samuel Richardson, the well known novelist, and Mr. Richardson was a very charitable man, who had often helped others in distress. Only recently he had rescued the great Samuel Johnson, author of the famous dictionary, from the sponging house. (A sponging house was the last stop before jail, a place where a debtor was held for a day or two to raise money from friends before being sent to prison.) If there was any need, he was sure Mr. Richardson would help the doctor and he would be very glad, as payment of his fee, to get an introduction to Mr. Richardson for Dr. Goldsmith.

For a moment Goldsmith hesitated, for his pride was involved. But when he saw how he could do nothing but starve to death, practicing medicine among the penniless, and realized that he must find some other work, he thanked the man and said he would be very glad of an introduction to Mr. Richardson.

So a few days later, Goldsmith called on Richardson, one of the most famous novelists in England at the time, who was also a bookseller (booksellers were also all book publishers). Richardson, an intense, small, plump man, as nervous as a wet sparrow, was a great writer of letters and at the age of thirteen had earned money by writing love letters for ladies who were incapable of the task themselves.

His letter writing had led to his first novel.

He had been persuaded to write a series of model letters dealing with personal and intimate problems which could be used as a guide for people who didn't know how to handle such things.

Richardson hit on the idea of writing the letters in the form of a romance entitled *Pamela: or Virtue Rewarded.* He was a fast writer and completed the novel in two months. It was an immediate best seller, and praised by some surprising people. Alexander Pope, for instance, thought it excellent. The novel was recommended from the pulpit and, at Slough, where the heroine in the end gets her just reward, the church bells were rung for hours out of sheer delight.

The novel, in short, became must reading for anybody of taste. The plot was utterly tedious, an eighteenth century soap opera, and the sentimentality is beyond the stomach of most present-day readers. But the eighteenth century, bathed in cruelty and callousness in everyday life, for relief turned hungrily to sentiment and even bathos in its literature. Edition after edition appeared and the delighted Richardson followed *Pamela* up with *Clarissa, or the Adventures of a Young Lady,* which was equally successful. Again the story was told in the form of letters; a novel in seven volumes in which the fair heroine is seduced by her wicked lover, who plies her with drugs to get her into bed. The story plunges on from misfortune to misfortune until eventually the heroine is exonerated and all ends well.

Johnson said of Richardson's novels that anyone reading them for the plot would soon hang himself from sheer frustration. They were to be read for the sentiment only.

To be fair, despite the soap-opera plots, Richardson managed to dig pretty deeply into the ego of his heroines, and Sir Walter Scott said of them that no one before had ventured so far into the human heart—Scott had forgotten about Shakespeare. The books, however, hold a place in English literature, marking a turning point from paper-thin heroines to characters in the round, though there was a reaction against their pious moralizing with the writing of such books as *Tom Jones* and *Tristram Shandy*.

At the time Goldsmith called on him, Richardson was sixty-seven, and his two triumphs twenty years old or so. But he was still living in a welter of praise for writing them and maintained a heavy correspondence with readers (mostly women) who wrote him from all parts of the country asking his advice on their problems. He loved praise and flattery and had got to the point where he could not live without them.

Despite that, he was a kind and generous man, and he hired Oliver to read manuscripts and correct proofs. He gave him a reasonable salary and often invited him to dinner at his fine London house, where Goldsmith met other writers. Yet he did not stay with Richardson long, and it is difficult to find out why he left. Possibly his own literary ambitions and Richardson's love of flattery provided the reason. Goldsmith started to write a play, and when it was still incomplete he was tactless enough to ask Richardson to read it. There is a suspicion that the play was a thinly disguised version of *Pamela* or *Clarissa* prepared for the stage, and that is not improbable. Whatever the facts, Richardson never read the play and maybe this was enough to anger Goldsmith to the point where he quit the job.

Before quitting he miraculously saved some money and bought himself a second-hand suit of clothes without a patch on the coat. The suit was of green cloth, trimmed with tarnished gold braid, and in it he called on another fellow student from Edinburgh named Farr who he found was also living in London.

Goldsmith had a copy of his incomplete play stuffed in his pockets and wanted Farr to listen to it. But Farr didn't want to hear the play and ducked by saying his opinion would not be worth having as he knew nothing of the theater. A little put out but still eager to impress his friend, Goldsmith said that he was soon to go to Syria to attempt the translation of the inscriptions on the Written Mountain at Wadi Mekatebb and Jebal Serbal. These were an eighteenth-century wonder, and someone had guaranteed a salary of three hundred pounds a year to whoever would attempt the translation.

"But you don't know a word of Arabic," protested Farr.

"Pooh," said Goldsmith. "There was a time when I didn't know a word of Latin or Greek, French or Dutch. I have a gift for languages and Arabic will not defeat me." But he was merely boasting. He never went to Syria to translate the curious inscriptions on the rocks, written from right to left, and extending over a distance of nine miles. When Goldsmith was feeling the need for a boost, he supplied it himself with this kind of fantasy, and, Farr having said he did not want to hear his play, he had to do something to bolster his ego on the moment.

Instead of going to Syria, Goldsmith went to Peckham as an usher or assistant schoolmaster at the Academy for Non-Conformists established by a Dr. Milner, of whom little is known. Milner was the father of one of Goldsmith's Edinburgh friends and that is how he made the contact. Edinburgh may not have given Goldsmith his medical degree but it gave him a lot of friends at the right moment—far more than he had made at Trinity in Dublin.

The Peckham position was a foolish one for Goldsmith, sensitive as he was, to take. He cut an awkward and laughable figure in his second-hand suit, which didn't fit him, capped by a wig which didn't fit either and kept sliding off his head. He was ridiculed by the students, which was something he should have expected but apparently didn't, for he always had a secret belief that, despite his appearance, his true worth would be recognized.

He suffered agonies of embarassment at the school; yet, despite the mocking and the teasing, he spent a great deal of his small salary buying treats for his students—not with a desire to bribe them, but out of genuine good-heartedness. Also whenever a beggar called at the school, Goldsmith, well trained by his father, was sure to give him something, so that he was always short of cash and Mrs. Milner suggested that she handle his money for him, as she handled the money of many of the students. Goldsmith thought it would be a good idea; that he stood in need of that service. But he continued to buy sweets for the boys and give pennies to beggars, to whose stories he always listened, knowing that beggars have need of companionship as well as cash.

His time at Peckham was not entirely miserable, though he later tended to remember the miserable rather than the good parts. He remembered, for instance, his mortification when, on teaching flute to a class, he said that the ability to play music was a necessary accomplishment of any gentleman.

"Surely you don't think of yourself as a gentleman, do you?" asked one of the pupils to shouts of laughter. He caned the boy, then bought him some candy and tried to forget that in the eyes of the whole student body, he had no dignity at all.

Among the servants of the school was a man called Williams who seemed to have a need of drawing attention to himself not unlike Goldsmith's own need. Williams was constantly challenging people to eat or drink something revolting—a handful of worms collected wriggling in the garden, or a foul bowl of kitchen slops.

Goldsmith decided to cure him.

"Williams," he said one day, "here's a dare for you. I'll eat this candle down to the nub if you will eat the other one." He picked a candle off the mantelpiece, took a big bite, chewed and swallowed it and went on until the whole candle was gone.

Williams stared in amazement. When Goldsmith had done, to save face, he opened his mouth and swallowed the other candle with one gulp.

"Why did you chew yours?" he asked. "It's quicker to get it down in one swallow."

"Oh, I enjoyed mine," said Goldsmith. "You see, it wasn't a real candle at all. I made it myself of Cheshire cheese." Everybody roared and Williams took the lesson to heart and cut down on the number of dares he issued each day.

At Peckham, Goldsmith had another burden to bear, beyond the mockery of the boys. The school boasted a French master who was something of a dandy. He shared Goldsmith's room, and would spend an hour before going to bed dressing his hair with rancid pomatum. All night long Goldsmith had to endure the smell of the stuff.

So the days dragged by. Milner became impressed with Goldsmith's learning and his travels despite the ludicrous figure he cut. Goldsmith had a surprising knowledge of ancient and modern literature, for he read every book he could lay hands upon. He talked of French and English novels and plays with deep insight and intelligence. The two had many discussions of poetry and plays and essays and novels and Milner mentioned that he sometimes wrote an article for a highly successful London bookseller and publisher, Ralph Griffiths.

"No reason why you can't do the same," he said. "You certainly can't spend the rest of your life as an usher at this or any other school."

Griffiths came down from London one day to talk with Milner, who saw to it that Goldsmith was present at the dinner which followed.

Now Griffiths was the publisher of a magazine called *The Monthly Review* to which Milner contributed pieces. But another publisher, Archibald Hamilton, had started in March, 1756, a rival publication called *The Critical Review* and it was giving the *Monthly* very severe competition. The editor of the new *Critical* was the popular Scottish novelist Tobias George Smollett, and there were some curious, though superficial, parallels between the careers of Smollett and Goldsmith. Both, for instance, were doctors—or claimed to be—

and Smollett had been a surgeon in the Royal Navy. Both had traveled about Europe on foot and in poverty. Both were widely read and highly educated.

Griffiths probed Goldsmith with questions about his travels and education and concluded the evening by asking him whether he would care to produce a few pieces of literary criticism for him to look at.

That was very easy for Goldsmith, who finished them in short order. He wrote almost as readily as he breathed. Griffiths liked the articles and offered him in 1757 an excellent job—board and room and a small salary (the amount is uncertain) in return for writing for *The Monthly Review*. Goldsmith accepted and left Peckham to start his career as a writer.

He'd been forced into it, having failed in all else.

CHAPTER VI

RALPH GRIFFITHS WAS TEMPERAMENTALLY THE PRECISE opposite of his newly hired hack, Oliver Goldsmith. He was a shrewd, tight-fisted businessman, his head entirely occupied with accounts and profits. His appreciation of any piece of writing was measured in pounds and shillings (without which, of course, a publisher will not long survive), and he would alter anybody's work to put it in the form which he thought was most marketable. He regarded himself as a foremost authority on what that form should be.

In this he was joined by his wife, a formidable egoist who believed her literary ability the equal of any author's in the world. She was a big, heavy-set, somewhat masculine woman who insisted on wearing "a neat and elevated wire-winged cap."

Griffiths was a Welshman who had set up in Staffordshire as a watchmaker. Once a member of the Presbyterian Church he had quit watchmaking, come to London with a little capital, and set up as a publisher. It wasn't so risky a venture for there was then, as there is now, a plentiful supply of material from unknown and unestablished authors. From this flood of manuscripts, a shrewd man could choose material that was likely to sell, buy it for a pittance, and make a profit. This is precisely what Griffiths did, and there is nothing villainous about it for the method is used to this day and how else is an unknown writer to get published?

One of Griffiths' great finds (in fact his greatest), made

eight or ten years before his meeting with Goldsmith, was a manuscript by a half-starved writer named John Cleland. Cleland had written a book called *Fanny Hill—The Memoirs of a Woman of Pleasure*. It is the most elegant account in English literature of an utterly free sexual life, related in rich but delicate prose by Fanny, who comes as a young girl to London looking for work as a domestic and is soon in a genteel brothel undergoing her apprenticeship in prostitution.

Fanny likes being a prostitute and makes no bones about it. Nothing gives her greater pleasure than the sight of an erection, and she describes in detail the excitement and pleasures of intercourse in noble prose and without one coarse word. But she had lost her heart to a young man, Charles, to whom she had also surrendered her virginity, and after a great variety of thoroughly enjoyable sexual bouts and orgies, she is reunited with Charles whom she still loves and presumably lives happily and virtuously with ever after.

Cleland probably wrote *Fanny Hill* as a sort of antidote to Samuel Richardson's *Pamela* and *Clarissa* (is it possible that it is from Cleland's title that we developed the noun *fanny*?). Richardson extolled virtue, by which he really meant chastity, which in the end must have its reward, however sullied by a wicked world. Cleland writes of the delights of promiscuity but he has a theme too, for Fanny comes to realize that sexual pleasure, for all its delight, is not fulfilling unless love goes with it. In a sense he is a moralist also. True love is true fulfillment—though he doesn't berate sex for the sake of sex.

Griffiths bought Cleland's book for twenty guineas, which wasn't a bad price and was indeed generous in Griffiths' scale. In his lifetime he is said to have been made ten thousand pounds out of it. The book paved his way to become a "respectable" publisher though it is difficult to find out precisely how he brought out *Fanny Hill* and escaped being sentenced to the pillory or the stocks. (Another publisher who brought out a pirated edition did go to the pillory.) With the money from Cleland's novel he brought out his successful *Monthly Review* and he used *The Monthly Review* to praise a watered-down version of *Fanny Hill* which he brought out more publicly later, so that, as it were, his clean hand washed his dirty hand.

Fanny Hill through the centuries went through scores of editions (sold under the counter), and it is only recently that it has been openly published and sold in the United States. Griffiths' profits were such that he soon owned two coaches and built himself a fine house on the outskirts of London near Turnham Green (it was typical of Griffiths that he chose for his house an area which was really a dismal swamp but where land was cheap). He gave lavish dinner parties, collected a great store of tales of authors and books with which to entertain his guests, and died respected and prosperous.

Cleland, a writer of talent, was an expert on philology rather than pornography—indeed, it is a big mistake to think of *Fanny Hill* as a pornographic novel. He wrote treatises and books pleading for the development of a universal language. He was given a government pension of a hundred pounds a year to encourage him not to write any more *Fanny Hills,* lived to be almost eighty, and died utterly forgotten and quite poor in Westminster.

This then was the man (and his wife) for whom Goldsmith went to work on Grub Street—the fictitious abode of struggling writers, though there was an actual Grub Street in the poorer part of London. He believed he was following in the footsteps of Dryden and Otway, but does not seem to have reflected that Dryden lived and died in poverty and that Otway (Thomas Otway the dramatist), starving, got hold of a piece of bread, stuffed it into his mouth and strangled in trying to swallow it.

Griffiths and Goldsmith soon fell out.

Goldsmith found he was expected to be at his desk at nine in the morning and write without a break until two in the afternoon. Sometimes he had to write all day. He had to write on subjects which Griffiths or his wife picked for him, and he had to work at times with Mrs. Griffiths peering over his shoulder to see how he was coming along. Whatever he wrote was sure to be revised by one or the other of them, his best paragraphs mutilated, and often his viewpoint ignored in order to substitute that of Mrs. Griffiths.

Goldsmith could never last under such conditions. He couldn't write by the hour. He couldn't sit for a stipulated period at his desk. He couldn't tolerate everything he wrote being interfered with. He was humiliated by the snide remarks of Mrs. Griffiths at mealtimes that he was eating more than he was producing. He found no dignity in his position. Indeed, he was looked upon as a somewhat inferior servant. His salary was sometimes late in being paid and even then handed over with reluctance. In short, with one of the most talented writers of the times on their staff, the Griffiths did everything possible to break his spirit and ruin his work.

In his free time, Goldsmith met other writers and grumbled at what was being done to his copy. Smollett, editing *The Critical Review,* heard how he was being treated. Maybe Goldsmith told him. Griffiths unwisely decided to attack *The Critical Review* and wrote a piece hinting that it was written by "Physicians without practice, selected authors without learning, men without decency, gentlemen without manners, and critics without judgment." Smollett replied to the effect that Griffiths' paper was produced by "a parcel of obscure hirelings, under the restraint of a bookseller and his wife, who presume to revise, alter, and amend the articles occasionally." His own staff, he said, were unconnected with booksellers, unawed by old women, and independent of each other.

This kind of quarrelling was the practice of the day. Weeklies and monthlies appeared and disappeared like mushrooms, spawning their little puffs of town gossip, comment and recrimination, and then vanishing forever. They produced a laugh or two in a coffeehouse or a tavern, but that didn't help to keep the publications alive.

For five months Goldsmith drudged on. He reviewed a translation of the *Edda*, a collection of Norse mythology by a Professor Mallet of Copenhagen, remarking that, "The learned on this side of the Alps have long labored at the antiquities of Rome and have almost totally neglected their own; like conquerors who, while they have made inroads into the territories of their neighbors, have left their own natural dominions to desolation."

Mrs. Griffiths let that go by.

He reviewed plays and pseudo-epic poems and even a history of England in four volumes by Smollett, saying of it that "it is impossible for a reader of taste not to be pleased with the perspicuity and elegance of his manner." (Smollett and Goldsmith admired each other's work.)

This was all hack writing—writing in the polished, prissy, "elevated" style of the day. In part, Griffiths demanded it of him, and in part Goldsmith believed that this was the way to write for publication, and indeed even in private correspondence.

One adopted an attitude of elegance and learning, wrote English as if it were Latin, aimed for a slight smile rather than a loud laugh, and always preserved, though clothed in rags and unbathed for a month, the manners of a gentleman. Smollett, Sterne, and Fielding were pioneers in destroying this brittle container into which all writing had to be poured. It was only later that Goldsmith learned to throw the pretenses out and write in a way that was natural to him.

One of the books Goldsmith reviewed was a volume of travel by Jonas Hanway. Hanway was very good at writing of foreign travels and very poor at writing of journeys in England so that Johnson said of him that he acquired a reputation by traveling abroad but lost it by traveling at home.

He is most noted, however, for securing for Englishmen the liberty to carry an umbrella, a privilege which received a severe setback under Neville Chamberlain. Umbrellas at the time were respectable for women, and men might carry them in wintertime. But to be seen with one on a summer's day brought down the scorn and taunts of carters, porters, chairmen, and all the vagabonds of the London streets. Drivers of hackneys often tried to run down a man who carried an umbrella out of season. Hanway insisted on carrying an umbrella whenever he wanted to, endured the ridicule, assaults, and threats and eventually made the umbrella so respectable that there came a time when an Englishman was not reckoned properly attired unless he was carrying one. Not, however, while wearing pajamas.

Hanway did other things as well, for he was a man with a social conscience. He tried to reform the treatment of prisoners and abolish the exploitation of children as chimney sweeps. Many of these children were blinded or suffocated in chimneys, lost their way, became terrified in the darkness, and were smoked out by a fire lighted in the grate below.

They were covered with sores, their lungs were soon as black as the chimneys they swept, and most of them died young and in misery. But London hung on sentimentally to its child chimney sweeps for fifty years or more, ignoring the appalling cruelty of the job. It taught the little boys manliness, while helping them earn a living. That was a popular view.

Reviewing a volume of odes by Gray, Goldsmith gently warned the poet not to waste his talent writing for the learned few, with their affected emotions, but to study the people. It was, of course, exactly what he needed to do himself, which is not to be wondered at, for the advice we need for ourselves, we first of all give to others.

Eventually, matters came to a head. Griffiths, probably egged on by his wife, said Goldsmith was lazy and too independent, leaving his desk before his day's work was done. The charge was undoubtedly true.

Goldsmith said in return that he had had enough of Griffiths' impertinence and his wife's niggardliness. So they parted and Goldsmith started his struggle as a free-lance writer in a city teeming with free-lance writers.

He gave his address as the Temple Exchange Coffee House, near Temple Bar (it was common, as already noted, for writers to use coffeehouses as places to receive mail), and rented a garret near Salisbury Court, a few blocks away. It is possible that it was at the coffeehouse that Goldsmith first ran into Johnson, though they would be mere acquaintances at that time.

Before leaving the Griffiths, Goldsmith had written a cheerful letter to his brother Henry in Ireland, saying he was a staff writer on the important *Monthly Review*, that his articles were widely read and commented on, that he was now a literary figure and acquainted with many of the great men of the city. As a result of these letters there was a knock at the door one day and in came his youngest brother Charles. Charles had got tired of hanging around in Ballymahon and doing nothing, so he had decided to visit his famous brother in London and start on a career himself.

He soon learned the truth of the matter, stayed a day or two, and then left, returning to Ireland and migrating years later to Jamaica.

As the year 1757 dragged to its close, Goldsmith sank deeper and deeper into poverty. Utterly depressed, he once decided to burn all his manuscripts, but reflected that whether he did or not, nobody would know and nobody would care. So he kept them. Eventually, without anything to eat and no money to pay the rent of his garret, he dragged himself back to Peckham and asked Dr. Milner for his old position as usher.

Milner was now the only friend he had. He was sick and glad to take Goldsmith back. Milner felt sorry for him, and told him he had a friend in the East India Company. Since Goldsmith was a physician Milner said he would ask his friend to see if he could get him an appointment as a doctor at one of the company's factories in the East Indies.

He would have to pay for his passage, of course, and ten pounds for the appointment, and there would be other incidentals to take care of. But if the appointment came through, Goldsmith could become what he always wanted to become —a doctor with a practice worth perhaps a thousand pounds a year.

Purely to raise the needed money, Goldsmith started work on a book. It was to be called *An Enquiry into the Present*

State of Polite Learning in Europe. He had all the material he needed from his travels and his visits to many European universities. He intended a survey of philosophy, literature, poetry and plays, of education and universities, criticism, and the rewards of the writer and thinker, and what was being done about all this. He settled down to write in his leisure time, and then either because Milner died or because Goldsmith couldn't stand the ridicule of the students any longer (or their tears when he was required to flog them) he quit again and in August of 1758 went once more to London.

He had a grubstake of sorts from the money saved out of his tiny salary. He believed he could find a publisher for his book, which was almost finished. He believed also he would soon be on his way to India, where he would have a spendid carriage and fabulous clothes and establish himself as a brilliant physician and surgeon.

He was dreaming again, of course, and his dream dissolved gradually.

In London, the small amount of money he had saved was soon gone. His book remained unpublished though Robert Dodsley was interested in it, said he would bring it out, but wanted more work done. He gave Goldsmith, it would seem, no advance.

There was nothing to be done but start seeking a magazine market for his work again. He went to Archibald Hamilton—the publisher of *The Critical Review* mentioned earlier—and asked for an assignment. Hamilton gave him a little advance and assigned him to write three full-page articles on the Roman poet, Ovid. Goldsmith loved Ovid, soon wrote the articles, and got the money. It was little enough but it enabled him to move from whatever unknown hovel he had been living in, into what were for him better quarters.

This was perhaps the worst period in Goldsmith's life in London—the time when he hit bottom and came close to despair. His mood fluctuated, often within the hour, between cheerfulness and hopeless melancholy. He wrote to Bob Bryanton in August, 1758, just after returning to London from

Peckham; and his letter is a mixture of nostalgia and bravado but ends with the cry, "O Gods! Gods! here in a garret writing for bread and expecting to be dunned for a milk score [bill]." His supper at these times, and often his only meal of the day, was a bowl of boiled milk. He had only two projects to give him hope. The first and brightest was the post of doctor with the East India Company, for which he had scraped together the ten-pound deposit required though he had still to produce his passage money, his chest of clothes, and his medicines to go with the appointment. The second, on which the first depended, was the publication of his book *Polite Learning*, which he was still revising though he was now so poor that he had to water down his ink to save the expense of buying more.

Books published in England were often reprinted in Ireland without any payment to the author or the English publisher. Because he needed for his East India appointment every penny he could get out of *Polite Learning* when it was published, Goldsmith wrote to his friends in Ireland asking them to obtain subscriptions for the book—that is, advance orders or sales which would scoop up some of the illegal reprint sales.

He wrote to Edward Mills, who was a cousin of his, asking him to get subscriptions and send them to a Mr. Bradley, a bookseller in Dublin who would handle the accounting. He wrote to Jane Lawder, with whom he had often played flute and harpsichord duets, asking her for the same favor. But the Lawders, as noted, had turned against him and did not reply to his letter although he explained he had stopped writing because he thought "my letters might be regarded as the petitions of a beggar and not the offerings of a friend, while my professions instead of being considered as the result of disinterested esteem might be ascribed to venal insincerity." (By that he meant that if he said he loved them and sympathized with them over Uncle Contarine's illness, they might think he was only saying these things to stay in their good books and receive more favors from them. Also he may have had a guilty conscience over the amount of help he had received from his uncle at the expense of his cousin Jane.)

He wrote to his brother-in-law Daniel Hodson to explain the whole of the East India medical appointment. He would be going to one of the factories of Coromandel (on the lower southeast coast of India). He would be a physician and surgeon. He had already paid the ten pounds needed for the post, but he had to come up with fifty pounds for his passage and ten pounds more for sea stores—the total cost to him would be somewhere between sixty and seventy pounds.

His annual salary would be a mere one hundred pounds, but the practice was worth a thousand pounds a year. He admitted that at times he was dubious about leaving London and his friends and hopes to go to such an outlandish part. But the prospect of making his fortune for life overcame all his hesitations. (It's an odd admission because he had very few friends and was living in grinding poverty.) He hurriedly squelched a plan that his younger brother Maurice should accompany him to India, saying it would cost a hundred pounds in passage and expenses and Maurice ought to learn to write and spell properly first.

The letter contained a touch of bravado perhaps summoned up to raise his own spirits. "I suppose," he wrote, "before I return I shall find all the blooming virgins I once left in Westmeath shrivelled into a parcel of hags with seven children apiece tearing down their petticoats. Most of the Bucks and Bloods whom I left hunting and drinking and swearing and getting bastards, I find are dead. Poor devils they kicked the world before them. I wonder what the devil they kick now?"

He did not forget to ask Hodson to sell subscriptions to his book and send the money once again to Mr. Bradley in Dublin. That paragraph was, of course, the purpose of the whole letter.

Finally, he wrote to Henry, saying he was going to send him two hundred and fifty books to sell. He'd had no reply from the Lawders or from Edward Mills and he was desperate for advance sales in Ireland. In writing Henry he dropped some of the pretenses and spoke about his true condition.

"You scarce can conceive how eight years of disappointment, anguish and study have worn me down," he wrote. "Imagine to yourself a pale, melancholy visage with two great wrinkles between the eyebrows, with an eye disgustingly severe and a big wig, and you may have a perfect picture of my present appearance. I can neither laugh nor drink, have contracted an hesitating disagreeable manner of speaking, and a visage that looks ill-nature itself . . . in short I have an utter disgust of all that life brings with it."

Toward the end of the despondent letter, in a mercurial change of mood, he mentioned a comic poem he intended to write about a hack writer, and quoted a few lines which gave a picture of his state:

A window patched with paper lent a ray,
That feebly shewed the state in which he lay.
The sanded floor that grits beneath the tread
The humid wall with paltry pictures spread . . .

The morn was cold he viewed with keen desire
A rusty grate unconscious of a fire.
An unpaid reck'ning on the freeze was scored,
And five cracked teacups dressed the chimney board.

None of these letters produced a single sale of his book in Ireland. Hodson and his brother both tried to get sales but his friends were not interested in Goldsmith as a writer though he had been amusing enough singing songs and telling stories in the drawing room or tavern.

His new lodgings, to which he moved after writing the articles on Ovid, were at 12, Green Arbor Court, off Fleet Street. They were close to the stinking Fleet ditch full of offal and the bodies of dead dogs, which had not yet been covered up.

The court was a rectangle of tottering buildings three

stories high, so dilapidated that they were pulled down later in the interest of public safety and replaced by a stables. The center was cobbled and used by laundresses for washing and drying clothing on trestles. Pools of dirty water from the washing lay about, to which was added the slops thrown out of the windows by tenants. Children played games among the wash tubs and trestles, adding their shouts and screams to the quarrelling of the laundry women over the right to use a tub or hang their clothing up.

The windows were also draped with laundry hung out to dry. The court was reached from Fleet Street by a flight of worn steps, called "Breakneck Steps," for the water from the courtyard froze on them in wintertime. In summer they were coated with green slime.

Goldsmith's room was funished with a single chair, a trestle bed, and a window bench. He made friends with the washer-women, played his flute for the children, sometimes bought them a pennyworth of sweets, and spent hours with an old watchmaker talking of whatever came into his head.

He also worked away revising his book. He sold what pieces he could to whatever magazines would buy them. The market was overcrowded and few wanted his work. His clothing became more and more ragged until at last he dared not go out in the daylight, and could only walk the streets after dark.

There was no way to patch his clothes anymore for the cloth was too thin to take stitching and his behind showed through his breeches. His shirts were in tatters and his stockings full of holes. He was in such a ragged condition that he dared not face an editor to ask for work. He was, in fact, on the verge of disappearing for lack of clothing in which to present himself.

In this condition he one day received a letter from the East India Company dashing his hopes of making his fortune in India as a doctor. The letter notified him that there was no position open now or likely to be open in the near future at the company's factory at Coromandel. Reading between the lines, Goldsmith realized that in effect the appointment was about to be canceled or so long postponed as to be of little benefit to him.

This change was not Goldsmith's fault. What had happened, though few in England knew of it at the time, was that the French had attacked the East India Company's holding in southeast India, captured Fort St. David nearby, and laid siege to the city of Madras. It looked as though the East India Company might be driven out of that part of the land; then, of course, there would be no job at all for Goldsmith. But the news was suppressed for the time being.

Desperate, for he needed money urgently if he was not to starve, Goldsmith decided to apply at Surgeon's Hall for a position as a hospital mate. An examination had to be passed but it was so simple that a butcher's apprentice could have got through it with honors. Maybe Smollett told him of the post and persuaded him to apply. First, however, Goldsmith had to have a suit of clothes to present himself to the examiners. Down to his last resource, he swallowed his pride, went to Griffiths and begged him to give him something to write that would earn him enough money to buy a new suit—and something to eat.

Griffiths thought about it and gave Oliver four books to review. In payment he said he, Griffiths, would go surety with a tailor for a suit of clothes for Goldsmith. But Goldsmith either had to pay for the suit within a given time or return it. In short, in return for the review of the books, Businessman Griffiths didn't part with a penny, and he didn't even send Goldsmith to the tailor to be measured until the reviews had been written.

When he got the suit, Goldsmith went cheerfully down to Surgeon's Hall and sat for the examination. He was sure that he would pass, after his medical studies at Edinburgh, Leyden, Louvain, and Padua.

Four days before Christmas, 1758, he got the results of the examination. He had achieved the impossible. He had failed.

CHAPTER

ON CHRISTMAS DAY, 1758, MRS. MARTIN, GOLDSMITH'S landlady at Green Arbor Court, came to him in tears. Her husband had been arrested for debt on Christmas Eve and was now in the sponging house, with debtor's jail ahead unless his creditors were paid off. Goldsmith was behind with his rent, having been allowed to fall in arrears because he had amused the landlady's children with playing the flute, had bought them apples and candy when he had a penny to spare, and anyway was desperately poor himself. The poor do not oppress the poor.

"Mr. Goldsmith, sir," said the landlady, "can you raise any money at all? I have to get my poor husband out of the sponging house, and I'm desperate."

"Madam," said Goldsmith, "I haven't a penny but I soon will have."

"I need the money today," said Mrs. Martin.

"You shall have it today," said Goldsmith. He changed back into his rags, which he fortunately had not thrown away, bundled up his new suit, and went from pawnshop to pawnshop until he got the highest price he could for it. He brought the money back to the landlady, telling her that she must look on the bright side of things and that he was sure that her husband would soon be restored to her. He had a gift for encouraging people and he was loved for this more than for his generosity with money. He was now, of course, without a penny himself, so he took the four books that

Griffiths had given him to review and left them with a friend as security for the loan of a few shillings.

It wasn't long before Griffiths heard that the suit was gone and the books too. He wrote Goldsmith demanding either payment or the return of both. Goldsmith wrote back begging for a little time. Griffiths refused. Goldsmith, he said, was a cheat and a sharper and he would have the law on him. Goldsmith wrote again saying, "I know of no misery but a jail to which my own imprudencies and your letter seem to point. I have seen it inevitable these three or four weeks and by heavens request it as a favour, as a favour that may prevent something more fatal." He insisted that he was not a villain, that he suffered only from poverty, and his greatest fault was his own generosity and good nature. He ended by saying that he had a book with Mr. Robert Dodsley which would be brought out soon, and when paid he would be able to return to Griffiths the four books he had left as security for the loan and pay for the suit of clothes as well. The book was his *Polite Learning*, which Dodsley had now agreed to publish.

Griffiths didn't put Goldsmith in jail. Above all he was a man of business, and a writer in jail meant only an unpaid debt. The obvious way to get his money back was to give Goldsmith some work to do. There was no denying the fact that the man was a good writer and a fast one. And Oliver wasn't in any position to grumble if his copy was altered. Griffiths was about to bring out a pirated translation of the *Henriade* by Voltaire—an edition for which the French playwright would not receive a penny. This was a common practice at the time, in all countries, and does not make a villain out of Griffiths. Much of the work of Charles Dickens, for instance, was reprinted in the United States without a cent being paid to the author, who revenged himself by visiting the country and writing a book about it.

To go with the *Henriade,* Griffiths needed a life of Voltaire, a book-length life for which he was prepared to pay Goldsmith twenty pounds—out of which would be deducted the cost of the pawned suit.

Goldsmith had boasted of meeting Voltaire during his travels, and readily agreed to write the life. It could be said that he wrote his first book, *Polite Learning*, to get a job as a doctor with the East India Company. He wrote his second book, on Voltaire, to pay for a suit of clothes. Not only did he turn out a good life of Voltaire, he also finished the work in four weeks. He had, before his return to Dr. Milner's academy at Peckham, done a translation for Griffiths of a work called *Memoirs of a Protestant Condemned to the Galleys for his Religion* by Jean Marteilhe. In the original French the book was very rough and wordy. As translated by Goldsmith it was concise and well written. (The translation was attributed, for reasons known only to Griffiths, to one James Willington.)

These two works gave Griffiths and other booksellers a new view of Goldsmith. Here was a man who understood French perfectly, who could translate from French with grace (which many who understood French perfectly could not do), who wrote with elegance, charm, and humor and who wrote fast. He was something more than a scribbler, then.

Now the booksellers began to take an interest in him. Dodsley had the *Polite Learning* on which so many of Goldsmith's hopes rested, Griffiths had the Voltaire, and John Newbery approached him about writing something for children. This was the same John Newbery, publisher of children's books as well as books for adults, whose name is remembered today in the Newbery award for children's literature. He was a kind and good-natured man with a red pimply face, and he was always in a tearing hurry. For him Goldsmith is said to have written *Goody Two Shoes* but that he did so is not certain. He was still writing anonymously or under pen names. It is beyond question that he did some writing in the children's field for Newbery, who was one of the earliest to recognize the charm and clarity of Goldsmith's style, and *Goody Two Shoes* may have been written by Goldsmith later.

A number of writers of note wrote for Newbery, all anonymously, among them the great Sam Johnson, who called Newbery "Jack the Whirler" because he could never stop anywhere for a moment's rest or gossip, never sit down at leisure, but was always compelled to dart off somewhere else on some other piece of pressing business. He shovelled his meals down even at social dinners, often got up from the table with some excuse about business matters, and constantly complained that there just wasn't enough time to do all the things that had to be done.

Besides his publishing activities, Newbery wrote juveniles himself and had a very profitable sideline in the sale of Dr. James' Fever Powders, which were the miracle medicine of the day.

Dr. James was an eminent physician but so heavy a drinker that a friend said he had never seen him sober in twenty years. He brought out a medical dictionary (of solid worth) in three volumes with which Johnson helped him, and Johnson in the process picked up at least as much medical knowledge as Goldsmith had amassed at Edinburgh, Louvain, Leyden and Padua combined. As to the fever powders, they were given to George III, who survived into his dotage and to Goldsmith, who died young.

Gradually, then, things began to improve for Goldsmith. He was able to turn out a few essays, reviews, travel notes, translations, or whatever else might be commissioned and be sure of a pound or two a week. The suit of clothes was his at last—paid for by his hero, Voltaire. He was still seeing a few patients, who consulted him at the Temple Exchange Coffee House, and with careful management he probably earned enough money to take care of his needs—his rent, food, and laundry.

But he was incapable of careful management.

When he had money, he gave it away to others in need, and soon became known as a soft touch. When he had no money, he went without meals or ran up bills and then spent miserable days avoiding his creditors while making the rounds of the magazines looking for work. The money he earned, then, was gone as soon as it was received. But more valuable than the money was the reputation as a writer which he was building up. That reputation grew quickly and to such a degree that he began to be talked of among other writers as someone with a big future ahead of him. Smollett knew and admired his work and so did Samuel Johnson though they were still only casual acquaintances.

Then, having heard so many mentions of Goldsmith from Griffiths and Dodsley and Newbery, Johnson and Smollett and others, Dr. Thomas Percy, a prosperous clergyman very much interested in writing and writers, decided that he must call on him.

Percy was later to become famous as the editor of *Reliques of Ancient Poetry,* which was based on an old manuscript collection of ancient poetry which he rescued from a housemaid, who was about to light a fire with it. But at this point he was just a prosperous and influential clergyman with strong literary leanings.

In March, 1759, he inquired for Goldsmith's address and went to Green Arbor Court, where he found Goldsmith in his wretched and dirty room, which still had but one chair. He was working away at the proofs of *Polite Learning* (which was at last in type) while from all around came the shrill quarrelling of the laundry women, and the shouts and cries of children playing up and down the stairs and around the courtyard.

Goldsmith gave the neatly dressed clergyman the only chair in the room and seated himself upon the windowsill.

"I interrupt you, I fear," said the clergyman.

"You rescue me, sir," said Goldsmith. "Proofreading of the work of others is tedious enough. But proofreading one's own work is a task scarcely to be borne."

They talked about the book. Goldsmith explained that it was a survey of the state of learning and literature in the various nations of Europe as it stood at that time. It dealt not only with great works and authors, but also with the problems of authors and men of learning in changing times, when profit rather than merit was becoming the criterion for acceptance, and reverence for their work replaced by a superficial criticism. Patrons who would provide a writer with money while he produced something of merit were gone. Alexander Pope had had a patron who had supported him while he did his translation of *The Iliad*, which was one of the great works of English literature and had incidentally made a fortune for Pope. But Johnson had been unable to find a patron to sustain him while he put his dictionary together. With patrons no more to be found, writers were in the hands of publishers, who obviously paid as little as they could, so that the writer was forced to produce as many words as possible to earn more—payment being presumably by the page. Quality then, in both learning and art, was bound to decline. This was the situation as Goldsmith saw it and wrote of it.

While they were talking there was knock at the door and a ragged little girl entered. She made a curtsy to the two gentlemen and said to Goldsmith, "My mamma sends her compliments and begs the favor of you to lend her a chamberpot of coals." Goldsmith now had enough money to buy a sack of coal occasionally. He gave the little girl the chamberpot full and went on with the conversation.

That first meeting with Goldsmith made such an impression on Dr. Percy that he became Goldsmith's close friend and decided to help him in every way he could. One way would be to introduce him to other eminent men of letters, and thus raise the level of his acquaintances.

Despite his need for money (not now as pressing as it had been, though still there) Goldsmith at times had attacks of indolence. He wrote fast and well with the wolf at the door. But when the wolf was gone, there were days when he could hardly bring himself to pick up his quill, and editors began to discover that it was not always wise to give him a big advance against copy. He tended to spend the advance and postpone the work.

One day his landlady saw a man enter Goldsmith's room after angrily inquiring whether he was in and heard the man lock the door behind him. Soon she heard the two quarrelling violently. She was on the point of interrupting when the argument died down and there was silence, which lasted for a couple of hours. Then the door of the room was unlocked, and the man reappeared and sent her out for a hot dinner for the two of them. The explanation was that Goldsmith had been paid for an article which he had not written. The editor had locked him in his room until it was done and then, pleased, sent out for some dinner, for Goldsmith was as broke as usual.

Polite Learning, on which he had started work two years before, was published at last on April 2, 1759. It was published anonymously though Goldsmith had pleaded that it be brought out under his name. The full title, *An Enquiry into the Present State of Polite Learning in Europe*, is far too sweeping and although the book is still active among his works today, its main interest lies in what he had to say about the plight of the writer in his time. He has a trenchant chapter on the rewards of genius in England (of which he found but few) and there is a lengthy attack on incompetent critics who can make or break an author's work. "I fire with indignation when I see persons wholly destitute of education and genius indent [write] to the press and thus turn bookmakers, adding to the sin of criticism the sin of ignorance also; whose trade is a bad one, and who are bad workmen in their trade." So Goldsmith wrote.

As for the author, compelled to hack work to live, he wrote, "A long habit of writing for bread thus turns the ambition of every author at last into avarice. He finds that he has written many years, that the public are scarcely acquainted even with his name; he despairs of applause and turns to profit which invites him. He finds that money procures all those advantages, that respect and that ease, which he vainly expected from fame."

The complaint is an old one and exists to this day.

The book did well—far better than its subject matter perhaps warranted, for there were not that many people who were interested in the fulminations of authors against book publishers and critics. It was again Goldsmith's clarity of style that sold the book, the aptness of his allusions and the conciseness of his argument. His was a conversational style—an easy, graceful chat with friends, and it was this that made the book popular. He picked a subject both academic and dull and made it glow with the light of his own mind. Several editions came out, his fame increased (for it was known that he was the unnamed author) and the work survived the criticism of *The Monthly Review* and *The Critical Review*.

On *The Monthly Review* his place had been taken by a writer named Kenrick (first name unknown) who, either out of personal jealousy or under orders from Griffiths, lambasted the book. Griffiths was still smarting over the pawning of the suit of clothes and his hack, Kenrick, made oblique allusions to Goldsmith as a sharper and one who, while criticizing others for lack of ethics, was "conscious himself of laboring under the infamy of having, by the vilest and meanest actions, forfeited all pretensions to honor and honesty." Kenrick's venom was to be poured on Goldsmith again and again in the years to come. It would be too much to blame it all on that suit of clothes, but certainly Goldsmith's pawning of the suit to help his landlady was the start of it.

Goldsmith now received news from Ireland that his mother was almost blind. He had been her favorite son. She had been bitterly disappointed in him, put him out of her house, and refused to have anything to do with him. It was perhaps up to Goldsmith (if he loved his mother) to heal her hurt. He didn't. After leaving Ireland for Edinburgh, he had never written to her, though he had asked others to remember him to her, made very few inquiries about her, and never sent her as much as a few shillings from his earnings. Now he wrote his brother that the thought of her blindness was one reason for his not returning to see her, for he could not bear to find her almost deprived of sight.

It is odd that the same Goldsmith who took the children of paupers into his room at Green Arbor Court to get them out of the cold and give them sweets or a piece of cake, or have them dance to his flute, wouldn't go to Ireland to comfort his mother in her blindness and her old age.

It is odd but it is true.

When she died a few years later the evidence is that he put on only half mourning for her.

Something had plainly snapped between the two of them when she turned him away from her house after he had squandered his money on the expedition to Cork. Whatever had been lost was never restored, and his brother Henry remained the only one of his family whom he truly loved. One explanation may be that for Goldsmith to love he had to be tolerated. When his mother and his cousin Jane withdrew their tolerance and understanding, they lost his love. Henry always understood him, whatever his failings.

Polite Learning greatly increased not only Goldsmith's reputation but also the demand for his work. He had written for Griffiths, Newbery, Dodsley. Now a new bookseller, Wilkie, whose offices were at the sign of "The Bible" in St. Paul's Churchyard, approached him with an idea.

Since he wrote so well and wrote so fast, why not produce a magazine which Wilkie would bring out once a week? At this time, probably because of the demand for coffeeshop reading, magazines were proliferating in London. New magazines were announced every month and new magazines died every month, if not every week. They were most of them short-lived. Among them were *The Babbler, Friends, The Adviser, The Bachelor, The Scrutator, The Skeptic,* and on and on. There were enough hacks to fill them and many of them depended upon reprinted translations from foreign publications. There was, however, not enough difference in their point of view and character for the reading public to prefer one over the other. And so they died for lack of loyal support, though they often tried to keep themselves going by picking quarrels with each other.

Bookseller Wilkie thought that a magazine from Goldsmith's hand would have a distinctive style and viewpoint which might catch on and survive. The magazine would be of thirty-two pages and contain half a dozen essays. There is a general assumption that Goldsmith wrote them all though it is entirely possible that he accepted and perhaps rewrote the contributions of other writers. He was certainly not above borrowing. An essay, for instance, on eloquence was taken without the slightest acknowledgment from a work of Voltaire.

The idea of having one man produce the greater part of the contents of a magazine was not new. Johnson had written, or at least been responsible for, the contents of a magazine called *The Rambler*, which came out twice a week. He then brought out *The Idler* for John Newbery on condition that he got two-thirds of the profits. The major content of these two magazines are acknowledged to be Johnson's work, but it is still possible that he accepted contributions from others, which he rewrote or edited heavily.

Goldsmith's magazine was to be called *The Bee*. He wrote on every subject that came into his head and he always wrote well. He wrote about spiders that had their webs in the corners of his room, about fashions, manners, and acting, about Addison, Swift, Steele, Pope, and Congreve. He reviewed again the history of England by Smollett and praised Smollett's *Peregrine Pickle* and *Roderick Random*. He wrote on philosophy, poverty, and philology; on clubs and wandering the streets at night and how victories are celebrated. While churning out pieces for *The Bee,* he also wrote for *Busy Body,* which came out three times a week, and for *The Lady's Magazine*. All this produced a competence but no great wealth because, for all his efforts, *The Bee* failed after eight issues. Still, he was making enough to eat, pay his debts, and replenish his wardrobe, buying new shirts and stockings and giving them to the laundresses, who were his neighbors, to wash.

Because his clothes meant a great deal to him, he sometimes got angry with the washerwomen over a spot they had failed to remove or a tear they had not repaired. His temper would flare up and he would stalk away full of wrath. But within a few moments he would be back, repentant, apologizing, asking forgiveness, and then he would pay them extra for the laundry. They got to know him well and they liked him. Sometimes they would deliberately provoke him with an eye to the extra payment.

He still walked about the London streets after dark, talking with beggars, comforting shivering and ragged children and their mothers. He might go out with a pound in his pocket and return without a penny, and the pound would be needed to pay some bill or maybe his rent. He couldn't help this. Throughout his life Goldsmith suffered far more for others than for himself. He could endure hunger, cold, and want of money. He couldn't bear to see others endure it. He had put his mother out of his mind, but the sore-covered, starving London beggars were there before his eyes. They could not be ignored.

After weeks of work, producing huge amounts of copy, he was finally in a position to move to better quarters. But he stayed for a while in the squalid room with the one chair in Green Arbor Court for a reason which to him seemed quite sufficient.

The landlady needed the rent.

CHAPTER

WEEK AFTER WEEK AND MONTH AFTER MONTH, GOLDSMITH did nothing but write for magazines. It was a catchpenny existence, with no stable market for, as noted, magazines appeared and disappeared like mushrooms. His performance with *The Bee* had further increased his reputation. There was still no guarantee that what he wrote would be printed, but he had a much better chance now of selling his articles and reviews than when he had first come to London.

Some weeks he made two or three guineas. Some weeks he made only two or three shillings. But he was incapable of averaging his income and what he made was gone as soon as received. He thought that if he could only be sure of a regular amount per week, all his problems would be solved.

Newbery and Smollett thought the same thing. Newbery, one of God's gifted optimists, decided that if he brought out a magazine with Smollett as editor and Goldsmith as a regular contributor, it couldn't possibly fail—this in the face of all the magazines dead and dying that lay all over London.

The two called on Goldsmith with the proposition. The new publication was to be called *The British Magazine*. It was to be dedicated to William Pitt, the Prime Minister, to be staunchly patriotic, and published under a royal license. This was remarkable in that Smollett had just been released from a royal prison after serving a three months' sentence for a libel of Admiral Knowles. But then there were no hard feelings either on the part of Smollett or on the part of the King.

Goldsmith was delighted with the new market. He'd written a few pieces for *The Critical Review*, of which Smollett was the editor, and in so doing incurred the further enmity of Griffiths, who could never think of Goldsmith anyway without thinking of the pawned suit of clothes. Copy was needed right away and as soon as the two gentlemen left, Goldsmith picked up his quill and started writing, for he was never at a loss for a subject.

The British Magazine did well. It actually lasted through some twenty issues before going under, and to each issue Goldsmith contributed some notable essays—anonymous, of course, so that it has taken much scholarly research to establish what was his and what was someone else's. He drew his material from his own wanderings about London and on the Continent and from the books he'd read, the plays he'd seen, and the people he'd met.

He wrote a spirited piece about a beggar, filthy, shivering, and undernourished, who was a fount of cheerfulness. The beggar thanked God that, although he had lost a hand and a leg and had a wound in his chest from his years as a soldier (no pension, of course), he hadn't lost both legs and an eye. Telling how he had been thrown into a French prison and given a bed of boards on which to sleep, he praised the blanket that went with it and kept him warm. As for being in jail, though people grumbled about it, he himself had been put in Newgate for being too poor to pay his debts and he'd found it as agreeable a place as he had ever lived in all his life. He'd fought the French in six pitched battles, and he really believed that his captain would have promoted him to a corporal but on the other hand there was probably some very good reason why he hadn't. In the Navy, which he joined later, he had been cruelly flogged by a boatswain, but then the boatswain had not stopped to consider just what he was doing. Of course, it would have been better if, when he had lost his hand and leg, he had been serving on a King's ship instead of on a privateer. But then one man was born with a silver spoon in his mouth and another with a wooden ladle and he shouldn't grumble. He concluded by saying, "Blessed be God, I enjoy good health."

That particular essay set the whole of London laughing and was widely reprinted in France (though without any payment to Goldsmith). Voltaire had published *Candide* in the same year, 1759, and Goldsmith's unconquerable beggar has a close resemblance to Voltaire's unconquerable Dr. Pangloss. But Pangloss is a buffoon and Goldsmith's beggar is not. Two great writers had treated the same subject matter —blind optimism—from two different points of view. It would be fascinating to know if Voltaire ever read Goldsmith's essay. Almost certainly, Goldsmith had read *Candide* and may have got his model from Dr. Pangloss.

The British Magazine failed after twenty or so issues as stated. Newbery, however, probably didn't lose money on it. He owned the editorial contents of the magazine and could reprint the contributions of Goldsmith and others in pamphlets later on. Undaunted, and even before *The British Magazine* had gone under, Newbery had decided that London was ready for a new daily newspaper. Johnson and Goldsmith would be regular contributors, and as soon as he had obtained Johnson's agreement he hustled around to Goldsmith.

"*The Public Ledger,* sir," he said. "An excellent title. That is to be the name. I would require from you a minimum of two articles a week for which I will pay you a guinea an article. You can then, by a trifling expenditure of your time, be assured of two guineas a week regular income."

"Done," cried Goldsmith, delighted with the prospect of a regular basic income to which he could add whatever else he could earn. He decided that now at last he would move from Green Arbor Court, where it was very difficult for him to receive or talk to visitors, to better lodgings, and, later in 1760, rented two rooms in a house in Wine Office Court, also off Fleet Street but a little removed from the stinking Fleet ditch, the shouting washerwoman, and the clamoring children. The house, it is suspected, belonged to a relative of

Newbery, and that suspicion adds a little interest later on in the story.

Goldsmith did not, however, wholly desert his old landlady, Mrs. Martin. He went around to see her frequently, took sweets for the children and food for her, and often lent —or rather gave—her a little money though he pretended to lend it. He took his laundry back to the same washerwomen for a while at least. He hated to think that they should lose money as a result of his own good fortune.

Before he left Green Arbor Court, Goldsmith had, naturally, parted with his last penny to help someone else. A man called Jack Pilkington, also Irish and a fellow hack, called on him, greatly excited, and said his fortune was made for life if he could only get hold of a very small sum of money, which he hoped Goldsmith could give him. He knew, he said, of a certain duchess who had a passion for collecting white mice. She had two of them and would pay a huge sum to anyone who could supply two more. Pilkington had sent all the way to India for a pair, and the East Indiaman, with the two white mice worth thousands of pounds aboard, had just come into the Thames. Could Goldsmith come up with two guineas—a miserable two guineas—with which Pilkington could pay for the mice and buy a decent cage in which to take them to the duchess and collect his thousands of pounds?

Perhaps there wasn't another man in the whole of London and indeed in the whole of England who would have believed such a tale but Goldsmith did.

"My dear Pilkington," he said, "I have only ten shillings on me but you are welcome to that."

"What about your watch?" said Pilkington, spotting it on the writing table. (Goldsmith had bought himself a watch though he could not afford it. He needed it to support his self-image.) "If you could let me have your watch for just a few hours, I could pawn it, get the white mice, collect the money, and bring the watch back to you this very day."

Goldsmith gave him the watch and Pilkington went off

with it and then ten shillings. Goldsmith didn't hear of Pilkington again for a long time. Then at last, telling a friend the story as a joke played on him, he learned that Pilkington was dying. He sought him out, found him very sick in bed, and pressed a guinea into his hand. No mention was made of the duchess and the white mice. Pilkington died shortly afterwards.

Goldsmith was known to everyone, and particularly among his fellow countrymen arriving in London, as an easy touch. He was constantly being taken in for, as with Pilkington, he had a childish belief in any story that was told him. He never thought to check on anything. Much of the reputation he gained later for being a simpleton in conversation came of his readiness to accept any story he had heard as gospel and repeat it. Someone told him that horses were far more sensitive than people realized and if, for instance, a bucket of blood was put in a stable, the horses became nearly frantic with fear. He maintained in company that this was so and everybody laughed at him. But he would not deign to check it out by actually putting a bucket of blood in a stable, which would have been very easy to do.

Again, later, when he was writing a history of Greece, he asked the historian Gibbon who was the Indian King who had given Alexander the Great so much trouble. "Montezuma," said Gibbon, joking, and Goldsmith said, "Of course," and made a note of the name, so Gibbon had to quickly correct the error.

He was everybody's dupe. It was easy to fool a man as trusting as a child. Once, as a member of a club of which more will be said later, he arrived for dinner and discovered that he had accidentally tipped the coachman a guinea instead of a shilling. He mentioned his mistake to other members and passed it off. At the next meeting, when they were all enjoying their dinner, a coachman turned up at the door and asked for Goldsmith.

"Sir," he said, "you gave me a guinea the other night and I think you intended only to give me a shilling."

Beer Street and Gin Lane. From the original design by Hogarth.
BETTMANN ARCHIVE.

"Why, you honest fellow!" cried Goldsmith, touched almost to tears. "You are a monument to the hidden goodness of mankind. Come. You shall not go unrewarded." He dragged the coachman into the dining room, told the story to his fellow members and suggested they then and there take up a collection to reward the coachman for his honesty. This was done, and the coachman went away, overflowing with humble thanks.

When he'd gone one of the members suggested to Goldsmith that he take a look at the guinea the coachman had returned. Goldsmith did. It was a counterfeit coin.

They all burst out laughing and finally explained that the whole thing was a hoax. Whatever coachman he'd given his guinea to had gone off into the jungle of London and he'd never see him again.

People traded on his good nature too, and on a queer kind of humility which overcame him whenever he received unexpected recognition. Once, a writer named Charles Lloyd introduced himself to Goldsmith in a coffeehouse and invited him to dinner at a tavern where they would have an evening of fun with other writers. Goldsmith was highly complimented to be recognized as a writer of sufficient importance to be invited to such a gathering. Everybody ate all he wanted and drank all he wanted as well. But when it came time to pay the bill, it turned out that Lloyd hadn't a penny. Goldsmith felt that in return for the compliment of having been invited to dinner, the least he could do was to come to the rescue of his new friend. He didn't actually pay the bill, but guaranteed its payment. Whereupon Lloyd ordered another cask of wine.

Not all such evenings were pleasant. At another meeting with writers, the company got into a violent quarrel about Sterne's *Tristram Shandy*. Goldsmith didn't like the book, insisted on saying so, and had his eye blacked for stating his viewpoint.

In January, 1760, Goldsmith started earning a regular

two guineas a week writing for *The Public Ledger*, and it was this income, as noted, that enabled him to move to Wine Office Court. At that time England and particularly fashionable London were in love with China and its culture. Chippendale was turning out Chinese-style furniture. Chinese fans, vases, screens, and scrolls were in high demand. It was fashionable to have whole rooms decorated in Chinese style. Dr. Thomas Percy, Goldsmith's friend, was working on the translation of a Chinese novel into English—or rather rewriting the translation into acceptable English. And Horace Walpole had (in half an hour) written a highly successful satire in the form of a letter from a Chinese philosopher, Xo Ho, in London to a friend in Peking. The letter dealt with the execution of Admiral John Byng, who had been shot for losing a battle (*"pour encourager les autres,"* as Voltaire wrote).

It is not possible to put a finger on precisely why there was so much interest in China at that time, for there were undoubtedly many causes. One was the widespread popularity of tea from China, imported by the East India Company. Everybody drank his dish of tea, which was the most profitable cargo the East Indiamen brought back from their long voyage.

Other cargoes included silks and cottons. Chinaware—dishes from China—was eagerly sought and widely imitated. Chinese customs, being often the reverse or made to appear the reverse of English, were reckoned quaint and deeply wise. Again, Catholic missionaries had been in China for more than a century, and a great deal was now being written about China, its history and customs, on the Continent and being translated and reprinted in English magazines. Finally, China was under the control of an enlightened Manchu emperor, Ch'ien Lung, who encouraged foreign commerce, with the London-based East India Company leading the field. But if one word was needed to explain the Chinese cult in England it would have to be "tea," which produced polite chatter in London and outright rebellion in Boston. (The present-day

American fondness for coffee dates from the 1770s when tea-drinking became un-American.)

Goldsmith, in writing for *The Public Ledger,* could have produced each week two disconnected articles. Instead, he decided to give them a continuity of interest and of point of view by copying Walpole—by writing his articles in the form of a letter from a Chinese philosopher in London. Such a man would take a dispassionate and critical look at any English customs and entice the reader to do the same thing—to question that which he had always accepted as reasonable and right.

The name Goldsmith chose for his Chinese philosopher was Lien Chi Altangi—this last very un-Chinese. But it didn't matter. The letters constituting what we would today call a "column" poured out twice a week and were the most widely read feature of *The Public Ledger.* In fact, without them, the paper would have gone under. But soon everybody in London was talking about the Chinese philosopher. Reprinted later in two volumes under the title *Citizen of the World,* the letters are reckoned among the greatest of Goldsmith's writings even today.

There is good reason for the opinion. His satire and irony were always gentle and good-humored, never bitter or malicious. His reasoning was always simple and clear, and he dealt not only with ridiculous fashions and manners but also outrageous customs and cruel and oppressive laws which out of sheer habit had come to be accepted as just and humane. There were more than a hundred of these letters, and since they were written at the rate of two a week while Goldsmith was writing other things as well, some of them are trivial and some are obviously contrived and written under pressure. But many of them are excellent, anticipating some of the work of his yet unborn countryman, G. Bernard Shaw.

A sample is worthwhile. In one letter, Goldsmith's Chinese philosopher writes that he had overheard an astonishing conversation in London between a porter staggering under a heavy load, a prisoner talking through the grating of a debtor's jail, and a soldier. The subject had been the threatened French invasion of England, for the war with France still raged.

"For my part," says the prisoner seriously, his face pressed against the bars, "the greatest of my apprehensions is for our freedom; if the French should conquer, what would become of English liberty?"

"Aye, slaves," says the porter, wearily resting his heavy load for a moment. "They are all slaves, fit only to carry burdens, every one of them." He takes a drink from a cup and says, "Before I would stoop to slavery, may this be my poison—I would sooner enlist for a soldier."

The soldier (no shrine of piety) says hotly, "It is not so much our liberties as our religion that would suffer by such a change; yes, our religion, my lads. May the devil sink me into flames if the French should come over; our religion would be utterly undone."

Again, a friend called The Man in Black (taken to be a picture of Goldsmith himself) is showing the Oriental around Westminster Abbey, which he takes to be the burial place of the most famous men of the land. But The Man in Black explains that many are buried there merely because, being wealthy, they had been able to persuade others that they were also worthy. The tombs and monuments, then, were often the reward of nothing more than a man's being wealthy and having a high opinion of himself.

Goldsmith also showed deep political insight though that is often a matter of luck. Maybe he was just lucky when he warned that Russia was the natural enemy of Western Europe. But he was thinking more deeply than the statesmen of his day when he warned that the thirteen American colonies might very well break away entirely from rule by Britain, and added that England would not thereby lose her prestige and her standing and influence among other nations.

With the unbiased philosopher as his mouthpiece he pondered over clergymen getting all the money they could, while encouraging others to do all the good they could, marveled at the fashion that sent boys to school wearing wigs and cocked hats and at the sale of women into marriage while pretending that love conquers all.

There was scarcely a subject which he did not touch upon, but his social criticism was never angry. Not only is The Man in Black Goldsmith, but so also is the Chinese philosopher, for he is gentle, kindly, and entirely honest. In real life Goldsmith lost his temper very often, though he quickly followed up his outbursts with heartfelt apologies. But the true Goldsmith came out in his writings, and there is not in them a line of anger or a cruel remark. Nor did he ever preach. The way in which he held up to view the foibles, fashions, and customs of which he wrote made preaching unnecessary.

Quietly, he defended all who needed defending, and he even put in a word for dogs. There were thousands of dogs all over London, half-starved, garbage-fed mongrels for the most part. There was no licensing of dogs, no attempt to control dog populations, and no dog catcher. Sometimes the animals were fierce and attacked people; then there would be an upsurge of fear of them and even hatred. One or two dogs biting people was thought natural enough, but a report swept London that very many people had been bitten by dogs, without cause, and that hundreds of dogs roaming London's streets were suffering from hydrophobia. Hysteria and panic gripped the city in a day, with the result that dogs were stoned, clubbed, and shot to death in such number that piles of carcasses were soon lying about, sometimes blocking passage in the narrower alleyways.

Goldsmith attacked the cruelty, gently ridiculed the hysteria, and put in an eloquent plea for man's best friend—even though he be a starving London mongrel.

"Of all the beasts that graze the lawn or hunt the forest," he wrote, "a dog is the only animal that, leaving his fellows, attempts to cultivate the friendship of man; to man he looks in all his necessities with a speaking eye for assistance; exerts for him all the little service in his power with cheerfulness and pleasure; for him bears famine and fatigue with patience and resignation. No injuries can abate his fidelity, no distress induce him to forsake his benefactor; studious to please and fearing to offend, he is still a humble, steadfast dependent; and in him alone fawning is not flattery. How unkind then to torture this faithful creature who has left the forest to claim the protection of man! How ungrateful a return to the trusty animal for all his services!"

He was very fond of dogs, indeed of all animals, and wrote an elegy on the death of a mad dog which he used to pad out *The Vicar of Wakefield*. The elegy had not a thing to do with the text of the novel but it is excellent Goldsmith and here it is:

Good people all, of every sort,
Give ear unto my song,
And if you find it wondrous short,
It cannot hold you long.

In Islington there was a man
Of whom the world might say
That still a godly race he ran,
When'er he went to pray.

A kind and gentle heart he had,
To comfort friends and foes;
The naked every day he clad
When he put on his clothes.

And in that town a dog was found,
As many dogs there be,
Both mongrel, puppy, whelp and hound,
And curs of low degree.

The dog and man at first were friends;
But when a pique began,
The dog to gain some private ends,
Went mad and bit the man.

Around from all the neighboring streets,
The wondering neighbors ran,
And swore the dog had lost his wits,
To bite so good a man.

The wound it seemed both sore and sad
To every Christian eye;
And while they swore the dog was mad,
They swore the man would die.

But soon a wonder came to light,
That showed the rogues they lied;
The man recovered of the bite,
The dog it was that died.

With the publication of the Chinese letters and his removal to new and better lodgings at Wine Office Court, the great day came when Goldsmith was introduced formally to the greatest of all of London's literary figures, Dr. Samuel Johnson.

Dr. Thomas Percy, Goldsmith's earliest friend of any literary importance, was the one who arranged the meeting between Johnson and Goldsmith. They'd met briefly but never socially, though Johnson was well aware of Goldsmith's great talent. Percy now arranged to bring Johnson to dinner (something that would have been impossible at Green Arbor Court) at Goldsmith's new lodgings and the date fixed was May 31, 1761.

Johnson lived at the time at Inner Temple Lane, several blocks up Fleet Street from Goldsmith's lodging. Percy went to fetch Johnson and found him, to his surprise, very neatly dressed, for Johnson normally dressed in anything he could find to put on—clean or unclean, mended or torn. He had on a new suit and a clean shirt, his shoes were buckled, his hose without holes and well pulled up, and his undersized frowsy wig had been replaced by a new one which fitted his huge head.

"My dear doctor," said Percy, "I trust you will forgive me

remarking on it, but I am surprised to find you so neatly attired. Is there some special reason?"

"There is indeed," replied Johnson. "I hear that Goldsmith, who is a great sloven, justifies his disregard for cleanliness and decency by quoting my practice; and I am determined this night to show him a better example."

It is a great pity that nothing further is known of this first meeting between Johnson and Goldsmith, who were fast friends from that moment. But not a single anecdote of the dinner, at which other writers were present, has survived. Johnson turned up in his new suit and it's a good guess that Goldsmith had a new suit too. It wasn't necessary to teach Goldsmith to dress well. He dressed as well as he could and he often overdressed to compensate for his unprepossessing appearance. So maybe they laughed at each other's special clothes and then got down to Johnson's *Idler* and *Rambler* and Goldsmith's *Bee* and *Polite Learning* and Chinese letters and what was the matter with the publishing business, which is the stock talk of writers to this day.

In the matter of dress, Goldsmith became interested in Beau Nash, an eighteenth-century dandy, who was then eighty-nine years of age and living in genteel poverty in Bath. He became so interested, in fact, that he took a post chaise down to Bath to interview him. There he listened with deepest interest to all that Nash had to say on the subject of manners and clothing.

It was part of Nash's philosophy that good clothing and good manners produced esteem. Esteem was something that Goldsmith craved. Nash, in his heyday, had been the ruler of the "bon ton" at Bath, had worn a huge white hat, a richly embroidered coat, waistcoat and breeches, and traveled about town in a coach drawn by six gray horses, the outriders equipped with French horns.

Goldsmith, interviewing him at length, was more than impressed. He wrote Nash's life story and was confirmed in his belief that to dress well, even extravagantly as Nash had done, would bring him the prestige for which he yearned. He never stopped to consider that he had neither Nash's aplomb nor taste.

A fashion for extravagance in dress was being established in London at the time by members of the Macaroni Club—a group of exquisites who dined on exotic foreign foods (including macaroni, then little known in England) and dressed like fops. (The puzzling line about the feather in the hat in "Yankee Doodle Dandy" was sung by English soldiers in the War of Independence originally to mock the uniforms of the rebels. The rebels were Macaronis.)

Goldsmith admired the Macaronis and dreamed of the wonderful clothes he would soon be wearing, which would make him the talk of the town. His book on Beau Nash ran to some two hundred and thirty pages and was sold for fourteen guineas. It was published when Nash died at the age of ninety, having in his last years sold his collection of snuffboxes to support himself.

Goldsmith did more than describe Nash as a dandy; he delved into his character and pointed to his many moral qualities. He said of him that, born poor, Nash had spread out the little gold he had thinly and as far as it would go. Like Goldsmith, Nash could not be indifferent to suffering and had often borrowed money to give to those who needed it.

To the essays for *The British Magazine,* and the Chinese letters in the *Public Ledger,* and the *Life of Nash,* Goldsmith now added a *Life of Christ,* and was working also on a translation in several volumes of Plutarch's Lives. He fell ill from overwork and irregular meals before the fifth volume was completed and asked the publisher (Newbery) to let another writer by the name of Collier finish the job for him. Newbery objected, but in the end agreed, and Goldsmith gave part of his fee to Collier and rested for a little while.

But he was always in need of money. He took on assignment after assignment, spent the advance, and then had to produce the work while looking around for another advance to keep him going. With all the success he was having, and with all the fame that was coming to him, Goldsmith still looked upon writing as a last resort. He would much rather have done something more exciting, something which would allow him to travel to exotic places such as Syria with its Written Mountains.

When a group of Cherokee chieftains (they were called kings) came to London, Goldsmith waited three hours to see them and then charmed them to the extent that they embraced him, leaving their ceremonial paint all over his face and clean ruffled shirt. They were exciting people and aroused in him again some thoughts of getting to the American frontier or any other place where fame and adventure lay waiting.

He wrote to Lord Bute, who was the new Prime Minister, suggesting that he should be sent (at government expense) to the East to explore the interior of Asia where many valuable inventions and techniques, unknown to the Western World, could be studied and brought back by a trained observer. In the Chinese letters he had written of such things, saying, "In Siberian Tartary, the natives extract a strong spirit from milk which is a secret probably unknown to the chemists of Europe. In the most savage parts of India they are possessed of the secret of dyeing vegetable substances scarlet, and that of refining lead into a metal which, for hardness and color, is little inferior to silver." The spirit obtained from milk was, of course, the fermented mare's milk of the Mongols. Goldsmith also described the kind of man who should be sent on such a journey of discovery. "He should be a man of a philosophical turn," he wrote. "One apt to deduce consequences of general utility from particular occurrences; neither swollen with pride nor hardened by prejudice, neither wedded to one particular system, nor instructed only in one particular science; neither wholly a botanist nor quite an antiquarian; his mind should be tinctured with miscellaneous knowledge, and his manners humanized by an intercourse with men."

In short, Oliver Goldsmith.

Lord Bute ignored Goldsmith's letter (probably the most

sensible decision of his undistinguished term in office). When Johnson heard of it he said, "Of all men, Goldsmith is the most unfit to go out upon such an inquiry for he is utterly ignorant of such arts as we already possess and consequently could not know what would be accessions to our present stock of mechanical knowledge. Sir, he would bring home a grinding barrow, which you see in every street in London, and think that he had furnished a wonderful improvement."

Back to writing then. Goldsmith wrote on and on and on. And spent and spent and spent.

CHAPTER

JOHNSON PROVIDED A MAJOR TURNING POINT IN GOLDsmith's life. Up to then, Goldsmith had been the friend of beggars and down-and-outs, washerwomen, street vendors, waiters, a few hack writers, and editors though these latter were business acquaintances rather than real friends. He had no place in society; no company with a talent comparable to his own.

Sordid, drab, penniless, hungry, drunken London was all about him, and he knew it well. But the other aspects of London—the London of elegance, manners, and intelligence, striving to rise above the money-hungry mass—had been closed to him.

Johnson opened the golden door, and Oliver was welcomed into this London with introductions to such people as Sir Joshua Reynolds, the great portrait painter, who alone did so much to raise the whole tone of London society above what was seamy on the one hand and what was purely ostentatious on the other. Putting aside his painting, Reynolds' great gift to eighteenth-century England was a sense of values—a sense of real quality and real worth outside the struggle for bread and social prestige.

The man who now took Goldsmith under his wing was a hulking, shambling figure of such huge strength that a publisher once suggested to him that instead of writing he would do better to hire out as a porter, carrying heavy loads on his back around the town. His eyesight was so poor that, peering over a book, he often singed his wig in the flame of his candle. He refused to wear spectacles.

As a boy his eyes had been so dim that at times he had to cross the road on his way to school on his hands and knees. His face was marked with scrofula, from which he suffered all his life, the result of his having been put out to a tubercular wet nurse. His mother had taken him as an infant to London to be touched by Queen Anne in the hope that this would cure him, for the touch of the sovereign was supposed to be able to achieve this miracle. It didn't.

Goldsmith soon found that Johnson suffered not only physically but also mentally, for he was subject to fits of depression during which he despaired of his work, the value of his life, and the salvation of his soul. He often told Goldsmith that he feared he was going insane.

It was useless for Goldsmith, when he got to know Johnson well, to try to argue him out of these moods. He, who had been brought up in the church, knew it from the inside and was not awed or overwhelmed by Christian doctrine. His Irish sense of fun and humor helped him to keep his religious balance. But Johnson's religion weighed him down, giving him far more suffering than comfort. He was a sensual man, strongly attracted to women, and because of his strict religious upbringing, he fought against his sexuality all his life.

Johnson had written a play, *Irene,* which had been produced by the actor-manager David Garrick some years before. As author, Johnson had had complete freedom to go back stage any time he wanted, and this seemed to Goldsmith a tremendous privilege, for he was deeply interested in the theater.

"I would love to have such a liberty," he said. "To be able to share in the excitement of the cast as they wait for the curtain to be raised. That must have been a great joy for you, sir."

"So it was," said Johnson. "But I gave it up, for watching the actresses pull on their black stockings, and seeing their often bare bosoms proved too much for me. Such sights jeopardized my soul."

Goldsmith noted that Johnson always perked up in company when he sat next to a pretty woman (he usually managed to sit next to one). He adored, among others, the Irish actress Kitty Clive. Bookseller Tom Davies had a pretty wife to whom Johnson was attracted; but in her presence he sometimes started mumbling prayers. Davies told his wife that she was responsible for this.

Johnson, some time after his meeting with Goldsmith, struck up a friendship with a wealthy brewer, Henry Thrale, and his wife Hester. The friendship was so close that the Thrales in a sense adopted Johnson and often had him for long periods as a member of the family in their house at Streatham.

Once, calling for him, they found him on his knees, imploring God to save his soul from eternal damnation. He was perhaps repenting a night on the town, drinking and keeping company with prostitutes. Johnson often rambled about London after dark talking with them. He would sometimes buy them a meal. He asked one what she thought was her purpose in life. Her reply, "To please men," touched him deeply. He seems to have got pleasure from the temptation they aroused, the erotic possibilities they stirred in him without succumbing. If the temptation proved overpowering, he would spend hours muttering prayers of repentance.

There were, of course, plenty of prostitutes in London. The higher priced were fashionably dressed and they solicited their customers in Vauxhall Gardens or St. James's Park or in the streets. Goldsmith knew them well. With his ungainly figure and his ugly pock-marked face, he had no mistress and no love affairs so that his sexual needs could only be appeased by professionals. But Goldsmith did not have the conscience of Johnson and repented neither his sexual adventures nor his drinking. Johnson fought a long battle with alcoholism and eventually gave up wine, spirits, and beer altogether for a while. As a young man he used to drink heavily, and he once said that the only time a man was happy was when he was drunk. But he admitted that he could never drink just a little—social drinking was beyond him. Finally, he concluded that drinking for a while to overcome dejection might result in madness, and he gave up the bottle altogether, saying that abstinence was easy for him but temperate drinking was difficult. In his later years he returned to drinking, but by now he had achieved control. Drinking never troubled Goldsmith. He had none of Johnson's quirks and so no tendency to alcoholism.

Reynolds once argued with Johnson that drinking made for better conversation, but Johnson would have none of it. "No, sir," he said. "Before dinner, men meet with great inequality of understanding; and those who are conscious of their inferiority have the modesty not to talk. When they have drunk wine, every man feels himself happy, and loses that modesty, and grows impudent and vociferous; but he is not improved. He is only not sensible of his defects."

Johnson's superstitions (he was full of them) made him an eccentric. Not only would he start mumbling prayers in company but sometimes he got up at dinner, stood behind his chair, and recited the Lord's Prayer. He developed the habit when walking of hitting with his stick each lamppost he passed and, if he missed one, he would go back and hit it. Often he counted his steps and if the number came out wrong, he would go back to the beginning and start counting again. He walked briskly, moving his head from side to side, mumbling to himself, and often bumped into people, continuing on too deep in thought to bother about the collision. At times while he was walking he would suddenly stop for no apparent reason and then after several moments of mumbling and gesturing go on again. Once, on his way to dine with a friend, he stopped and on some whim decided it would be unlucky to go to dinner that night and returned home.

Often, out in the crowded London streets, he made strange gestures with his hands and arms, holding his hands in front of him and jiggling them as if he were a jockey riding a horse, or crooking his fingers as if seized by a spasm, or holding his arms suddenly above his head.

Sometimes when Goldsmith and he were strolling about London together, which they often did, Johnson would halt and put either his toes or his heels together so that his feet were in the form of a V, go through curious motions with his hands until some required combination had been achieved, and then take off again.

Johnson could control these convulsions, if that was what they were, if anyone spoke to him. They certainly surprised Goldsmith, but he was too sensitive to make any comment. In his own wandering life he had met many eccentrics, so he would wait until Johnson had worked his way out of whatever fit had overtaken him, and then they would resume their walk. In fact, none of Johnson's friends commented on his eccentricities. He was a great man and entitled to them. That was their view.

Johnson suffered a great deal of physical pain, some of it perhaps from rheumatism, and at times lay in bed wrapped in flannel with a huge fire blazing nearby. He confessed to Goldsmith and others that he took opium at times to relieve himself of pain, but he never became an addict. Goldsmith, of course, approved of the opium taking, for the drug was often prescribed by doctors. In his short periods of practicing medicine, he often prescribed it himself.

All the while, plagued by his demons, Johnson's towering mentality continued to work. There was no subject or person on which he could not at any moment deliver a penetrating opinion. There was never an occasion on which he was at a loss for words—which often irritated Goldsmith, who was himself not so facile.

Johnson and Goldsmith had in common a carelessness in handling money, though Goldsmith was by far the worse offender here. Johnson lost money as a result of untidiness—that was the extent of his carelessness. He once hid five guineas in his study, strewed with books (mostly borrowed and rarely returned) and dust, so he could readily lay hands on the money when it was wanted. Then he forgot the hiding place and never found his five guineas.

Goldsmith never hid money. When he started earning it in quantities, he threw all his money in a drawer, out of which he or his servants (for he soon had some) paid any bills. He never knew how much money there was in the drawer or how much had been taken out, and he trusted his servants implicitly.

Goldsmith soon discovered that Johnson was pathologically afraid of being alone. He was always the last to leave a tavern, and he often begged Goldsmith to ride home with him in a coach. At first Goldsmith thought this a matter of friendship, but he later found that Johnson feared solitude even on so short a journey.

His fear of being alone, coupled with his charity to others in distress, resulted in Johnson's having three strange people to share his quarters at one time or another. The first and most honored of these was a Miss Anna Williams, who claimed to be a poet, who was three years older than Johnson, and to whom Johnson was so attached that he would call on her before going to bed, whatever the hour.

Goldsmith once asked Johnson whether Miss Williams, as she was always called, was really a poet.

"Why, sir," said Johnson, "she wishes to be known as such, and she has written a poem which I have rewritten. Let it rest at that."

Miss Williams had a strange history—as had the two others who lived in Johnson's house for long periods at one time or another.

Highly educated (she spoke French and Italian fluently), she was the daughter of an obscure apothecary, Zachariah Williams, who believed he had found a method of establishing longitude at sea by magnetism. To be able to establish longitude was one of the major problems of navigation at that time and was not solved until a completely accurate chronometer had been perfected. Williams, full of enthusiasm for his magnetic solution of the problem, came from the country to London with his daughter, determined to bring his method to the attention of the Admiralty and thereby gain fame and fortune. But nobody at the Admiralty was interested.

Williams, an old man, fell ill and, being also poor, was admitted to the charitable institution of Charterhouse. Anna, his daughter, had earlier become blind and, aged forty-two, went to Charterhouse with her father, for she plainly could not be left blind and penniless in London.

But the authorities disapproved of her presence and told her she must leave.

The story somehow came to Johnson's attention. His wife, Tetty, who died when Johnson was forty-three, was still alive and they were living in a house in Gough Square. They decided to take Anna in, and she made a contribution to the household with her needlework and translations. Perhaps Johnson also hoped that her presence would help control Tetty, who in her last years drank heavily and was also an opium addict.

When Tetty died a little later, Miss Williams remained with Johnson in the Gough Square house. She was with him, on and off, for the rest of his life.

There was never the slightest hint of a romance or affair between the two. He respected her and she understood his loneliness and provided him with company when his fear of solitude overwhelmed him. Thus, when she lived in his house he would visit with her before going to bed, or call on her, when she took separate lodgings. She would make him a cup of tea (he drank tea in oceanic quantities) and talk with him. Once, he called on her at five in the morning and pointed out that he was about to retire before others, for he had met a gang of bricklayers (coming home from their day's work, as he thought) on the corner.

"But, sir," said Miss Williams, "they have already been to bed and are now on their way to work."

"Is that really so?" cried Johnson. "I had not realized that the night was gone."

This was no affectation on his part. In his days of poverty he had often walked the streets of London all night with the brilliant Richard Savage, of whom he later wrote a biography, and never taken any notice of the time.

Goldsmith was curious to know how, since Miss Williams was blind, she could pour tea for Johnson. When he was invited to meet her—a mark of the greatest esteem—he found that she put her finger over the edge of the cup and so was able to judge the level of the tea.

The second occupant of Johnson's house, quite as strange as Miss Williams, was Francis Barber, a black from Jamaica, who had formerly been a slave and was the son of slaves. He had come to Johnson, freed, from a friend, and Johnson took him in and was very fond of him, though Barber had very little education. Still they often chatted together, and one day Goldsmith called on Johnson to find the great man almost beside himself with anxiety.

Barber had run away to sea, and Johnson not only missed him but was appalled at what might happen to him in the Navy of that time. He once said that no man would go to sea who had the contrivance to get himself into a jail, for being in a ship was being in a jail with the chance of being drowned.

Johnson set to work to use every ounce of his enormous influence to get Barber freed from the Navy and eventually succeeded. Smollett, who had been a surgeon in the Navy, was the first to help Johnson in his endeavor, which also called for the services of John Wilkes and Sir George Hay, one of the Commissioners of the Lords of the Admiralty. All for a black ex-slave whom nobody loved except Dr. Samuel Johnson. But Johnson needed Barber and Miss Williams and also his third companion—a strange man, Robert Levett, who lived with him too.

Levett was a gloomy, silent, dirty, ugly man of no literary pretensions whatever. He was a self-taught physician with whom Goldsmith was not averse to exchanging opinions—often to Johnson's amusement, for Johnson probably knew more about medicine than the two of them. Levett's practice was among the poor. He never turned down a patient and was often paid in pots of beer or bottles of wine, which he always consumed, whether he wanted them or not, as being his due. He had begun life as a waiter in a Paris coffeehouse frequented by doctors, and that had been his sole instruction in medicine.

Levett lived from hand to mouth the greater part of his life, and how he came to be acquainted with Johnson is not known. Possibly Levett prescribed for him in his days of poverty. It is not improbable, for Levett took almost the whole of London as his practice. He was unfailingly kind to his pauper patients and would go any distance to visit them. He lived with Johnson almost from their first meeting.

When he was sixty, Levett fell in love. He met a pretty prostitute in a coal shed off Fetter Lane, while still in Johnson's lodgings, lost his heart to her, and believed her story that she was the heiress to a small fortune which she was kept from possessing by a wicked relative. Levett married the girl. Then she was arrested as a pickpocket; Johnson intervened and got a legal separation. After that, the brokenhearted, gloomy Levett moved in again with Johnson, who did all he could to comfort him.

This relationship greatly puzzled Boswell, Johnson's biographer. Why such a friendship between this morose, ugly, strange man and the great Dr. Johnson? Why would Johnson have him in his house and undertake to support him?

Boswell put the question to Goldsmith, who replied, "Levett is poor and honest, and that is recommendation enough for Johnson."

But a man who had taken up with a whore and married her? Boswell persisted.

"He is miserable," said Goldsmith, "and that ensures the protection of Johnson." With that Boswell had to be content.

The truly great and good friend whom Goldsmith met as a result of his introduction to Johnson was Sir Joshua Reynolds, tolerant, warm, urbane—perhaps the most civilized man in the London of his day. He was a West of

England man, born in Plympton, Devonshire, and five years older than Goldsmith. All his life he had the easy-going West Country way, refined by years of London living.

He had never known the kind of poverty and squalor that Goldsmith and Johnson knew. His father had been a schoolmaster with a living worth a hundred and twenty pounds a year—three times what Goldsmith's father had earned when Oliver was born, and a farm on top of that. Reynolds came to London with a moderate allowance and lived first with an uncle and then in the house of Thomas Judson, the painter whose pupil he was. He was soon earning money in small commissions and, at the time Goldsmith knew him or shortly afterward, was at the height of his career, with an income of ten thousand pounds or so a year.

Reynolds never married, and his sister Fanny kept house for him for a long while though they did not always get along well. It was an elegant household that Reynolds kept. He bought a house (or rather bought a forty-seven-year lease on a house) in Leicester Fields (later Leicester Square) for sixteen hundred pounds and then spent a further fifteen hundred pounds building over the garden in the back a painting room for himself and for his assistants. His painting room was eight-sided and about twenty feet long and sixteen feet wide. There was only one window, high up in the wall, below which Reynolds placed himself when painting. He had a full-length mirror with a frame by Chippendale nearby. This perhaps increased the amount of light in the room, but also permitted his model to watch him painting, for he did not like his sitters to become bored. He worked very fast—walking backwards and forwards, staring at the painting and the sitter, and then rushing to the canvas to work furiously with his brushes and correct or add whatever he thought needed.

He spent his money lavishly on furnishing his house, largely in the Chinese motif which was so fashionable at the time. He had cabinets of gilt and lacquer, decorated with flowers and flying birds and imperial dragons. He had a Chinese Lowestoft dinner service of one hundred and fifty pieces

Sir Joshua Reynolds. Engraving by T. W. Hunt. BETTMANN ARCHIVE.

and he needed it, for he often invited eight or ten to dinner of an evening and was so easy with his hospitality that, when three or four more turned up, room was made for them without the slightest demur.

His dinner table was lit with silver candlesticks. His carpets were the best obtainable from Wilton, and the walls of his rooms beautifully paneled and hung not only with his own paintings but also with French and Italian landscapes, of which he was very fond. A cherished possession was a silver inkstand which he often used as a prop in his portraits. He fancied himself an author, and indeed he had room for such fancy, for he wrote elegantly and at the same time to the point. There was no more waste in his writing than in his painting. Everything served to convey what he had in mind.

This man then—this gentleman and artist with an open and inquiring mind—became the particular friend of Goldsmith and, almost alone among those he was to meet, understood his sensitivity, his curious innocence, his inferiority complex, which demanded that he push himself to the front at any gathering.

Reynolds never mocked Goldsmith or criticized him. His own perfect sense of harmony was never offended by Goldsmith's outlandish dress. He was never ashamed to walk with him though Goldsmith might be swaggering in a purple coat and red breeches. There is no firm record of Goldsmith's ever borrowing money from the wealthy Reynolds, who no doubt would have been glad to lend him whatever he needed. Reynolds probably enjoyed Goldsmith's improvidence.

Generously hospitable, he himself was a far better regulator of his affairs and at times showed surprising signs of penny pinching. He spent hundreds, if not thousands, of pounds a year on entertainment, yet seeing a mop handle in a cupboard, cautioned his servants to buy only the head of the mop next time so that the handle would not be wasted. And on one occasion a caller found a little girl sitting weeping on Reynolds' doorstep. It appeared that she had been modeling for him and he had given her a shilling. But the shilling had proved spurious. She had come back to tell Reynolds of his mistake, but he had refused to exchange the coin thinking the child was trying to cheat him.

His virtues far outweighed his minor defects, however, and one of his virtues was his constant effort to "civilize" London and, by extension, the whole of England.

One such effort was his part in the forming of the Royal Society of Arts under the patronage of that curiously disliked monarch, George III. And a smaller, but still significant effort was the founding of a club of eminent men which he proposed should meet every Monday evening at seven at the Turk's Head on Gerard Street, Soho. There were nine members originally (later extended to twelve) headed by Samuel Johnson. This was not a literary club (though it became known as the Literary Club later) but a group of men who were good talkers and deeply read. Prominent among the original members of Reynolds' club was Goldsmith.

Other members included Topham Beauclerk and Bennet Langton. Both of these had become friends of Johnson when they were young men. Langton had, in fact, come to London and taken lodgings there with the express purpose of meeting Johnson, whose *Rambler* he greatly admired. He had expected, reading the book, to find the author a philosophic, well-disciplined and moderate man. He met him at noon when Johnson had just tumbled out of bed and struggled into his brown suit, which hung loosely around him, his stockings nestling over his ankles. The shock was tremendous, particularly since Johnson was mumbling and rolling his head from side to side. But in a few minutes Johnson began to speak, and then his magnificent command of language and his ability to pick precisely the right word completely captivated Langton. He adored Johnson from then on. Langton came of an old English family which traced its ancestry back to Bishop Langton in the time of Henry II. That in itself was enough to impress Johnson, who in such matters was a snob with a deep regard for kings and the older nobility—not the new ones who had got their titles out of merchandising.

Langton was a learned and intense man, more ready to listen than to talk.

Topham Beauclerk (a friend of Langton before the two met Johnson) was not only the offspring of nobility but a descendant of royalty. His father was Lord Sydney Beauclerk (the name is sometimes spelled Beauclerc) and his grandfather was the first Duke of St. Albans, who was himself the son of Nell Gwynn by Charles II. Thus Topham Beauclerk was the great-grandson of Charles II, the Merry Monarch, and resembled him to a marked degree.

His character was utterly different from that of Langton and Johnson. His manners were elegant, he was easy in conversation in any company, he had his great-grandfather's taste for dissipation and women and seduced them, married or unmarried, with great charm and utter disregard of public opinion. He was tremendously rich and extremely well read. He lived in a mansion in Bloomsbury, then a London suburb, and had a library which contained thirty thousand volumes which he could read whether in French, Italian, Latin, or Greek.

Johnson said of him that his body was all vice and his mind all virtue and reprimanded him for the sharpness of his tongue. "You never open your mouth but to give pain," he said. Beauclerk might have replied that he opened it often to drink wine and kiss pretty women, but he didn't.

Beauclerk was in fact kind (as is the nature of a gentleman) but besides women, books, cultivated conversation, and good wine, he also adored a hanging. He never missed a Tyburn execution, taking along a party of friends and a hamper of food and drink, and reserving the best seats close to the gallows in the specially erected stalls. Once he journeyed all the way to Paris to see a man being hanged, drawn and quartered, a spectacle which was becoming rare in his day. He thoroughly enjoyed the performance.

These two younger men, wealthy in their own right, perhaps of all the members of The Club were least in awe of Johnson and least afraid to cross him. Once they woke him up, thundering on his door in the middle of the night, and invited him to make the rounds of the taverns with them. Johnson, who thought his house was being robbed, grabbed a poker but, recognizing his young friends, said he'd be glad to go for a "frisk" with the "young dogs."

"I love the young dogs of this age," he said. "They have more wit and humor and knowledge of life than we had." He admitted they had not the same learning, but then there was still time for them to learn.

Other members of The Club were Edmund Burke, a rising politician and orator soon to become a great statesman (he'd been at Trinity with Goldsmith but scarcely seems to have noticed him); Dr. Christopher Nugent, a physician and Roman Catholic, who was Burke's father-in-law; Anthony Chamier, who was then Deputy Secretary of War and subsequently became an Undersecretary of State; and John Hawkins, a Middlesex magistrate and author, who wrote a memoir of Goldsmith and his friends. Hawkins was seemingly a snob and a pedant. He didn't think much of Goldsmith when he was first introduced to The Club and said of him, "As he wrote for booksellers we at The Club looked on him as a mere literary drudge, equal to the task of compiling and translating, but little capable of original and still less poetical compositions."

At their meetings, the members had dinner together and talked on any subject. Johnson dominated the conversation, and Goldsmith was so hungry for esteem that he constantly made a fool of himself by challenging Johnson, rushing in with an opinion on a subject of which he knew nothing, or to which he hadn't given a moment's thought.

He couldn't help it. Remembering the figure he had cut as a boy in Ireland he just couldn't stand to be overlooked. He had to get himself into the limelight—talk brilliantly before these eminent people and dress magnificently so that they would respect him.

Johnson was an encyclopedia of knowledge and also had tremendous power of observation and an insatiable curiosity. "All knowledge is of itself of some value," he said, adding that, however minute a fact might be, it was better to know it than not to know it. Dogs, he announced for instance, have no ability to judge size for they would as quickly take a small piece of meat as a large chunk. They could not compare mass to mass. Millions had watched dogs eating without noticing that.

Searching for information, he had gone to a magistrate's court for a whole winter to hear how people were tried, and got permission to experiment in a china factory because he wanted to know how china dishes were made. He conducted endless chemical experiments in the upper room of his house until the constant explosions and stenches caused complaints. He went to a militia camp and asked to accompany the officer of the watch on his rounds so as to discover exactly what was done when the guards were changed.

Goldsmith was very careless with facts. Things were what he imagined them to be—what delighted him. If he needed to know something he looked it up in a book or asked someone, never for a moment pausing to consider whether the source itself was reliable. His facts were merely the stuff for dreams, and so in challenging Johnson at The Club, he was like a soap bubble daring cannon shot.

But sometimes, though admittedly rarely, it was Goldsmith who made sense and Johnson who produced mere verbiage. Thus, on one occasion Goldsmith spoke against the maxim, "The King can do no wrong." He pointed out that what was morally false could not be politically true and therefore the King might at times command and cause something to be done that was wrong and would have to be admitted wrong.

But Johnson, a monarchist through and through, thundered that the King was the constitutional head of the country. "He is above everything, and there is no power by which he can be tried." Johnson forgot in his fervor that Charles I had been tried for high treason, found guilty, and beheaded. And he did not seem to realize that he was attributing to the King of England the powers which the Papists attributed to the Pope. Had it been Goldsmith who produced such an argument he would have been laughed at.

Again when they were talking about writing fables, probably in reference to writing children's books, Goldsmith brought up the problem of getting animals to talk in character and little fishes to talk like little fishes. Johnson shook with laughter at the thought, but Goldsmith turned on him and said, "Why, Dr. Johnson, this is not so easy as you think, for if *you* were to make little fishes talk, they would talk like *whales*." He epitomized Johnson's monopoly of conversation at The Club by saying that he had turned what was intended to be a republic into a monarchy. When Johnson pooh-poohed the idea of there being a third theater in London, holding two (which put a tremendous restriction on the production of plays) enough, the Goldsmith soap bubble turned for a moment into roundshot. "Ay, ay," he said, "this is nothing to you, who can now shelter yourself behind the corner of a pension." Johnson, stunned by the rebuke, was silent. He was receiving three hundred pounds a year from the government and didn't have to struggle to get a play produced to earn his living.

But Johnson said of Goldsmith, "Whether, indeed, we take him as a poet, as a comic writer, or as an historian, he stands in the first class."

And Goldsmith said of Johnson, who had been compared to a bear, "No man alive has a more tender heart. He has nothing of the bear but his skin."

He might have added his voice.

CHAPTER

NOT LONG AFTER MEETING JOHNSON, GOLDSMITH WAS introduced to a young man who was to become even more important in Johnson's life than Goldsmith was. A twenty-two-year-old Scotsman, James Boswell, had arrived in London, hoping to meet Johnson and hoping also that the fact that he knew the playwright Thomas Sheridan would provide an introduction. But Johnson, though once a friend of Sheridan, had made some sneering remarks when Sheridan received a government pension (pensions aroused many jealousies among writers) and that door was shut. Boswell then set out to make the acquaintance of London booksellers as another road to the door of the great man.

Tom Davies, as a kindness, invited Johnson, Goldsmith, Robert Dodsley, and Boswell to dinner, so that Boswell could meet the man he so eagerly sought. But Johnson had another engagement, and only Goldsmith, Dodsley, and one or two others turned up. It was at this dinner that Boswell and Goldsmith met for the first time. They neither of them were much struck with each other.

Goldsmith discussed poetry with Dodsley. He had an almost religious attitude toward poetry and hated to see it used for satire or political purposes.

"This is not a poetical age," said Goldsmith. "There is no poetry produced in it."

But Dodsley had just brought out a collection of works by contemporary poets and would not agree. There might not be palaces in the collection, he said, but there were some very pretty houses.

The talk of poetry bored Davies and probably Boswell. Davies heard that sort of talk around his shop all day. Since he had failed to produce Johnson for Boswell, he started to give imitations of Johnson, mouthing his words and rolling his head. One bottle was finished at the dinner and a second and a third called for, and Boswell could not resist pushing himself forward in the conversation.

He'd been in London only a short while, but related how he'd met John Wilkes; how Charles Churchill, the satirical poet, had shaken hands with him; how he had seen Samuel Foote, the dramatist and actor, at the Bedford Coffee House mimicking notables about town; and how he had peered over Hogarth's shoulder while he was sketching and watched his miraculous ability with his pencil.

A little drunk, perhaps, he then described how he had gone to the Drury Lane Theater, where sitting in the pit he had brought down the whole house by imitating the lowing of a cow.

" 'Encore the cow! Encore the cow!' everybody shouted," said Boswell. "And I tried then imitating other animals but did not do so well. My imitation of the cow was the delight of the galleries."

Goldsmith, twelve years older, wasn't much impressed by the brash young Scotsman. He had other and loftier ideas of the theater than as a place for making barnyard noises. Boswell on the other hand was a literary snob. Having discovered that Goldsmith had never published a line under his own name, and was basically a compiler of books and a journalist, he tended to dismiss him as a literary lightweight and could not understand why he should be a close friend of Johnson.

The two did not meet again until Boswell had at last managed to meet Johnson—which was without a doubt the greatest event in his life and which he did not achieve until a year later.

Again it was Davies who came to his aid. Davies had formerly been an actor and had a very wide acquaintance in London among actors, writers, and critics. He was a cheerful, pleasant man, who served tea or coffee to his special friends and customers in the back of his bookshop with the result that the bookshop had become a sort of club at which authors, editors, actors, and others met and talked. Johnson was frequently there. Davies knew the times of his visits and so invited Boswell to tea in the back parlor of the bookstore on May 16, 1763. From there it was possible to see through the shop out of the plateglass windows to the street beyond.

While they were chatting away, Davies suddenly said in dramatic tones, "Look. It comes."

Boswell looked up and there was the lumbering figure of Johnson at the front door of the shop accompanied by an Irishman of whom Johnson was very fond, the actor Arthur Murphy.

"Don't tell him where I'm from," Boswell begged in a panic, for he knew that Johnson disliked the Scots.

"This is Mr. Boswell, sir," said Davies, bringing him out into the shop. He added, to Boswell's dismay, "From Scotland."

"I do indeed come from Scotland," said Boswell anxiously, "but I cannot help it."

"That, sir, I find," said Johnson, "is what many of your countrymen cannot help."

They sat down in the back parlor to tea again.

Johnson was not in a good mood. "What do you think of Garrick?" he stormed. "He has refused me an order [seat] to the play for Miss Williams, because he knows the house will be full, and that order would be worth three shillings."

If there was one thing that Boswell lacked all his life it was sensitivity and, hoping to make Johnson feel better, he said, "Oh, sir, I cannot think Mr. Garrick would grudge such a trifle to you."

"Sir," snapped Johnson, "I have known David Garrick longer than you have done; and I know no right you have to talk to me on the subject."

Goldsmith, Boswell, and Johnson. Engraved for The Eclectic *by George E. Perine, New York.* BETTMANN ARCHIVE.

That shut Boswell up. He accepted the rebuke and for the rest of the session he just listened. But when Johnson had gone, and Boswell thought all hopes of becoming intimate with the man had been destroyed by his own brashness, Davies told him not to be upset. "I can see he likes you very well," he said.

After that Boswell started frequenting the places where he was likely to run into Johnson. He was so persistent that Johnson, who was very soft-hearted, finally agreed to dine with him at the Mitre tavern. They had a good supper and got through two bottles of claret. Boswell told Johnson of his tremendous admiration for him and how he had come to London with the hope of meeting him—as well as to study law. His father was Lord Auchinleck of the older Scots nobility and Johnson loved the old nobility. When the bottles were empty, Johnson suddenly leaned over the table and said, "Give me your hand. I have taken a liking to you." That was the start of the most famous friendship in the literary history of England.

One of the subjects brought up at this meeting was Goldsmith. Boswell just could not understand why Johnson should take up with Goldsmith.

"Goldsmith is one of the first men we now have as an author," said Johnson. "He is a very worthy man too. He has been loose in his principles, but he is coming around." The last sentence probably referred to Goldsmith's occasional relations with women.

But Boswell still could not appreciate Goldsmith's worth, particularly since Goldsmith was such a poor conversationalist, and conversation rather than literary merit was what Boswell most admired.

Time and again he returned to the puzzle of Goldsmith and in his *Life of Johnson* said of him: "He had sagacity enough to cultivate assiduously the acquaintance of Johnson, and his faculties were gradually enlarged by the contemplation of such a model. To me and many others it appeared that he studiously copied the manner of Johnson, though, indeed, on a smaller scale." (The passage quite accurately describes Boswell's own approach to Johnson though Boswell was unaware of it to his dying day.)

Goldsmith's mind, said Boswell, resembled a fertile thin soil. "There was a quick but not a strong vegetation of whatever chanced to be thrown upon it. No deep root could be struck. The oak of the forest did not grow there: but the elegant shrubbery and the fragrant parterre appear in gay succession." He was fair enough to add that, although Goldsmith was generally believed to have been a fool in conversation, his reputation for foolishness had been greatly exaggerated. . . . Ideas tumbled out of his mind in hurried confusion and that was his main fault.

The first supper shared by Boswell and Johnson was followed by many more in quick succession. They supped together again at the Mitre on July 1, they met again in Inner Temple Lane on the 5th, they had supper together once more at the Mitre on the 6th. They met again on the 9th, had another supper at the Mitre on the 14th, met once again on the 19th, dined together at Boswell's on the 20th, spent the whole of the next day together followed by dinner at the Turk's Head in the Strand, and so on until early in August when Boswell had to leave for Utrecht to study law. When he left, on August 5, Johnson took the coach with him to Harwich to see Boswell off on his ship to Holland.

Such a whirl of social activity with one man, and a brash young Scotsman at that, puzzled Johnson's older friends.

"Who is this Scots cur at Johnson's heels?" someone asked.

"He is not a cur," said Goldsmith. "You are too severe. He is only a burr. Tom Davies flung him at Johnson in sport, and he has the faculty of sticking."

At some of these early meetings between Boswell and Johnson, Goldsmith and others were present. From the start, Boswell belittled Goldsmith. He wrote of him that he was short and his countenance coarse and vulgar, and his deportment that of a scholar awkwardly affecting the easy gentleman. He didn't like Goldsmith though later on he came to have more regard for him and in the end perhaps affection. But in the beginning there was at least a tinge of jealousy in his feelings, and Goldsmith himself was jealous of Boswell.

It was at one of these early meetings that Johnson made his famous remark about the Scots. A Presbyterian minister, a Reverend Mr. Ogilvie, was one of the company dining with Johnson, and he unfortunately picked Scotland as his topic of conversation. He said that there was very rich land around Edinburgh and Goldsmith, who had studied medicine there, sneered at the claim. The Reverend Ogilvie plunged on and said that there were many noble prospects [views] in Scotland.

Johnson agreed but added that there were many noble prospects in Norway and in Lapland as well. Then he delivered the crusher. "But, sir, let me tell you," he concluded, "the noblest prospect which a Scotsman ever sees is the high road that leads him to England." There was a roar of laughter in which Goldsmith joined loudly.

"As usual," wrote Boswell in his famous life of Johnson, "Goldsmith endeavoured with too much eagerness to shine."

Putting aside the ruffled feelings that existed for a long time between Boswell and Goldsmith, Goldsmith got along very well with others to whom Johnson introduced him. Indeed, he later joined with Johnson in helping an author more unfortunate than himself, one equally gifted in his own way.

The man was Christopher Smart and he was the son-in-law of John Newbery. Smart had been an illustrious student at Pembroke College, Cambridge, and was a brilliant poet. In his youth he had been so highly thought of that the Duchess of Cleveland granted him a pension of forty pounds a year to enable him to write, and the pension was paid until her death in 1742.

But Smart was a heavy drinker who was financially incompetent and often compelled, even in college, to hide from his creditors. He left Cambridge, having become a fellow of his college at the age of twenty-three, and came to London to write under the curious names of "Midnight Mary" and "Pentweazle." He was at this time thirty years of age. He was a brilliant satirist as well as a poet, but he now showed signs of mental breakdown. He became intensely religious and would sometimes seize someone by the arm and demand that they both kneel and pray together. This religious fervor became so fierce and so annoying to others that Smart was eventually confined to the Bedlam madhouse.

While he was there, he was denied pencils, pen, and paper so he wrote the words of a magnificent religious poem, "Song to David," on the walls of his cell with an iron key—not the one that fitted the door, however.

He was not chained or fettered at Bedlam for he was not violent and Johnson occasionally visited him. That Smart had been sent to the madhouse because of his religious fervor must have been a torture to Johnson, who also was obsessed with a need to pray spontaneously, whatever the occasion. But he would not desert Smart and now and again he recovered his spirits sufficiently to make a joke about him.

Dr. Charles Burney, composer and authority on the music of his day, once said to Johnson that Smart was getting fat at Bedlam, probably as a result of a lack of exercise.

"No, sir," replied Johnson, "he has partly as much exercise as he used to have, for he digs in the garden. Before his confinement he used to walk to the alehouse, but he was always carried back."

Goldsmith, hearing of Smart's condition, went with Johnson to visit the mad writer and was struck by his genius and his plight. The two of them got up a petition to have Smart released from Bedlam which they circulated among their friends. Smart was released at the end of 1763 and by April of the following year had written an oratorio, "Hannah," with music by a Mr. Worgan. It was a great success when performed at the King's Theatre. Goldsmith was inspired by this to write the words of an oratorio in three acts on the subject of the captivity in Babylon. He sold it to Dodsley for ten guineas, and John Newbery quietly bought a share in it. But the oratorio was never produced and perhaps rightly for it is not among Goldsmith's better works.

As for Christopher Smart, his genius seems to have burned out, and he produced nothing of worth to follow "Hannah." He had outbursts of religious fervor followed by bouts of drunkenness and died in obscurity, supported by the charity of his friends.

The Chinese letters as stated had made Goldsmith even more famous. Now his reputation was the more solidly established when they appeared in the form of a book under the title *Citizen of the World*. But to make his living he continued with his prodigious output for magazines and newspapers and turned out pamphlets on any subject that might interest the public if only for a moment. He wasn't, in short, writing to write but writing to earn, and it was all catchpenny work.

There is no need to sympathize particularly with Goldsmith, for Johnson had been compelled to do the same. Despite the fact that his *Dictionary of the English Language* had been finished in 1754 and since published in two volumes, Johnson was still living on what he could earn with his pen—writing, for instance, fictitious parliamentary reports based on the merest gossip. (The press at this time was not permitted to publish the debates in Parliament, and whatever bits of news dribbled out of Westminster were greatly elaborated on and distorted in an effort to satisfy public curiosity. Johnson's parliamentary reports, mostly imaginary, were presented as reported from the Parliament of Jonathan Swift's Lilliput.)

George III came to the throne in 1760 (a much more popular king in England than he was fifteen years later in his American colonies), and somewhat later Goldsmith whipped up a pamphlet on the history of Mecklenburg, which was the German principality from which Charlotte, George's queen, came. Goldsmith had the greatest talent as a compiler. Given any subject, he could quickly assemble sufficient facts and anecdotes to produce a pamphlet or a book. A great part of his genius here lay in his ability to decide quickly what facts and details were pertinent and should be used and what were not and so should be left out. With the *History of Mecklenburg* he also produced a pamphlet on the Cock Lane Ghost and another on the art of poetry. His earnings for the year 1761–62 were a very comfortable three hundred pounds. But by the end of the year it was all gone on gambling, on new clothes, on entertainment, and in cash gifts to whoever came by looking for money.

The Cock Lane Ghost was the talk of London at the time. It was reported to be the ghost of a Mrs. Fanny Kent, who had died at 33 Cock Lane in 1760. The ghost communicated by scratching and thumps with an eleven-year-old girl, daughter of Mr. and Mrs. William Parsons, who had rented the house after Mrs. Kent's death. Sometimes, the girl said, the ghost had a luminous form.

A woman called Mary Frazier, who was a friend of the Parsons, claimed that she could interpret the thumps and knocks and scratchings. Her interpretation was that the dead woman, reported to have died of small pox, had actually been murdered by her husband, who had fed her arsenic.

All this was the kind of stuff that Goldsmith, brought up on tales of banshees and hauntings, loved. He wrote his pamphlet in a few days—Cock Lane was but a short distance from his previous lodgings at Green Arbor Court so he was well familiar with the ghost—and it was a best seller for a few weeks. But then Johnson put an end to the haunting. He was appointed to a committee to investigate the Cock Lane Ghost, which had all London in an uproar. The pragmatic Johnson soon decided that the story of the ghost was a fraud, the object of which was a plot by Parsons to blackmail the dead woman's husband. He had the evidence to prove it.

Parsons was put in the pillory, where he was pelted by disappointed Londoners. He did not die in the pillory, however, for the crowd was annoyed rather than angry with him. Others less fortunate were pelted to death with stones, or blinded. Favorite missiles for throwing at pilloried men or women were oyster shells, which almost invariably blinded the victim.

John Newbery by this time had come to know Goldsmith well. He realized that Goldsmith, in matters of money, was an irresponsible child. Oliver realized it too, and in one of his Chinese letters he drew a portrait of himself, saying, "If the author be, therefore, still necessary among us, let us treat him with proper consideration, as a child of the public, not a rent-charge on the community. And indeed, a child of the public he is in all respects; for while so well able to direct others, how incapable is he frequently found of guiding himself. His simplicity exposes him to all the insidious approaches of cunning, his sensibility to the slightest invasions of contempt. Though possessed of fortitude to stand unmoved the expected bursts of an earthquake yet of feeling so exquisitely poignant as to agonize under the slightest disappointment. Broken rest, tasteless meals, and causeless anxiety shorten his life, or render it unfit for active employment. . . ."

Newbery decided in his brisk businesslike way to put some order into Goldsmith's affairs. Not only were his finances completely out of control, but he was constantly interrupted in his writing by callers. People dropped in on him every hour of the day without ceremony and he put his work aside to talk with them. He couldn't shut his door to anybody, and the strain of trying to write while being kind to callers was beginning to impair his health. He got further and further behind in his work until at last in 1762 Newbery persuaded Goldsmith to take rooms in Islington, then a country village, where he would get plenty of fresh air, be able to go for rambles in fields and lanes, and be free of all the interruptions. The arrangement was that Newbery would pay the rent and give him a cash account to draw on. The bookseller would recoup the money out of Goldsmith's writing. This worked well enough for a while, though Goldsmith seems to have become Newbery's captive, and did not earn much. However, he always enjoyed the country. His mind became more rested and therefore more active and he was still able to get to London every Monday for meetings of The Club, to which he looked forward. He didn't give up his rooms at Wine Office Court by any means, but the fact that he was often in the country reduced the number of callers there, and provided a hideaway from his creditors. Indeed, there is evidence that he had another hideaway, this one in London, where he shared a room at the top of the Library stairs in the Temple with a butler known only as Jeff. He would then have had three residences—at Islington, at Wine Office Court, and the use of a room in the Temple.

He decided now to start on a work of his own, in short, to write a novel. Recalling the generosity, good nature, and simplicity of his father, he created a character, Dr. Primrose, rector of a village called Wakefield, who, through his own trust and goodness, sees his family destroyed, his fortune gone, and winds up in debtor's prison, though all is restored in the end. This novel, *The Vicar of Wakefield,* Goldsmith probably worked on at Wine Office Court and he soon had the manuscript completed.

Then the inevitable happened. Goldsmith got behind with his rent at Wine Office Court, ignored the matter, and went deeper into debt. Finally, his landlady summoned the bailiff, who arrived to take him off to the sponging house, with jail just one step ahead. She is thought to have been a relative of Newbery, and Newbery, perhaps discontented with the amount of copy Goldsmith was producing while drawing upon him, may have encouraged her in this step.

Goldsmith was outraged.

He stormed at the landlady and the bailiff too. Hadn't he always paid his rent in the past? (He hadn't.) Wasn't he a writer capable of earning four, five, or ten pounds just by scribbling some lines on a few sheets of paper? What did she think she was doing—arresting a friend of the great Dr. Johnson, and Reynolds and Burke, for a few paltry pounds? The landlady was unmoved. The rent was long in arrears. He had promised again and again to pay and had failed. He must settle the account now or go to jail.

Desperate, Goldsmith sent a message around to Johnson, explaining the situation. Johnson, who lived nearby, was not yet out of bed (the incident occurred before noon, Johnson's normal time for rising). Johnson sent Goldsmith a guinea, and Goldsmith as soon as he received it sent the bailiff out for a bottle of Madeira, which he proceeded to drink. Johnson arrived, spotted the bottle of wine, thumped the cork back into it, and told Goldsmith to calm down and let him handle the situation.

"Have you got anything written?" he asked. "Anything I can raise some money on?"

"I have a novel," said Goldsmith and produced the manuscript. Johnson took it over to the window, peered at it, holding the pages close to his nose, asked the bailiff to wait, and took it around to Francis Newbery, nephew of John.

(This may have produced a rift between Goldsmith and John Newbery, who perhaps thought he had the right of first refusal of anything Goldsmith wrote.)

Johnson was gone quite a while and, according to one story, the landlady proposed that Goldsmith settle the debt by marrying her. Goldsmith refused. At last, Johnson came back with sixty pounds, having sold the novel to Francis Newbery. Goldsmith paid off the landlady and dismissed the bailiff with a tip. He then sent out for more wine and some food with which to celebrate.

Goldsmith's first and only novel was thus sold for cash to pay his arrears of rent. Johnson actually didn't think very much of it and thought the sixty pounds he had obtained for it a very good bargain indeed. Francis Newbery didn't think very much of the novel either. It was not completed and it was too short. Goldsmith completed it and then padded it out with the *Elegy on a Mad Dog* already quoted and another poem called "The Hermit," which was certainly not first class and had been inspired by his reading Dr. Percy's *Reliques of Ancient Poetry*.

Goldsmith had a charming way of lengthening manuscripts by having his characters sing songs or tell tales which had nothing whatever to do with the plot but did help to round out the personality of whoever was involved. He padded so well that the novel eventually made two volumes. Francis Newbery was still dubious about its appeal, and to cut his losses (for he expected to lose money on the novel) sold one-third of his share in it to Benjamin Collins of Salisbury, who was to be the printer.[1] Newbery stalled over publication and did not bring out *The Vicar of Wakefield* until 1766, fifteen months after he had bought it.

When he did publish the novel, three editions were sold out in the first year, and thereafter edition after edition was

[1] The *Encyclopedia Britannica* states that Goldsmith sold a one-third share in the novel in October of 1762 to Collins—this on the basis of later research. But the story as set down was told by Johnson to Boswell. It is difficult to see how Goldsmith would have dared withhold this information from Johnson, since the facts would very soon have come out.

produced and each one sold out. The book swept England and Europe and entranced Goethe, who fell in love with it. Two centuries later and in an utterly different world, new editions are still being produced. *The Vicar of Wakefield* has earned a fortune for publishers in many countries though Goldsmith never received a penny more than the sixty pounds for which it was originally sold.

One day, a little before the publication of *The Vicar of Wakefield*, Reynolds called on Goldsmith at Wine Office Court. He entered the apartment without knocking on the door and found him not in the throes of meditation or composition or even reading, but squatted down trying to teach a dog to beg. Goldsmith had the dog in a begging position and was admonishing it by wagging his forefinger. Reynolds glanced at Goldsmith's desk and found that he was working on a poem and had just written two lines of it. The lines were:

By sports like these are all their cares beguiled,
The sports of children satisfy the child.

Reynolds laughed. Goldsmith laughed too. "I did get the idea from playing with the dog," he admitted. "But the lines refer actually to the nature of the people of Italy. I'm writing a poem about all the nations of Europe and I got to Italy when I started teaching the dog to beg."

Goldsmith had started this poem, which was to be called *The Traveller*, while he was journeying through Europe with his flute. He had sent some trial verses, summarizing the characteristics of the people of the different countries he passed through, to his brother Henry. Then he had shown some of the verses to Johnson. Johnson had admired them and told Goldsmith to go ahead and complete the poem.

Although from childhood he had loved writing verse, Goldsmith had become so inhibited as a man after reading the works of Pope, Gray, and Congreve that he had not had the courage to attempt to write a poem of his own for publication. It was Johnson who gave him that courage, and told him to show John Newbery what he had written. Newbery, who had perhaps the keenest eye in the eighteenth century for literary merit, was delighted and promised to publish the poem when completed.

So Goldsmith continued to work on it, aided at times by his muse and at times by his dog. In its final form, *The Traveller* pictures a man on an Alpine peak, meditating on the people of the countries through which he has passed, which lie, as it were, at his feet. In a four-page preface Goldsmith explained the meaning of the poem. "I have endeavoured to show," he wrote, "that there may be equal happiness in other states though differently governed from our own; that each state has a peculiar principle of happiness; and that this principle in each state, and in our own, in particular, may be carried to a mischievous excess." He repeated that message in the poem itself, writing:

> Each to the favorite happiness attends,
> And spurns the plan that aims at other ends;
> 'Til carried to excess in each domain,
> This favorite good begets peculiar pain.

Goldsmith was paid twenty-one pounds for the poem, which was published in December, 1764.

Its success was astonishing.

Everybody read it. It was the first work to be published with Goldsmith's name on it. Nobody would believe that Goldsmith, who was reckoned nothing more than a competent journalist and compiler, could produce such a work.

The word went around that the poem was really written by Johnson, and even some of Goldsmith's close friends doubted that he was the author. Anthony Chamier, Deputy Secretary of War and a noted member of The Club, just couldn't swallow the idea that Goldsmith was the author of so deep and elegantly constructed a work. At the first meeting of The Club following the publishing of the poem, which all the members had read, Goldsmith was rattling away as usual, made no reference at all to its publication, and went home early. The talk turned to the poem and Chamier said that to believe that Goldsmith had written the poem was believing a great deal. At the next meeting rumors that Johnson had written the poem were thicker than ever though Johnson denied them. Chamier decided to get at the truth of the matter by indirection.

"Tell me, Dr. Goldsmith," he said, "in the first line of your poem describing a river, you write, 'Remote, unfriendly, melancholy, slow.' Now what do you mean by *slow*? Do you mean *slow-moving*?"

"Yes," said Goldsmith, "that is exactly what I mean."

"Oh no you don't," said Johnson. "You mean the sluggishness of mind which comes upon a man in solitude."

"Why, of course," said Goldsmith, reflecting. "Of course. That is what I really mean."

This naturally convinced Chamier and others that the poem was actually Johnson's since Johnson understood the meaning of the lines, and Goldsmith didn't. But Johnson vigorously and continually denied that he had written the poem though he admitted contributing a few lines to it (nine in all).

Boswell was absent from England on the Continent when *The Traveller* was published. He was astonished on returning to London to find the fame that now attached to Goldsmith's name and the reverence and awe which was aroused by mention of the work. It was too much for him also to admit that Goldsmith was really the author, and he tried time and again to get Johnson to claim a large share in it. He speculated that a great deal of the sentiment and of the expression of the poem was derived from conversation with Johnson.

"He imitates you, sir," said Boswell.

"Why no, sir," replied Johnson. "Jack Hawkesworth is one of my imitators, but not Goldsmith. Goldy, sir, has great merit."

"But, sir, he is much indebted to you for getting so high in the public estimation," Boswell persisted.

Johnson wouldn't agree. Goldsmith might have become famous a little sooner by his association with him, he said, but the fame would have come to him anyway because of his great talents. Only slowly and grudgingly could Boswell admit Goldsmith's talent. But admit it he did in the end, for, whatever his shortcomings, Boswell was, at bottom, candid and honest. (One of his worst shortcomings was an eternal prodding and pushing of people into situations which they wished to avoid just to see how they would react. Johnson bloodied him several times about this tendency, but poor Sir Joshua Reynolds, goaded by Boswell, went to one of the Tyburn hangings for the first time in his life, and his balance and harmony were destroyed for many days afterwards. This effect did not bother Boswell, who had satisfied his curiosity by inflicting spiritual pain on the great painter.)

Reynolds adored *The Traveller* and so did his sister Fanny, who had not initially adored Oliver Goldsmith. She snubbed him when he first appeared at her brother's house, saying that he dressed like a mechanic and had no poise. No conversation. No address. . . . Nothing. In fact, she heartily joined in a toast, laughingly proposed at a dinner party, to "Oliver Goldsmith, the ugliest man in London." But when later Johnson insisted on reading the poem aloud at the dinner table, Fanny Reynolds said, with tears in her eyes, "I shall never more think Dr. Goldsmith ugly."

CHAPTER

FAME THEN, INSTANT, OVERWHELMING, AND LASTING FAME, was the immediate reward Oliver Goldsmith received for *The Traveller.* He was a poet of classic worth. The cash payment of twenty-one pounds, representing about a shilling a line, was by no means niggardly. It was soon gone, to be sure, and there was no more to come although the editions of the poem poured out one after the other. Still, every door was now opened to the man who up to this point had been reckoned at best an outstanding journalist, and among those doors was that of the Earl (later Duke) of Northumberland, who had just been appointed Lord Lieutenant of Ireland—that is to say, the King's representative in that country.

It was Dr. Thomas Percy who put Northumberland in touch with Goldsmith. The clergyman, who had seen the poet give a chamberpot full of coals to a ragged little girl, now had the pleasure of introducing him to the great Earl, who told Dr. Percy that he understood Goldsmith to be an Irishman, and he would like to meet him and would do him any favor that lay in his power.

So Goldsmith dressed himself in a new suit of clothes, put on a new wig, picked out his finest walking stick, and presented himself at Northumberland House, where he was quickly shown into an antechamber by a servant who told him that the Earl would be with him directly.

Here's Goldsmith's version of the meeting:

"I dressed myself in the best manner I could, and after

A view of Northumberland House, Charing Cross, in 1753. From a picture by Canaletto. BETTMANN ARCHIVE.

studying some compliments I thought necessary on such an occasion, proceeded to Northumberland House and acquainted the servants that I had particular business with the Duke. They showed me into an antechamber where, after waiting some time, a gentleman, very elegantly dressed, made his appearance; taking him for the Duke, I delivered all the fine things I had composed in order to compliment him on the honor he had done me; when, to my great astonishment, he told me I had mistaken him for his master, who would see me immediately. At that instant the Duke came into the apartment and I was so confounded on the occasion that I wanted words barely sufficient to express the sense I entertained of the Duke's politeness and went away exceedingly chagrined at the blunder I had committed."

But there is another version told by Sir John Hawkins which just may be nearer to the truth. Here is what he wrote of the affair in his *Life of Dr. Johnson*:

"Having one day a call to make on the late Duke, then

Earl of Northumberland, I found Goldsmith waiting for an audience in an outer room: I asked him what had brought him there; he told me, an invitation from his Lordship. I made my business as short as I could and, as a reason, mentioned that Dr. Goldsmith was waiting without. The Earl asked me if I was acquainted with him. I told him that I was, adding what I thought was most likely to recommend him. I retired and stayed in the outer room to take him home. Upon his coming out, I asked him the result of his conversation.

" 'His Lordship,' said he, 'told me he had read my poem [meaning *The Traveller*] and was much delighted with it; that he was going to be Lord Lieutenant of Ireland, and that hearing I was a native of that country, he should be glad to do me any kindness.' 'And what did you answer,' I said, 'to this gracious offer?' 'Why,' said he, 'I could say nothing but that I had a brother there, a clergyman, that stood in need of help: as for myself, I have no great dependence on the promises of great men; I look to the booksellers for support; they are my best friends, and I am not inclined to forsake them for others.' "

"Thus," Hawkins continued, "did this idiot in the affairs of the world trifle with his fortunes, and put back the hand that was held out to assist him."

The probability is that Goldsmith did rebuff the Earl, making a boorish answer to what very well may have been a sincere offer of help. But a man who has come so far on his own efforts, without anyone giving him any help at all, is likely to be touchy and what Goldsmith did actually was assert perhaps unnecessarily his own independence as a writer. He did the same later when approached with an offer of money to write for the government. Another point is that some of the Irish (even of English stock) were getting a little tired of the condescending patronage extended in Ireland by high officials appointed from England. Northumberland may not have been condescending in the least, but given his Irishness and his struggles, Goldsmith might have thought he was.

Finally, Goldsmith may have been influenced in his reply by recalling how Lord Chesterfield had utterly ignored Johnson, who had needed his patronage while compiling his dictionary. When the dictionary was published, Chesterfield praised it to the skies and acclaimed Johnson's genius. Johnson rejected the praise and in a famous letter likened Chesterfield to a man who sees someone drowning in a river and does nothing to aid him until he reaches shore, when he overwhelms him with congratulations and offers of help.

In any case it says a great deal for Northumberland that he remained friendly to Goldsmith, who was often a guest at his house. His wife privately published Goldsmith's poem *The Hermit,* which, as stated, he used as padding in *The Vicar of Wakefield*, and was very fond of it. If there was a victim at all it was Goldsmith's brother, who never received the slightest help from the new Lord Lieutenant.

This tremendous fame, indeed worship, was all very heady for Goldsmith and upset his balance. He had been mocked at the Peckham school, had been bullied at Trinity, and had starved on Grub Street. He had walked the streets of London in filthy rags. Now he was lounging elegantly and talking in the elaborate drawing rooms of the great of the land. The Honorable Robert Nugent of Carlanstown, Ireland, who later became Viscount Clare, became a friend of Goldsmith and invited him to stay for days at a time at his country seat at Essex. Certainly it was splendid, grand, and exciting. It went so much to Goldsmith's head that at a meeting of The Club, where he was undoubtedly doing a little name-dropping, he complained that at Viscount Clare's great house, Lord Camden, to whom he had been introduced, treated him "as if I were just an ordinary person."

Everybody laughed. What did he expect? But Johnson defended him, saying that the poet was by no means an ordinary person and the nobleman was wrong to treat him as such. A poet was something more and something rarer than a nobleman. (Beethoven took the same view—namely, that talent was of far greater value than mere rank.)

It was a curious aspect of Goldsmith's character that when people did treat him with reverence and awe, when they hung on his every word and made room for him as he moved about, he felt uncomfortable and played the clown, sang songs, danced, told jokes, did card tricks—did anything at all to get rid of the admiration and be accepted just as an ordinary human being. Yet, when little or no respect was shown to him, he became irritated and petty and pushed himself to the fore to gain the attention he felt he deserved.

Reynolds knew this. He knew that Goldsmith was often intentionally absurd in order to rid himself of the homage which another part of him demanded.

But nobody else understood that about him.

Shortly before this sudden burst of fame, Goldsmith had been doing hack jobs for Newbery at Islington. While his brother Henry was alive, he often wrote of returning to Ireland for a visit. He had a great nostalgia for the meadows and water around Ballymahon and Lissoy. He yearned for the countryside, for the quiet creaking of loaded carts, for the sound of rain on deep grass and the blue cloud shadow passing over the sunlit fields. But he could never bring himself to go back to Ireland, to be so far away from the exciting activities of London. He was fearful, perhaps, that with an absence of a month or two, everyone would forget about him.

At Islington, however, he found some kind of substitute—a needed relief from overcrowded, smelly, jostling London, which held him prisoner. London has been called a devourer of men. It devoured Goldsmith's yearnings to go home to Ireland.

The hack work for Newbery didn't worry him. The delights of the country compensated for the drudgery of the writing. He wrote a little book called *Description of Millennium Hall*—a humorous proposal for government by women—or it was reckoned humorous at the time. The idea was Newbery's. He made some additions to four volumes for children in a series called *Wonders of Nature and Art*—much the same kind of series that publishers of juveniles are putting out today though without the splendid artwork. He revised a book by a Dr. Brookes called *System of Natural History*; in fact, he rewrote it and produced a preface for it and got from it some ideas for a book of the same sort of his own. For this last work he was paid nearly thirty pounds. He wrote several prefaces for other people's work and probably some juveniles for Newbery. This is an area in which the research is not conclusive.

There was nothing of any great importance in all this work, nor did it put a great burden on Goldsmith. He was well used to it by now and for a while, with Newbery to a degree in charge of his finances, at least as far as living in the village was concerned, life went by very pleasantly. Mrs. Elizabeth Fleming, stout and elderly, Goldsmith's landlady at Islington, took a liking to him and often provided teas and dinners for his friends without making any charge. He liked to drop in at the local tavern to gossip with farmers and tenants, talking of crops and weather, livestock prices, and the French War now coming to its close. An easy country life, then, during the week, interrupted by weekend visits to London to see friends, write at Wine Office Court, and go to The Club on Monday nights. So he wouldn't be forgotten.

At Islington he produced only one work of note during this period. It was a *History of England in a Series of Letters from a Nobleman to His Son*. Goldsmith, of course, was not a true historian. He never consulted original sources. But he was a tremendous correlator and compiler of material and a fast reader. Over and above that, his own personality, viewpoint, philosophy, wisdom, and wit pervaded everything he wrote. Since the history was to be in the form of a number of letters, Goldsmith's charm and viewpoint were more important than the facts he related. It was this which made his history of England a great success, going through many editions and thought solid enough to be translated into French.

Of necessity, the work was published anonymously. The author was rumored to be Lord Chesterfield, Lord Orrery, and Lord Lyttelton. Newbery was quite happy with these wrong guesses for they increased sales. Eventually, everybody agreed that the author was Lord Lyttelton, who was so complimented that he made little attempt to set the record straight. As for Goldsmith, he was delighted too that three such eminent men, all of them great literary stylists, should have been thought to have written his book.

He had established an agreeable routine for writing the history. In the morning he would read in the current authorities about all the events with which he proposed to deal in the letter to be written that day. He made notes of this material on sheets of paper, and added his own comments to the notes—the comments being really the more important. Then he went for a walk, sometimes alone or more often with an Islington acquaintance or someone who had dropped in to see him from London.

If his friend or friends stayed over for dinner, Goldsmith was quite happy and was never in a hurry to get his company to go home so that he could get down to work. He ate and drank moderately. When he dined alone his invariable supper was a bowl of hot milk, sprinkled with sugar, with bread broken up in it.

Finally, when it was time to go to bed, he took his notes, his reference books, and his candle into the bedroom, and, either in bed or more often at a writing table, he wrote whatever was needed for that day. The writing, he said, was always the easiest part of his day's work, for he had all the material in his head and had only to put it down as if he were in fact writing an ordinary letter.

William Hogarth, whose engravings with a moral such as "A Rake's Progress," "A Harlot's Progress," and "Marriage a la Mode," had made him famous, was one of those from London who visited Goldsmith in Islington.

How they met is not known but there was a natural affinity between the two. Hogarth was a sharp, unbending moralist;

Goldsmith, a gentle one. Hogarth regarded himself not as an artist primarily but as an author—his pictures were intended to tell stories and instruct.

The two took an immediate liking to each other, and Hogarth called on Goldsmith often enough to paint his portrait—not the spiritual, thoughtful, gentle portrait which Reynolds produced, but the portrait of a working author at his desk, with a stocking on his head in place of a nightcap.

Reynolds' portrait is that of a man suffused with inspiration.

Hogarth's is that of a man working hard for his living. That is the difference between the two paintings.

Hogarth also did a portrait of Goldsmith's landlady, Mrs. Elizabeth Fleming. Some have suggested that he did it to appease her, because the poet was behind with his rent and she was irritated with him. It's more likely he did it out of friendliness or in return for one of the free dinners which she often supplied out of her regard for the poet.

At this time, 1763, Hogarth was in great need of a friend. He was sixty-six years of age and within a year of his death. He had just quarrelled bitterly with his two greatest friends—John Wilkes and the poet Charles Churchill—quarrelled to the extent that they were attacking each other in public and there was no hope of reconciliation.

Goldsmith was not fond of Churchill, who used poetry solely for satire and invective—an unpardonable abuse of talent in Goldsmith's mind. Churchill, thirty-two years of age at the time, was a clergyman who had been married at eighteen and separated from his wife but two years before—that is to say, in 1761. He lived in poverty up to the time when he published, anonymously, and without any fanfare, a pamphlet called the *Rosciad,* a biting satire in verse of all the leading actors and actresses of the London stage.

For a week or so his pamphlet lay unnoticed on the booksellers' stalls. Then miraculously it started to sell, and sold in such quantities that Churchill became overnight wealthy and famous. He paid off all his debts, made a generous allowance for his wife, and started a life as a profligate so that he was forced by his bishop to resign his living. He became a friend of both Hogarth and Wilkes, two outspoken champions of the liberties of the people as opposed to the privileges and deceits of the ministers of the King.

Hogarth had been appointed sergeant painter to the court in 1757, and the appointment was reconfirmed when George III came to the throne in 1760. In a moment of weakness (or perhaps not even considering what he was doing), Hogarth agreed to execute some engravings which were thinly concealed government propaganda. Wilkes, an unrelenting foe of the monarch, engaged in a bitter struggle against the Prime Minister, Lord Bute, accused Hogarth of turning traitor, and bitterly attacked him as a man and an artist in his paper, *The North Briton.*

Churchill joined in denouncing Hogarth and also published an attack on the old artist.

The quarrel flared up so suddenly and so venomously that there was no possibility of explanation or reconciliation.

Hogarth was terribly shaken.

His health broke down but he was a man of pride and courage. He fought back, painting a portrait of Wilkes, squint-eyed and leering, which has lasted to this day. He did another picture of Churchill as a bear (Churchill was a huge man), and he said cheerfully that the money he earned from these engravings "together with occasionally riding horseback restored me to as much health as can be expected at my time of life."

But it wasn't true. He died in October of the following year, 1764, broken-hearted over the quarrel. Churchill died a few weeks later. But the last year of Hogarth's life was cheered to some degree by his friendship with Goldsmith.

The bait of government patronage—at times in the form of a pension and at others in the form of a salary or sinecure—was a temptation that writers and artists had to resist unremittingly if they wished to preserve their reputations and keep their friends, as Hogarth had found.

Edmund Burke in his early thirties had been given a pension out of the revenue of Ireland of three hundred pounds a year. Burke found that there were so many strings attached to the pension that he shortly afterwards gave it up. He learned that he was expected to become the lackey of William Gerald Hamilton, secretary for Ireland. Hamilton, who was described as "a sullen, vain, proud, selfish, canker-hearted, envious reptile," was known as Single Speech Hamilton, for he made but one brilliant address in the House of Commons and was thereafter silent. There is a strong suspicion that someone else wrote it.

Goldsmith was later sufficiently well known to be offered a government salary in return for writing propaganda for the administration.

Parson James Scott, chaplain to the Earl of Sandwich, then a principal Secretary of State, was sent around to Goldsmith to make the offer, perhaps in the year 1767. Sandwich, who was known as Jemmy Twitcher, was notoriously corrupt in an age of widespread corruption. His name is remembered today in the Sandwich Islands and in the sandwich itself, which he invented so as to have something to eat without having to leave the gaming table.

He was a prominent member of the Medmenham Monks, a secret fraternity organized by Sir Francis Dashwood which met in the ruins of St. Mary's Abbey on Sir Francis' estate at Medmenham in Buckinghamshire. The members parodied the rites of the Roman Catholic Mass, pretended to worship Satan, dressed as monks, and had sexual orgies with women (many of high society and some their own sisters) who were dressed as nuns.

Wilkes, who was also a member of the Monks, was unwittingly responsible for breaking the organization up.

He released from a cage, unexpectedly, a large baboon dressed as Satan just as Lord Orford had finished a prayer to the devil. Orford nearly went out of his mind, thinking his prayer had been answered, and that was the end of the Monks of Medmenham.

Later, Sandwich turned on Wilkes and took a leading part in prosecuting him, for which he was pilloried in *The Beggar's Opera* and never forgiven by the London mob which delighted in chasing his coach through the streets and pelting it with mud.

Parson Scott then called on Goldsmith and recounted the story of their interview himself. "I found him," he said, "in a miserable set of chambers in the Temple. I told him my authority; I told him that I was empowered to pay most liberally for his exertions; and would you believe it, he was so absurd as to say, 'I can earn as much as will supply my wants without writing for any party; the assistance you offer is therefore unnecessary to me.' And so I left him in his garret."

Pensions, though they carried a taint, sometimes were given for real merit. Cleland had received a pension to encourage him to write books of a sort different from *Fanny Hill.* In July of 1762, Johnson was offered a pension and, although he was desperately in need of the money, he was very hesitant about accepting it. In his Dictionary he had defined a pension as pay given to a State hireling to betray his country, and a pensioner as a slave of the State, hired to obey a master. If he accepted the pension, surely, he argued, his own definition would be applied against him.

He therefore first inquired whether the offer of a pension was seriously intended and whether there were any strings attached to it. He was assured that the offer was firm and the pension was given purely in recognition of his work—he would never be called upon to write for the ministry, at that time headed by Lord Bute.

Author and actor Arthur Murphy, a friend of Johnson, was the one sent to make the offer to him. Johnson said he would have to have time to think about it and agreed to meet Murphy for dinner the next day with a decision.

Johnson went around to Reynolds' house to ask his opinion. Reynolds assured him that Johnson's Dictionary definitions could never be applied to him and said that he should accept the pension with a clear conscience. It was his due. So Johnson decided to accept and, having told Murphy so, was taken to Lord Bute.

He still had some doubts. "Pray my Lord, what am I expected to do for this pension?" was almost his first question.

Bute replied, "It is not given you for anything you are to do, but for what you have done." He repeated that statement and Johnson was satisfied.

Johnson, however, complained later that he was asked by the administration to write political pamphlets and was so irritated by the request that he almost gave the pension up. But he didn't and remarked that the only real restriction resulting from the pension was that he could not curse the House of Hanover (if he wished) or drink a health to King James of the dispossessed House of Stuart.

"But," he added, "I think that the pleasures of cursing the House of Hanover and drinking King James' health are amply overbalanced by three hundred pounds a year."

The pension made a great change in Johnson's life. He largely gave up writing after receiving it, being content with becoming a conversationalist. And it is as a conversationalist rather than as a writer (his Dictionary aside) that he is remembered.

One of the people Goldsmith made friends with at this time was Peter Annet. He met Annet at the Robin Hood Club, a debating society which Goldsmith had joined because he was eager to make a name as a public speaker. His first attempts at debating were a fiasco. Rising to make a point, he rambled and stuttered and forgot in his nervousness what it was he wanted to say and eventually sat down in confusion.

Annet was an atheist or at least a fighting opponent of the Bible. He had published some articles attacking the Book of Genesis, had been put twice in the pillory in one year for disrespect to the Bible, and had also been imprisoned.

One day Goldsmith called on Annet with John Newbery. Newbery wanted to buy a child's grammar which Annet had compiled, and he took Goldsmith along because he knew the interview was going to be sticky and he thought Goldsmith would calm things down, being Annet's friend.

The interview was sticky indeed as a result of a small but important point. The price was agreed on and other details settled except the matter of to whom the grammar should be attributed. Newbery, a prudent man, didn't want to publish a children's grammar under the name of a man who had been pilloried for attacking the Bible. Annet was furious. He called the publisher a coward, said he was unworthy to handle the book, and, despite all Goldsmith could say, he ordered the two of them out of the room and refused to sign a contract.

Goldsmith liked him all the more for sticking to his principles at the expense of his purse, for Annet was in sharp need of money.

As for Goldsmith, he was now in quite a prosperous way, having completed for Newbery a compilation entitled *A Survey of Experimental Philosophy, Considered in Its Present State of Improvement*, a book on what we now call the sciences.[1] He received sixty guineas for this and with other commissions felt wealthy enough in 1765 to give up his Wine Office Court lodgings and his room at the head of the Library stairs in the Temple, move into better chambers at Garden Court, also in the Temple, and hire a manservant.

He was prosperous indeed and had bright visions of a new field in which to write. He contemplated, and may in fact have started upon, a play.

[1] This book was not published until 1776, two years after Goldsmith's death. He was again working on it the year he died. Presumably, his first effort was not satisfactory.

CHAPTER

The theater had always fascinated Oliver Goldsmith and, however poor he was, he would manage somehow to get together a shilling or so to see a play.

In the days of his vagabondage in Europe he went to plays in Louvain and Leyden and in Paris and Padua or wherever a new show offered. When he returned to England with but a few pennies in his pocket he tried to put on a show in a barn —some stage performance in which he recited bits of poetry or speeches from popular works, or sang songs, and played his flute. But the thing was a failure for his diction was poor, his accent strongly Irish, and his speech hesitant though he had a good Irish tenor when singing.

Much playgoing made Goldsmith into an excellent critic with a great deal of experience from which to draw his conclusions. One particular piece of criticism cost him heavily, however.

In writing his *Polite Learning* he chose as one subject the condition of the stage and, narrowing his general remarks down to the theater in London, said, "The actor is ever in our eye, the poet seldom permitted to appear; and the stage, instead of serving the people, is made subservient to the interests of avarice. Getting a play on even in three or four years is a privilege reserved only for the happy few who have the arts of courting the Manager as well as the Muse, who have adulation to please his vanity, powerful patrons to support their merit, or money to indemnify disappointment."

David Garrick, 1768, by Gainsborough. BETTMANN ARCHIVE.

David Garrick took this as a personal attack, which it very probably was, for Garrick was not only the outstanding actor of his age, but also the manager of the most important theater in London, the Drury Lane, the other being the theater at Covent Garden. Garrick was a very handsome man, small of figure, vastly talented, witty, a born actor, well read, cultivated—and highly sensitive. He adored flattery and could not get enough of it. He could not tolerate criticism.

He had been a pupil of Johnson for a while (they both came from Lichfield, Staffordshire) in a classical academy Johnson opened and which was soon closed for lack of pupils. His father, Captain Peter Garrick, was stationed for a long time at Gibraltar and rarely saw his family. (Johnson was eight years older than Garrick and about twenty years older than Goldsmith. He took a proprietorial attitude toward Garrick in later years which was the cause of much friction between them.)

Johnson and Garrick came to London together to seek their fortunes after the academy closed. Johnson said he had twopence halfpenny in his pocket at the time and Garrick a penny halfpenny. Garrick stayed with Johnson for a while and then, when an uncle died and left him a thousand pounds, went into the wine business with his elder brother, Peter.

He didn't like the wine business, of which he knew very little, and began to look around for sparetime work as an actor. He was afraid of his brother's finding out and so he appeared on the stage under an assumed name. He played the part of a harlequin, joined a company of players, and in a short while was playing the principal role in *Richard III.* His first performance brought the audience to its feet, stamping, shouting and blowing horns so that the poet Gray said the whole town was "horn-mad" about him. After that, Garrick quit the wine venture and was in a few years the most famous actor in England and manager and part owner of the most famous theater in London.

In that position he was the man who had to decide what went on the stage and what didn't. He decided, of course, on the basis of his professional judgment of what the London theatergoers wanted to see.

He couldn't afford flops. Not only did they cost him money at the box office, but also a flop usually meant the wrecking of the theater. The audience would surge onto the stage, rip up the scenery, manhandle the actors and actresses, tear up the seats, and smash the harpsichord. Sometimes they smashed it even when the play was merely indifferent, for there was a great public delight (lost with the introduction of the stronger piano) in smashing harpsichords.

This roughhousing had at least part of its origin in the fact that many in the audience were either half-drunk or wholly drunk during performances. Bottles of wine were brought into the theater and sometimes a bottle would be flung at the actors followed by loaves of bread, beef bones, oranges, and tomatoes.

In the boxes that lined the sides and back of the theater, drunks leaned over the railings to spit or vomit on those below, or sometimes they played rowdy games of cards. If the theater was wrecked, it was a day or two before it could be opened again, and there was no way at all of policing the mob. This sort of behavior was not limited to the rougher elements. Everybody took part in it, and Johnson himself, disappointed because a display of fireworks was not to be given at Marylebone Gardens because of rain, proposed to wreck the lamps illuminating the place and was only dissuaded when an attempt was made to light the damp fireworks anyway. They would not light.

From Garrick's point of view then, Goldsmith's criticism, which he took personally, was grossly unfair and in fact vicious. Goldsmith didn't have to deal with an outraged mob or salvage a wrecked theater and lose hundreds of pounds in the bargain. So even before they met, Goldsmith was an enemy as far as Garrick was concerned, and Garrick got an early opportunity to pay Goldsmith back at least in part.

The secretaryship of the Society of Arts fell vacant and Goldsmith wanted the job. He wrote to Garrick asking the actor to support his application for the post. Garrick replied that Mr. Goldsmith having taken pains to deprive himself of his assistance by an unprovoked attack upon his management of the theater in his *Polite Learning*, it was impossible he could lay claim to any recommendation from him.

Goldsmith didn't apologize. He said what every critic would say—he had spoken his mind and he believed that what he said was true. He did, however, remove some of the more offensive passages from the second edition of *Polite Learning* but the enmity between the two cost Goldsmith heavily for the rest of his life.

One immediate result was that Goldsmith was discouraged for a long time from attempting a play. But as noted he eventually set to work and completed a play which he called *The Good Natur'd Man*. It was really a play about himself, for he was certainly the good-natured Mr. Honeywood, always at the disposal of his friends or even chance acquaintances and never putting himself first. It was a play in a usual form—the plot depending on mistaken identities and intrigue with the audience aware of what was going on, and the characters gradually discovering the truth until the whole entanglement was resolved with everybody happy in the end. Molière had used these ingredients and so indeed had Shakespeare. Yet *The Good Natur'd Man* was a new play to the extent that the characters were people drawn from life. They were real people rather than theatrical stereotypes. The humor produces real laughs, rather than smiles soon followed by sentimental tears. Goldsmith included in the cast two bailiffs readily recognizable as bailiffs—a theatrical outrage. He broke away from the formula for genteel and sentimental comedy, the direct descendant of which today is the soap opera of television, and filled out a well-known mold with genuine characters.

He took the play to Johnson, who agreed to write a prologue for it. Johnson was now so important a figure in London that the King wanted to meet him privately. He had been given the privilege of using the royal library, and George, hearing of this, instructed the librarian to let him know the next time Johnson paid a visit so that he could drop in on him. He wishes to meet you."

Johnson went to the library one evening and was reading a book seated by a good fire (it was February) when the librarian sent a message to His Majesty that Johnson was present. The King had retired for the evening, but immediately hurried over to meet Johnson. He entered the library by a private door, using his own key, carrying a candle, and the librarian whispered to Johnson, "Sir, here is the King. He wishes to meet you."

Johnson started up out of his chair, but the King quickly put him at ease. He asked the question put to all authors—was he writing anything at that time? Johnson said he wasn't for he had pretty well said all he wanted to say, though constant reading might give him some more ideas. The King said he didn't think that Johnson borrowed much from other writers, and Johnson said he thought he had done his part as a writer in giving new material to the world and it was time to stop.

"I should have thought so too," the King replied, "if you had not written so well."

The conversation went on for an hour or more with talk about Oxford and Cambridge universities, the best-selling *History of the Life of Henry II* by Lord Lyttelton, *The Monthly Review,* and *The Critical Review.* The King even suggested that Johnson undertake to write a literary history of the country, to which Johnson replied that he thought it a good idea and he would attempt it. (He never did.)

Johnson liked the King and the King liked Johnson, and the story of their chat together was soon all over London.

A prologue for Goldsmith's play by the King's friend, Johnson, would then have great box-office appeal. The prologue was written (it was a bad one) and then came the problem of finding a producer. As we have seen, there were only two theaters—Garrick's Drury Lane and John Rich's Covent Garden. Rich was dead and the management of the

Covent Garden had been taken over by a certain Mr. Beard, who in addition to being deaf had no real theatrical talent.

Goldsmith decided to try his luck with Garrick. Reynolds arranged a meeting between the two at his house.

The meeting went badly.

Garrick still thought an author somewhat inferior to an actor. His attitude was that any writer should regard the acceptance of his play as a great honor. Goldsmith would have none of this. He refused to flatter Garrick and refused to persuade him. From his point of view, the actor made his reputation from the work of the writer.

The interview ended with a shaky agreement by Garrick to produce the play, and Goldsmith remarked to Reynolds afterwards that "he could not suffer such airs of superiority from one who was only a poor player." To which the even-tempered Reynolds replied that Garrick could hardly be called a poor player—a reference not only to his talent but also to his wealth.

Garrick, to be truthful, didn't like Goldsmith's play. He thought it would flop but he wasn't frank enough to tell Goldsmith so.

Months went by, and Goldsmith, short of money, grew impatient. He badgered Garrick into giving him an advance and Garrick started talking about alterations and cuts. Goldsmith took the money but would not consent to a line being touched. Garrick might know how to act, but he, Goldsmith, knew how to write a play and that was all there was to it. That was his point of view.

Garrick couldn't afford to risk the possible wrecking of his theater by an audience infuriated by the innovations in the play, particularly the scene involving the bailiffs, which he knew would be hooted as "low." He suggested that the two refer their differences to William Whitehead, a not very talented man whom Garrick employed as a reader. Goldsmith was furious. Garrick wanted one character, Lofty, the perfect picture of a name-dropper, left out of the play since he argued that this character distracted the audience's attention from Honeywood, the hero, and Mr. Croaker, his foil. Goldsmith wouldn't hear of it. The argument got so hot that it took all the efforts of Burke (who was brought into the discussion) and Reynolds to restore some degree of politeness between Goldsmith and Garrick.

At about this point in the negotiations the Covent Garden Theater was taken over by George Colman, himself an essayist and dramatist, who had written a comedy, *The Jealous Wife,* founded, at least in part, on the novel *Tom Jones.*

Colman was a friend of Garrick and had been a partner in Garrick's production of a highly successful piece called *The Clandestine Marriage.* Ignoring the friendship between the two and what might be its effect on his own work, Goldsmith took *The Good Natur'd Man* to Colman, who said he'd be very glad to produce it. Goldsmith told Garrick and Garrick graciously agreed to release the play, although, as noted, he had given Goldsmith an advance on it.

But Garrick was no fool. He didn't want a new play by a famous poet cutting into the receipts of his theater. He, therefore, brought out a play by a popular Irish dramatist, Hugh Kelly, who had been a staymaker, a literary hack, and finally a journalist in the pay of Lord North and was also a friend of Goldsmith.

Kelly's great talent was that he could write what the audience wanted, and *False Delicacy* was ready-made for the tastes of the day. Garrick persuaded Colman not to produce Goldsmith's play at the Covent Garden until he had opened with Kelly's play at the Drury Lane.

Two Irishmen were then pitted against each other, Kelly versus Goldsmith. The contest was the talk of London drawing rooms. Both had struggled hard to earn a living as writers and although Goldsmith had the greater reputation among literary men, Kelly was the more popular outside of that circle.

Garrick was to play in Kelly's piece and indeed wrote the prologue for it. This, of course, was a great box-office draw.

The publisher announced that the play, in book form, had sold three thousand copies by two in the afternoon of the day of publication. It went on to sell ten thousand copies. The play was an overwhelming success—the talk of London and of the Continent. It was translated almost immediately into German, Portuguese, and French. There were mobs outside the theater jostling to get tickets. Nothing so popular had appeared in London in many seasons. Kelly had, then, won the contest before Goldsmith's play was on the stage. His delighted publisher gave him a public breakfast and a piece of plate worth twenty pounds.

Goldsmith's play opened six days after the tremendous success of *False Delicacy,* on January 29, 1768. The theater was crowded too, for Johnson had rallied all of Goldsmith's friends to cheer the performance and drown out any opposition. But there were no mobs fighting for seats.

Goldsmith had ordered from his tailor an expensive new suit for the opening night. The coat was of purple satin and the breeches of blue silk, which splendidly set off the white ruffles of his shirt, his gleaming white silk stockings, and shoes with big silver buckles.

The play started very badly. The opening lines of Johnson's prologue were:

Pressed by the load of life, the weary mind
Surveys the general toil of humankind.

so the audience was put in a heavy mood right away.

The actor playing the hero, Honeywood, had complained at rehearsals that the part gave no opportunity for acting, so when the curtain went up he didn't act but rather recited his lines.

When a minor character complained that the French (with whom England was at war) had raised the price of beer to threepence halfpenny a pot, there were shouts of "low" and "vulgar" from the patriot pit. A scene in which Honeywood, heavily in debt, persuaded the bailiffs, who had called for him, to give him a break and dress up in his livery, pretending to be footmen, was hissed, and the new harpsichord was momentarily in danger.

In fact, it wasn't until the fifth act that the public warmed to the play. When the curtain came down, it was plain that *The Good Natur'd Man* had scarcely survived its opening night.

After that first disastrous performance, Goldsmith rushed backstage to congratulate those of the cast who had done well, and then suffered through the overhearty congratulations of his friends. He had to put a good face on things. He went off to The Club and chatted happily as if nothing had gone wrong. He didn't eat or drink much, but he did consent to sing his favorite song, "An Old Woman Tossed in a Blanket, Seventeen Times as High as the Moon," which he sang only on very special occasions. Johnson alone knew that when everybody had left the theater but him and Goldsmith, Goldsmith had burst into tears, and Johnson, whom everybody took for an old bear, had put his arms around him and consoled him.

Despite that terrible first night *The Good Natur'd Man* managed to survive. Goldsmith took out the bailiff scene (which marred his play but saved the harpsichord) and the piece was staged for another nine days, for some of its worth came through despite the bad acting. (The King ordered a command performance on the fifth night to everyone's surprise, and stayed to the end. But the house was by no means packed as had been the case with *False Delicacy*.)

It was the custom, instead of paying a royalty to a playwright, to give him the total box office on particular days. Goldsmith's days were the third, sixth, and ninth, and he made in all four hundred pounds from his play. To this was added a hundred pounds from the bookseller Griffin, who published the play in book form and said that the first edition had been sold out in a day or so.

This, though it didn't compare with Kelly's enormous

take, was a great deal of money that Goldsmith had earned in less than two weeks.

The obvious thing to do was to spend it.

Goldsmith moved into a quite sumptuous apartment at Brick Court, Middle Temple—two large rooms and a smaller one for sleeping in, though retaining his country residence at Islington. The lease cost him four hundred pounds, so he actually handed over his play profits to his landlord in an orgy of spending and then furnished his apartment in a manner that would impress everyone with his dignity as a poet, a novelist, and now a playwright.

London was devouring him.

CHAPTER

GOLDSMITH FURNISHED HIS APARTMENT AT BRICK COURT, where he was to spend the rest of his life, lavishly. He bought heavy woolen curtains of light blue (it was a favorite color, reminding him of the sky) for the windows. He ordered a Wilton carpet for the floor, and a mahogany table for the dining room with six chairs covered with blue wool and finished with an elegant double row of brass nails. He bought a fourposter with a feather mattress and bolster and two down pillows. He got a full-length mirror with a mahogany frame, a mahogany writing desk, and easy chairs. He hired a manservant and started to entertain his friends at dinners so lavish that his guests were dismayed. Garrick could afford such dinners and so could Reynolds, who was now getting a hundred pounds for a portrait. In silent rebuke they took to sending back one or two courses of Goldsmith's dinners, but Goldsmith didn't take the hint. He had money to spend, or thought he had, and he intended to spend it in style.

One day Reynolds called on Goldsmith in his beautiful coach the panels of which were decorated with pictures of the four seasons. (The coach was one means by which Reynolds publicized himself in driving about London.) They talked about money, and Reynolds, always kind and full of good sense, pointed out that what Goldsmith needed was a ready income, which was not obtained by merely promising to write something.

"You have a fine apartment now, beautifully furnished

and in a fashionable quarter," said Reynolds. "You are a man of eminence. Why not set up as a doctor again? Previously you had only the poorest of patients. But now the whole town will flock to be treated by Dr. Goldsmith, distinguished author of *The Traveller*."

"Capital idea," cried Goldsmith and went back to the practice of medicine. He bought an expensive new suit of clothes, a new sword, a new wig, and a gold-headed cane. Over his new suit he wore a splendid scarlet cloak, buttoned up to the chin. One suit he decided was not enough, so he ordered two more. But he soon found that one of the disadvantages of being a fashionable doctor was that he had to give up his visits to alehouses and coffeehouses, where in his own words, "I used to play the fool very agreeably."

Still, he stuck it out for a while, arriving in his scarlet cloak at the houses of fashionable patients and making a great play with his cane and his fine sword.

His glory ended, however, when he took a certain Mrs. Sidebotham as a patient. He wrote out a prescription for her which she sent to the apothecary. The apothecary sent it back, challenging the quantity of the drugs prescribed. Goldsmith said that the apothecary didn't know what he was talking about. The apothecary said that the prescription would kill the patient. Mrs. Sidebotham listened to both sides and decided in favor of the apothecary, and Goldsmith stormed out saying he would practice medicine no more. He would even leave off prescribing for his friends.

"Do so, my dear doctor," murmured Topham Beauclerk. "Whenever you undertake to kill, let it be only your enemies."

So he had to go back to writing again. He borrowed money from booksellers or got advances from them, and borrowed from friends, including a gentleman named Edmund Bott, a lawyer with an apartment adjoining his, with whom Goldsmith became very friendly.

William Blackstone, eminent English jurist, occupied the apartment below Goldsmith and complained that Goldsmith made so much noise that he could not work.

He had cause for complaint, for Goldsmith's parties included singing, dancing, and playing games like blind man's buff and forfeits. He often had parties for children, played hide and seek among the furniture, gave them rides on his back, taught them card tricks, put his wig on back to front to amuse them, and so on. "Men are never so much like men as when they look like boys," he said once, flinging his wig up to the ceiling in delight.

Once he was jiggling a little boy up and down on his knees but the child didn't enjoy this and smacked Goldsmith across the cheek. The father banished the boy off to another room, where he was to stay in the dark until he recovered his temper. This was too much for Goldsmith. He slipped out of the company with a candle and opened the door for the little prisoner. The boy was still sobbing and sulky. Goldsmith went off and got three cocked hats and put them on the floor, each with a shilling beneath. Then he made some passes and the shillings were all under one hat. The boy smiled and soon he was back in the company in Goldsmith's arms and Goldsmith was smiling too.

Goldsmith invited minor and unknown writers to his parties as well as famous men. It made no difference to him provided they were good company. Anyone who came over from Ireland was sure to be invited to dinner with him and he didn't mind at all if everybody, including his partner, burst out laughing when he tried to dance a minuet.

One of his friends at this time was a Dr. Glover, whose first name is not known. He came from Ireland and, like Goldsmith, had had little luck practicing in London and had become an actor. Glover, however, had a tremendous reputation as a physician for he had once been taken to a house in Cork where the body of a thief, cut down from the gallows but half an hour before, was lying. Everybody thought the man dead but Glover worked on him and brought him back to life.

"Had he his wits about him when you brought him around?" Glover was asked.

"He had indeed," was the reply, "for the rope mark on his neck was hardly beginning to fade before he had picked my pocket."

It was not only for his dinner parties that Goldsmith was known among his friends. He also started a Wednesday Club, meeting once a week at The Globe Tavern, and this club was a sort of corrective to the one founded by Reynolds to which only the famous were admitted as members. Goldsmith's Wednesday Club had minor writers, actors, and composers in its membership. They got together and sang songs and played pranks. There was little "elevated" discussion. It was a fun club. One member, a Mr. Gordon, a huge bladder of a man, sang a song called "Nottingham Ale" which was a great favorite with Goldsmith. Goldsmith wrote an epitaph for another, Ned Purdon, whom he had known at Trinity. Purdon was a struggling writer and in his last years Goldsmith was his principal support. He dropped dead, probably of a heart attack, in Smithfield market. Goldsmith's epitaph went:

> Here lies poor Ned Purdon, from misery freed,
> Who long was a booksellers' hack;
> He led such a damnable life in this world,
> I don't think he'll wish to come back.

Since Goldsmith was so naive it was easy for the members of the Wednesday Club to play jokes on him. Once, he arrived at the club late and found all the other members had finished their dinner. A plate of excellent lamb chops was put before Goldsmith. It was hardly on the table before the man next to him got up and moved to another part of the dining room. Another pushed his chair away. A third put his handkerchief to his nose.

"Before God," cried one, "how could the waiter have produced such a dish as that?"

"Those chops smell," said another. "The fellow ought to be made to eat them himself."

Goldsmith sniffed at the meat and looked around at his friends. The waiter was called.

"How dare you bring this tainted meat for Dr. Goldsmith's dinner?" he was asked. "Eat those things yourself. Come on. We're going to watch you."

The waiter realized what was going on and ate the chops, which were, of course, quite fresh. Goldsmith ordered a new dinner and a dram of whiskey for the waiter. "He'll need it, poor fellow," he said, "after you made him eat that bad meat."

Sometimes, however, Goldsmith would become sad during the merrymaking at the Wednesday Club and go quietly off to his chambers alone. His friends let him work out by himself whatever was troubling him.

Hugh Kelly was one of Goldsmith's friends at the Wednesday Club. Kelly was married and often invited Goldsmith to his home. He had a very pretty and adoring wife and Goldsmith was enchanted with the couple. How nice to have someone to come home to, with whom to share hopes and disappointments, someone to take care of cooking and mending, set up a budget and handle the eternal problem of money. Someone, in short, to share his life with and love. Ugly as he was, he had never experienced romantic love for though he might have himself fallen in love once or twice, he dared not speak of his feelings, knowing he would not be taken seriously and probably would be laughed at by his friends.

Kelly's wife had a sister who was often about during Goldsmith's visits, and Goldsmith decided he ought to marry her. He would then have a real home, someone to love, and someone to love him. Maybe they could even have children.

He spoke to Kelly about it and Kelly told him to forget the idea. His sister-in-law, he said, was a very different person from his wife. She was as much of a spendthrift as Goldsmith. A worse couple it would be hard to imagine. After a few weeks, they would be miserable together. Goldsmith took a lot of persuading, but eventually he dropped the idea. For him there was only the life of a bachelor, often alone in his room, at other times enjoying club and tavern life.

Another amusement of Goldsmith at this time was to organize what he called a shoemaker's holiday. He would invite a party of his friends to his apartment for breakfast. This was always a big meal, and when it was finished, Goldsmith gave whatever was left over to the poor—including some of the washerwomen he had known at Green Arbor Court.

After breakfast everybody went for a walk out of the city to the countryside, which was but a mile or so northward. The usual destination was Highbury Barn, where they had lunch. A good meal—two dishes and a pastry—was served at Highbury Barn for ten pennies and one of the objects of the shoemaker's holiday was to have a good time without spending much money. After lunch there was another country walk and then everybody met at White Conduit House to drink tea. The evening ended with supper at the Grecian or Temple Exchange Coffee House back in the city, or perhaps at The Globe, which was in Fleet Street.

The total expenses of the day never exceeded five shillings, and more often than not, three shillings and sixpence covered them. For this everybody got three full meals and plenty of fresh air and exercise.

One of those who went frequently on these outings was a man called Peter Barlow, who was a copyist. He was poor and always wore the same clothes. He insisted that he would not spend more than eighteen pence for his supper and Goldsmith used to pay the difference, for he was fond of Barlow. Another was a writer named William Cooke, who was also often without money. Once Cooke asked Goldsmith to lend him a guinea because he had a date to meet someone at Marylebone Gardens. Goldsmith hadn't got a guinea to lend, but Cooke would not believe him. Goldsmith, hurt, scurried around town until he found someone who would lend him the money and brought it back, but Cooke had already left. To prove his goodwill, Goldsmith wrapped the coin in a sheet of paper and stuffed it under Cooke's door. It was only when the door would not open on his return that Cooke found out the trouble Goldsmith had gone to to get him his guinea.

After a while Goldsmith gave up his country apartment in Islington, and the suspicion is that he had quarrelled with John Newbery, who had as noted arranged for the apartment for him and handled his financial affairs to a large extent. On the other hand Newbery was ill and this illness may have resulted in Goldsmith's leaving Islington.

Illness aside, a quarrel seems inevitable in any case, since Newbery was meticulous about spending money and kept excellent accounts and Goldsmith though wealthy enough was outrageously careless. Sometimes Newbery had to lend Goldsmith a few shillings, for which the poet gave him no receipt since the money was often borrowed on the spur of the moment. Newbery would note it down, however, and Goldsmith would, of course, forget it, which would produce a little friction.

Again Goldsmith perhaps began to wonder whether Newbery was not exploiting him, assigning him petty pieces to write for modest sums of money which didn't give him time to write something bigger for another publisher. In this connection Christopher Smart, Newbery's son-in-law, was the victim of a very lopsided literary arrangement. He had agreed with the publisher of a weekly pamphlet called *The Universal Visitor* to give him everything he wrote for ninety-nine years in return for which he would get one-sixth of the profits—if any. Poor Smart was absolutely forbidden to write a line for anyone else.

This, to be sure, was not the arrangement between Newbery and Goldsmith, but disagreements seem to have arisen, and Goldsmith left Islington and looked around for another country place.

The link between him and the country was very strong and his greatest works had a rural setting. He found a tiny cottage at Edgeware which had belonged to a shoemaker and with his lawyer friend, Edmund Bott, took a lease on it. The cottage was built on half an acre of land, and the shoemaker had tried to get the most for his money by erecting a gazebo (a sort of little temple very fashionable at the time) in the garden; had constructed walks so that they wound here and there to give a sense of great length; and had put in a small lake or pond with jetting fountains as another attraction.

It was just the kind of place to delight Goldsmith. He and Bott, who had a light carriage, would drive down to it over weekends. They often landed in a ditch, for Bott loved a bottle or two of wine and once managed (in the dark) to drive the carriage into a post on the side of the road, while assuring Goldsmith that they were going straight down the middle.

Following the decision to leave Islington, Goldsmith had soon engaged with Tom Davies to write a history of Rome which was to be a school text. The shoemaker's cottage in Edgeware provided him with a quiet place in which to do his research and then the writing. He did no original research, of course, though he was capable of reading the works of Polybus, Tacitus, and others. But this was basically a job of compiling from modern authors, condensing and commenting—the sort of thing at which he excelled. He followed the same routine as he had for his *History of England*. He would do his reading in the morning, make his notes, have breakfast and go out for a long walk, birdwatching, dozing under hedges, collecting wildflowers, and chatting with anyone he met. In the evenings he wrote his pages for the day and the work went smoothly and rapidly, so that he had it finished in time for publication in May of 1769.

The book was an instant success, even outside the schoolroom. The simplicity of Goldsmith's style and the charm of his approach again caught on immediately. Davies was so delighted that he asked Goldsmith in the summer of 1769 to write a new English history in four volumes (as distinct from the history in the form of a series of letters from a nobleman, which he had written for Newbery) for which he would pay him five hundred pounds—a tremendous sum in those days.

This, however, followed an even greater offer.

Griffin, another bookseller, asked Goldsmith in February of the same year to write a new natural history of animals in eight volumes for which he would receive eight hundred pounds. (This was the work which was subsequently entitled *An History of the Earth and Animated Nature.*) To this Goldsmith agreed without the slightest hesitation.

It was a massive undertaking to which he had assented. In effect he was to produce twelve books, four of which would cover the whole history of England from the Roman invasion to his own time, and eight of which would provide a description of all the animals on earth, together with a history of the earth since the Creation.

Goldsmith seems to have thought little of it. Life was good. He had plenty of money to draw upon now after the fallow years at Islington. He had fashionable lodgings at the Temple in London, and a country cottage in Edgeware. He was famous as a poet, dramatist, and novelist. He ought to celebrate.

He went to his tailor and ordered a new suit.

CHAPTER XIV

WHILE GOLDSMITH WAS AWAY AT EDGEWARE WORKING ON his new four-volume *History of England* and also getting some notes together for his natural history, which was to have the short title *Animated Nature,* London was often in the hands of the mob. John Wilkes, champion of liberty and one of the most profligate men of his time, returned to London and the mob rallied to support him.

Some years earlier he had brought out in his newspaper, *The North Briton,* an attack on the King's speech to Parliament, which he said was nothing but a collection of lies. He made it clear that it was known that the King's speech was actually his minister's speech, but the King chose to take the attack personally.

Wilkes was order to stand trial, for the House of Commons had voted his attack a seditious libel on the King. Wilkes realized that he wouldn't stand a chance in court and fled to Paris. In Paris he placed his daughter in a very strict boarding school, having first lectured the prim lady who ran it on the dangers to morals which faced a young girl in the kind of world in which they lived. He then seduced the schoolmistress (for ugly as he was, few women could resist him for long), left his daughter at the school, and set about seducing as many of the ladies of Paris as he might.

In 1768 he returned to England—now an outlaw—and boldly ran for election to Parliament as a member for London. He was defeated in that election and ran immediately for Middlesex, the county in which London is situated, and was elected. He was then brought to trial on the outlawry charge, found guilty, and sentenced to a year's imprisonment and a fine of five hundred pounds.

But the London mobs adored him for his bold challenge to the King (or rather his ministers, for they liked the King personally). A huge crowd collected outside the prison shouting, "Wilkes and Liberty." Soldiers fired into the mob, killing many—a foretaste of the Boston massacre—and the government congratulated the soldiers.

Boatmen on the Thames struck and there was not a boat to be hired along its length. Sailors not only refused to sail ships but took down their masts and rigging. Longshoremen refused to unload cargoes, warehouses were raided and set on fire, and well-dressed Londoners, meeting a mob, were forced to shout "Wilkes and Liberty" at the top of their voices. Irish coal heavers rioted, paralyzing the waterfronts for many hours. Troops were again summoned and nineteen persons were killed.

None of these rioters had the right to vote, and Wilkes had made them aware that they must have that right. He also demanded the reform of the election system, getting rid of rotten boroughs, where a few votes, readily bought, could elect a man to Parliament.

Wilkes' debts at one time amounted to twenty thousand pounds, but he never lost his nerve or his wit. Informed that one of his prominent followers had turned coat and deserted him, Wilkes replied that there must be some mistake for none of his followers had a coat to turn. The Earl of Sandwich prophesied of Wilkes that he would die either of clap or on the gallows.

"That, my Lord," said Wilkes, "will depend upon whether I embrace your mistress or your principles."

Wilkes became a hero in America, his example helping to fire the colonists in their stand against taxation without representation. They sent large sums to pay off his debts. Wilkes paid his accounts and drank up and gambled away the rest.

From all of this Goldsmith and most of literary London remained apart. Goldsmith never interfered in politics or uttered a political word.

Goldsmith's life had now undergone a profound financial change. He no longer borrowed money in sums of a guinea or two, but commanded thirty, fifty, and a hundred pounds from publishers. He became a spendthrift not of a few pounds but of hundreds of pounds, which went in lavish entertainment in London. He often took strolls about town dressed like a peacock, while Johnson, beside him in his usual plain brown, was dressed like a bear. Once they visited Westminster Abbey together and, standing in the Poets' Corner, Johnson whispered, *"Forsitan et nostrum nomen miscebitur istis."* ("Perhaps our names will be remembered here.") From the Abbey they strolled up Whitehall and along the Strand until they came to Temple Bar. On top of Temple Bar were the heads of Scots rebels of the Rising of 1745, fixed on pikes and sundried. Goldsmith pointed to them and said, *"Forsitan et nostrum nomen miscebitur istis."*

His lavish spending and entertaining were Goldsmith's method of trying to regain the attention that had been focussed on him as a child. Sometimes he was elated with his success and then did not feel the need to push himself forward. But then some minor incident would occur and he would be thrown down and desperately seek attention and adulation. He was painfully sensitive, indeed neurotic, but Reynolds and perhaps Dr. Percy were the only ones who, in the rough-and-tumble eighteenth century, realized this.

Johnson, despite his own inner turmoil, was seldom aware of Goldsmith's sensitivity, nor were the rest of his friends. Johnson, in fact, was often callous to him.

For instance, a Scottish writer, James Beattie, produced in 1770 a book, *Essay on the Nature and Immutability of Truth, in Opposition to Sophistry and Scepticism*, which was a best-seller overnight. Johnson and all London spoke in glowing terms of this *Essay on Truth* as it became known. Johnson embraced Beattie when they met and called him the long-delayed avenger of insulted Christianity. The author was awarded a government pension worth two hundred pounds a year.

Goldsmith was hurt. He complained that here was a man who had written one book and received a pension while he who had written several had had very little reward and no government recognition.

"Why, Goldy," said Johnson, "you have to bear in mind that there are forty-two sixpences in one guinea," meaning that all Goldsmith's work added up to only the one book this man had written. The thrust, from so close a friend, was cruel. It was made in public, at a dinner at the Thrales', and Mrs. Thrale and the rest of the company laughed heartily.

Sometimes, without a doubt, Goldsmith merited such a rebuke. One of his faults was that the envies and jealousies that others felt and kept to themselves, Goldsmith spoke out about. He had no power of dissimulation and his insecurity brought out the envy in him. Though he never criticized Johnson's work in front of Johnson, he often did when Johnson was not there. He was even envious of the dead and spoke slightingly of Shakespeare. He told Hawkins that to hear Johnson lavishly praised harrowed his soul. Praise for others threatened his own self-esteem. Yet he had a right to be hurt when he compared Johnson's much touted poem *London* with his own *The Traveller* or Johnson's somewhat pious novel *Rasselas* with his own *Vicar of Wakefield*.

His envy extended to people who were certainly not his rivals. Once, hearing a ballad singer, he complained that her singing was miserably poor. Challenged to do better, he sang the song beautifully and was very pleased with himself. Another time, when a puppet was applauded in a theater for jumping over a stick, he said he could do very much better himself and nearly broke his leg trying.

Yet it was Johnson who out of kindness decided to establish Goldsmith's claim to be a doctor of medicine more firmly, for he knew how sensitive he was on the subject—to the point that he insisted upon being addressed always as Dr. Goldsmith, and allowed only Johnson to call him Goldy.

Johnson arranged for Goldsmith to receive a confirmation of his medical degrees from Oxford University. But the records for the day on which this grant was made have been lost.

Oxford University was by no means then the center of learning and of thought which it is today. To exist at all, it had to attract the sons of wealthy men. To do that it had to cater to them rather than educate them. The curriculum was tailored to the student rather than the student shaped by the curriculum. The sons of merchants and noblemen were allowed to behave very much as they would when they left to enter fashionable life in London. (The poorer students, since their livelihood depended on it, stuck to the books.)

There were three ranks of students at Oxford—noblemen, gentlemen commoners, and commoners in that order. At the public schools which were really private schools, the word *Nob* was entered after a student's name if he were of noble blood and the notation, *S. Nob,* meaning *sine nobilite* (*without nobility*) if he were not. *Nob* is still used in England today to indicate someone of high station while *S. Nob* became *snob*—one not of high station but who acted as if he were.

The sons of the nobility, who were the greatest in number, rarely attended lectures, drank claret copiously, and spent their evenings in the taverns or gambling. While still in their teens at Eton, Harrow, or Winchester, they had had sexual intercourse with whatever women of inferior rank were available and continued to do so at Oxford. To no small degree it was expected of them, for wenching was part of the life of a gentleman. Marriages were business contracts entered into to increase family wealth, and although the bride was expected to be a virgin, a groom who was still a virgin would have been thought queer.

As for the dons at Oxford, many of them spent the greater part of their time soliciting funds and endowments from the wealthy, and gave few lectures. Some were not even qualified to lecture. Richard Watson, professor of chemistry at Cambridge in 1764, admitted that he had never read a syllable on the subject and had never even seen a chemical experiment performed.

It was no great effort then for the eminent Dr. Johnson to get Oxford University to confirm Goldsmith's medical degree. But that Goldsmith should be gratified by such a farce is a measure of how deeply he needed to have some kind of degree of learning attached to his name.

Goldsmith did not spend the whole of his time at Edgeware on the English history. His real love was poetry. He had been timid about trying his hand at it until encouraged by Johnson. The huge success of *The Traveller* gave him confidence, and he started work on a new poem about a village whose inhabitants, as a result of changing times, had all left so that it was now in ruins. The poem was to be called, when finished, *The Deserted Village*.

He took far more care with poetry than he did with prose and evolved a special method for writing this poem. He first sketched out what he wanted to say in prose, putting down any ideas that occurred to him. He then read the prose through and eliminated anything that seemed superfluous or was repetitious.

Then he set about putting these thoughts and pictures into heroic couplets, which were the recognized verse form of the time. He wrote about ten lines a day, in the morning, being very careful about word selection and meter. With ten lines done, he was ready for a shoemaker's holiday or some other amusement unless he had to work on something else in the afternoon.

All of Goldsmith's deep love of the country and country people came out in *The Deserted Village*. The poem was not published until May 26, 1770, two years after Goldsmith had started writing it. He sold it outright (sixty pounds is the usual price mentioned). It was an immediate success. A second edition was brought out on June 7, a third on the 14th, a fourth on the 28th. A fifth edition appeared on August

16. It has gone through uncounted editions in a score of languages since. Gray, who was to die within the year, on hearing it read aloud, said solemnly, "This man is a poet." Burke, now the most prominent statesman in England, said, "What true and pretty pastoral images has Goldsmith in his *Deserted Village*. They beat all—Pope and Philips and Spenser too in my opinion." Goethe was in transports when he came upon it and immediately undertook to translate it into German.

The poem went straight to the hearts of all who read it. Unlike *The Traveller* it did not comment on nations as a whole but on one village and the people in it, as a focus for the plight of rural England as Goldsmith saw it. The villagers were recognizable in their humanity in any country in the world. In the American colonies, *The Deserted Village* was so popular that a score of new settlements were called Auburn, the name Goldsmith gave to the idealized hamlet whose core was the Lissoy of his childhood so that every individual pictured has a counterpart in Goldsmith's own life. There is not one of them who is not treated with warmth and love.

Just after he started work on the poem, Goldsmith received news that his brother Henry had died, and went into mourning for him. The blow was so heavy that he never really recovered from it. He pictured his brother as the parson of his village and wrote a tribute to him now known throughout the world:

A man he was to all the country dear,
And passing rich with forty pounds a year;
Remote from towns he ran his godly race,
Nor e'er had changed, nor wished to change his place;
Unpractised he to fawn or seek for power,
By doctrines fashioned to the varying hour;
Far other aims his heart had learned to prize,
More skilled to raise the wretched than to rise.
His house was known to all the vagrant train,
He chid their wanderings, but relieved their pain;

The long remembered beggar was his guest,
Whose beard descending swept his aged breast;
The ruined spendthrift, now no longer proud,
Claimed kindred there, and had his claims allowed;
The broken soldier, kindly bade to stay
Sat by his fire, and talked the night away;
Wept o'er his wounds, or, tales of sorrow done,
Shouldered his crutch and showed how fields were won.
Pleased with his guests, the good man learned to glow,
And quite forgot their vices in their woe;
Careless their merits or their faults to scan,
His pity gave 'ere charity began.

His theme was the destruction of the village by the concentration of wealth in the hands of the few in a position of power. These, with the purchase of more and more lands and the passage of enclosure acts by a Parliament which they controlled, took away lands common to the villagers and destroyed the yeomen of England.

It has been argued that this was not actually the fact, and that there was no mass desertion of English villages, the villagers migrating to the big cities and especially to London. Yet even those who put forward these arguments admit that the yeoman farmer, hard pressed by fluctuating prices and land taxes, was compelled to sell his holdings and become the employee of the big landlord to whom he sold. His children, especially his daughters, migrated to the city, where the carts bringing them in at the rate of five thousand a year were met by agents looking for domestic servants and procurers from bawdy houses looking for prostitutes. And the big estates were growing, their holdings measured not in tens or hundreds of acres but in thousands. The Earl of Leicester built a magnificent home, Holkham Hall, and remarked that there was not another house to be seen around. He had gobbled them all up and had become the owner of Giant Castle.

Goldsmith was aware that a great number of people did

not believe that the English villages were being depopulated and some of them deserted. His friends, probably Johnson among them, warned him that the basis of his poem was fanciful and false, and in the dedication to Reynolds he wrote, "I know you will object (and indeed several of our best and wisest friends concur in the opinion) that the depopulation it [the poem] deplores is nowhere to be seen, and the disorders it laments are only to be found in the poet's own imagination. To this I can scarce make any other answer than that I sincerely believe what I have written; that I have taken all possible pains, in my country excursions, for these four or five years past, to be certain of what I allege; and that all my views and enquiries have led me to believe those miseries real, which I here attempt to display."

For Goldsmith, something of great value was being lost, and he summarized that loss in two powerful lines.

Ill fares the land, to hastening ills a prey,
Where wealth accumulates, and men decay. . . .

The couplet has the cold touch of truth for much of the world today.

But for all the truth the poem contains, it is sentimental in many places. It is full of nostalgia, and the real deserted village was in Goldsmith himself. For it was he who had left and gone to the city, where he dreamed of childhood and the cackling geese in a country lane. And while he denounced the Lords with their limbs clad in silk, he ordered from his tailor Filby satin suits and loved the very displays which he denounced. So *The Deserted Village* was a catharsis for him. He was torn between the excitement of London and the worth of the countryside and he knew, deep down, that the joys of London were false and that he was in the wrong place. Yet he could not help himself for he was not one man but two, and these two in opposition.

Both Goldsmith and Johnson were country bred, for Lichfield, where Johnson was born, was a small agricultural town.

But Johnson was all his life a city man and he died a little whenever he left London. His only poem of note was entitled *London.*

But Goldsmith belonged to the country. He could make a living as a writer only in London, but it was in London that Goldsmith died a little. He had constantly to return to the fields and the hedgerows at Islington and at Edgeware to bring himself back to life. He needed the hush of the wind, the chirp of birds, the clean rain and warm sun and the feel of soft grass under his feet to feed him and to nourish him. Without these things he grew into another and false self, playing the peacock, trying to excel in repartee and philosophical debate, having to impress others so that they would notice him and think him clever.

In the country there was no need for this kind of display—no need for anyone to think him clever. He lived with natural things and when he left the singing and pranks at the Wednesday Club to go quietly home and be alone, it was because some memory of lake water and meadows sparkling in the sun had returned to him.

He described this deep inner loneliness in *The Deserted Village,* writing:

In all my wanderings round this world of care,
In all my griefs—and God has given my share—
I still had hopes, my latest hours to crown,
Amid these humble bowers to lay me down;
To husband out life's taper at the close,
And keep the flame from wasting by repose:
I still had hopes, for pride attends us still,
Amidst the swains to show my book-learned skill,
Around my fire an evening group to draw,
And tell of all I felt, and all I saw;
And, as a hare, whom hounds and horns pursue,
Pants to the place from whence at first she flew,
I still had hopes, my long vexations past,
Here to return—and die at home at last.

Toward the end of the poem there is a farewell to Poetry, which dismayed his friends. He seemed to know that he would never write another poetic work (other than humorous verse, which he did not regard as poetry). Maybe he sensed that something was complete in his life and an end was drawing near. He wrote:

> Dear charming nymph, neglected and decried,
> My shame in crowds, my solitary pride;
> Thou source of all my bliss, and all my woe,
> That found'st me poor at first, and keep'st me so;
> Thou guide, by which the nobler arts excel,
> Thou nurse of every virtue, fare thee well. . . .

Johnson did not think as much of the poem as he did of *The Traveller* but then Johnson was a moralizer, concerned with principles rather than with people.

Goldsmith had ended the poem, addressing Poetry with the lines:

> Aid slighted Truth, with thy persuasive strain;
> Teach erring man to spurn the rage of gain;
> Teach him, that states of native strength possessed
> Though very poor, may still be very blessed.

The end is perfect. But Johnson added four lines more as follows:

> [Teach him] That trade's proud empire hastes to swift decay,
> As ocean sweeps the laboured mole away;
> While self-dependent power can time defy,
> As rocks resist the billows and the sky.

Good, skillful lines without a doubt. But Goldsmith had already made the point and they are repetitive.

There was a difference of view on the role of poetry between these two friends. Johnson held that the job of the poet was to examine not the individual but the species, to remark general properties and large experiences.

But Goldsmith's heart bled for the human heart. A sinner himself, he understood the sinner. Johnson would have made a Calvinist. Goldsmith was closer to St. Francis of Assisi.

CHAPTER XV

GOLDSMITH DEDICATED *The Deserted Village* TO JOSHUA Reynolds with the words, "The only dedication I ever made was to my brother, because I loved him better than most other men. He is since dead. Permit me to inscribe this Poem to you."

Reynolds, reflecting on the life of Goldsmith, to whom he was so close, seems to have realized that his friend was essentially lonely. In large part his trouble was that he had no home life—no wife, no children. There was no one to steady him down, to focus his affections and enforce some discipline. For entertainment he gave dinners for his friends or dined with them in taverns. Johnson at least had Miss Williams living with him for company. She was someone who was always there when Johnson came home, ready to make him a cup of tea and listen to him talk before he went to bed.

Johnson had made friends also with the wealthy brewer Henry Thrale, who took him into his house for long periods. Johnson had a family around him but Goldsmith had none. He needed the warmth of family life and could not find it in parties and the rounds of the taverns.

Reynolds then in 1769 decided to introduce Goldsmith into a family which admired his writing and might adopt him. This was the Horneck family, old friends of Reynolds, and it consisted of the widowed mother, Mrs. Hannah Horneck; her son, Charles; and two daughters, Catherine, who was nineteen, and, Mary, who was seventeen.

Charles, a fancy dresser, had just bought a commission in the Guards and was called "The Captain in Lace." Catherine, who was engaged to Henry William Bunbury, son of a baronet, was called "Little Comedy"—the family was fond of fanciful nicknames. Mary had been given the name "The Jessamy Bride." (*Jessamy* derives from jasmine and she seems to have had the sweetness and delicacy of the flower.)

Goldsmith fell in love with Mary Horneck. This was the first and only deep love of his life. It was unspoken on his part and shown only in the delight he took in her company. He was well aware of the age difference (he was forty years old at the time) and his own ugliness. He knew that if he mentioned anything of his feelings to Mary or to her family, relations between them might become strained to the point where he could not see her again. He adored her silently and possibly she loved him too for she did not marry until after Goldsmith was dead, and her face used to light up when, an old woman, she spoke of him.

This love turned Goldsmith into a boy again and he spent all the time he could with the family. He could, of course, never be alone with Mary and so was overjoyed when he was invited to dine with them, or stay at their country house in Devonshire, which was pure heaven. The tavern life dwindled to be replaced by family dinners or dinners with Reynolds at which the Hornecks were also guests.

He was so deeply in love that a year later he went with Mary, her sister, and mother to France, though he was terribly behind with his work and could not afford the journey. They sailed from Dover to Calais in the middle of July, 1770, shortly after the publication of *The Deserted Village,* and from there went through Flanders and on through Lisle to Paris.

At Lisle there was a military parade past their hotel, and the two Horneck sisters, with Goldsmith and their mother, watched it from the balcony.

The crowd soon noticed the two pretty girls and turned to wave and shout to them. Goldsmith, amused, pretended to be jealous and said that there were parts of the world in which he also was admired, which produced a laugh. (Later, the incident was reported as if Goldsmith were really put out that the crowd should notice the girls and not him.)

It was fourteen years since Goldsmith had been in France. Then he had been poor and now he was wealthy. The passage of time and the fact that he was now well-to-do made a great difference in his attitude. He complained to Reynolds about tough dinner meat and being cheated by postillions and landladies and having at times to lie in barns, which had been pure heaven for him when he was young and poor. He began to worry about money and work. Even his adoration of Mary would not keep these things out of his mind. They nagged at him constantly. But in Paris, hoping to prove that he really wasn't as old as he seemed and remembering his boyhood, he tried to jump from the edge of one of the fountains at Versailles to one of the islets in the center. He missed and landed in the water, disgraced, and knew that he was forty and Mary in her teens.

The plan was that after visiting France they would all go down to Devonshire to the Horneck home and spend some time there. But Goldsmith was too concerned over his affairs. He had overspent himself for the trip, which had naturally included a couple of new suits as well as a handsome new wig to make him look younger.

He bought a silk coat in Paris and wrote to Reynolds that when he put it on it made him look like a fool. It was hard to be forty years of age, to be in love, to not dare say a word about it, and feel like a fool for attempting a boy's jump and buying a young man's silk coat.

What made it worse was that an attorney named Hickey, Reynolds' lawyer, joined the party in Paris, witnessed the miserable leap at the Versailles fountains, and made jokes at Goldsmith's expense. Now he was no longer the sole squire of the three ladies but had the coarse Mr. Hickey butting in. This gave him less and less chance for a private word, or a hand touch, or a smile with Mary.

All in the party were Protestants and Mrs. Horneck was a confirmed churchgoer. It was not always possible to find a Protestant church on Sunday and many times she asked Goldsmith to read the service to them in their room. Goldsmith, who had been thought of as having no religious side at all, always replied that he would be glad to do so, but he did not think himself worthy to read the service publicly.

London was a village as well as a metropolis and lived on gossip about its more prominent inhabitants. It was not possible then that Goldsmith's love for Mary could be kept quiet. His friends said nothing but his enemies waited. Among them was the same Kenrick who had taken Goldsmith's place years ago when Goldsmith left Griffith. No matter what Goldsmith wrote, Kenrick attacked it and viciously.

Sometime after Goldsmith had returned to England, Kenrick wrote a letter which appeared in *The London Packet* and was printed under a pen name. It attacked Goldsmith's work and his vanity. The letter said that Goldsmith was like Narcissus, very pleased with himself and full of self-admiration, and the writer added, "was but the lovely H———k [Horneck] as much enamoured [as Goldsmith was with himself] you would not sigh, my gentle swain, in vain." This was an unpardonable piece of public mockery of Goldsmith's unspoken love. What made the matter worse was that Goldsmith dined with the Hornecks in their Westminster house almost immediately after they had read the article and found them disturbed. So when dinner was over he excused himself and went straight to the shop of Thomas Evans, a Welshman who was the publisher of *The London Packet.*

He demanded to see Evans, who was called from another room. Goldsmith waded into him immediately.

"I have called in consequence of a scurrilous attack in your paper upon me (my name is Goldsmith) and an unwarrantable liberty taken with the name of a young lady," he said. "As for myself I care little, but her name must not be sported with."

Evans said he didn't know what Goldsmith was talking

about and stooped down behind a counter to get the file of the paper. Goldsmith had a violent temper (Johnson said it was like that of a hornet). He thought the man was lying and as Evans bent down he struck him across the back with his cane. Evans was a sturdy fighter and returned the blow with interest. The two started pummeling and wrestling each other. An oil lamp overhead was broken and Goldsmith drenched with coal oil. Then Kenrick, who was in another room, appeared and separated them and sent Goldsmith home in a coach. He was without a doubt the cause of the trouble, but he'd kept out of sight as soon as he heard Goldsmith's voice.

Evans sued Goldsmith for assault. The scandal was all over town. In attempting to defend Mary's honor Goldsmith had instead publicized their whole relationship. The press sniggered over the incident and eventually Goldsmith settled out of court, agreeing to pay fifty pounds to a Welsh charity.

The Hornecks understood the whole unfortunate incident and forgave him. Ever after, however, Goldsmith had to be even more careful to keep his love hidden. He had thought to cut a fine figure and he had blundered as he did in attempting the leap at the fountain of Versailles.

While Goldsmith was away in France his mother died. He had long been estranged from her, and he did little about her but put on half-mourning (such is the report) for a while. This, after all, was but a physical death. The spiritual death between the two of them had occurred many years before. She was no longer a mother to him since she had not understood and forgiven him his Cork adventure. He was no longer a son to her since he had not realized what a disappointment he was to her and forgiven her her feelings. She had spent many bitter years thinking of him after he had left. His successes made her only more bitter. He had thought of her too, asking to be remembered to her in letters to his friends. But the love between the two had gone.

On his return from his expensive excursions in France Goldsmith started immediately looking about for sources of ready money. His Roman history, two volumes each of two hundred and fifty pages, had been published and had sold very well.

Johnson was delighted with it and at a dinner at Topham Beauclerk's announced that Goldsmith was not only a poet of the first class but an historian as well. This was too much for Boswell, who protested strongly against Goldsmith being described as an historian at all. The Scots historian William Robertson, he asserted, was a far better historian than Goldsmith. But Johnson would not have it. Robertson's work, he said, was too wordy. "Sir," he said, "it is the great excellence of a writer to put into his book as much as his book will hold. Goldsmith has done this in his history. Now Robertson might have put twice as much into his book. Robertson is like a man who packed gold in wool; the wool takes up more room than the gold. . . . No man will read Robertson's cumbrous detail a second time; but Goldsmith's plain narrative will please again and again."

But this was all in the past and Goldsmith needed money now. He had borrowed five hundred pounds from Davies against the eight-volume *Animated Nature*, of which scarcely more than a few chapters had been drafted. He still had the four-volume *History of England* to write. The good-natured Davies proposed that he abridge the Roman history and paid him fifty pounds for the abridgment. But at the rate at which Goldsmith was now spending money, this was little more than petty cash. Davies came once more to the rescue, suggesting that Goldsmith write a life of Bolingbroke to introduce a reprint of Bolingbroke's *Dissertation on Parties*. This was Henry St. John Bolingbroke, the eminent statesman and writer who had died in 1751. He wrote it well so that the style was fluent and the sentences, as always, clear in their meaning. But he hadn't had time to research his subject properly, and the life lacked anecdotes and detail. He also wrote a life of Thomas Parnell, who had been the archdeacon of Clogher, in Ireland, and also a poet.

Both these biographies were hackwork written for money and not out of love of the subject. They were the last biographies he was to write, and they could have been as well written by any competent compiler.

At the same time he was working on the *History of England* and *Animated Nature* and he was very tired. While he was engaged with all of this he received news that Colonel Nugent, son of his friend Lord Clare, was seriously ill. He took Nugent to Bath to be with his father and there Nugent died. Lord Clare was deeply grieved by the death of his son and Goldsmith stayed with him for a long while to comfort him.

In Bath, he made the same kind of mistake concerning houses as he had made as a youth in Ireland. The Duke of Northumberland had rented a house next door to Clare's and Goldsmith in deep thought went into the wrong house one morning, threw himself down perfectly at ease on a sofa in the dining room, and, finding Northumberland present with his Duchess, presumed that they too were visiting Clare. He chatted along about the news of the day and the work he was doing, and eventually the Duke and Duchess, who were getting hungry, invited him to breakfast. It was only then that Goldsmith realized that he was in the wrong house. He blushed, apologized and got out in a hurry.

When Goldsmith returned to London, Lord Clare sent him a haunch of venison with which he was so delighted that he wrote a humorous poem describing how it was taken by a friend who then invited him to dinner, intending to serve the venison as a pasty. The other courses at the dinner were tripe, liver, and bacon, dishes Goldsmith did not like. He saved his appetite for the deer meat, which, however, did not arrive, for his friend had forgotten to bake it.

That's a bald summary of the contents but the poem itself is one of lively fun. A sample:

At the top a fried liver and bacon were seen
At the bottom was tripe in a swinging tureen
At the sides there was spinach and pudding made hot
In the middle a place where the pasty—was not.

Now my lord, as for tripe, it's my utter aversion
And your bacon I hate like a Turk or a Persian.
So there I sat stuck, like a horse in a pound,
While the bacon and liver went merrily round.

He tossed off such poems (often doggerel) whenever he was in the mood. Meanwhile, he had to write his way out of the many commissions on which he lived and which put him deeper and deeper into debt.

He was, with his extravagance, writing himself into peonage, for which he alone could be blamed. The big project was the eight-volume natural history, *Animated Nature*, on which he immediately went back to work.

CHAPTER XVI

REYNOLDS OUT OF LOVE AND ADMIRATION FOR GOLDSMITH appointed him Professor of History to the Royal Academy. The Academy had been started as the Academy of Arts by a group of artists who promptly elected Reynolds its president, and in a short while it received the patronage of the King and became the Royal Academy. George III was genuinely interested in the arts. He read copiously, was knowledgeable on painting and statues, and liked to meet writers and artists on a man-to-man basis. He liked to meet farmers the same way and would often chat with a farmer about the grain crop or cattle sickness, leaning over a fence all the while and sometimes having a meal at the farmhouse. On one occasion he was so taken with an apple pie that he begged the farmer's wife for the recipe. Farmer George, as he was called, strolled about the countryside without ceremony, talking with whomever he met.

Goldsmith was delighted with the honor, which added to his dignity, but he pretended to pooh-pooh it, writing to his younger brother Maurice in Ireland that the post carried no stipend and was the equivalent of presenting ruffles to a man who was in need of a shirt.

Reynolds also painted Goldsmith's portrait, of which Oliver was very proud. Several prints were run off, and Goldsmith presented a number of them to his friends in Ireland. Indeed, meeting one of the pupils, now a grown man, whom he had taught at that wretched academy in Peckham, he

Oliver Goldsmith. Likeness from a painting by Sir Joshua Reynolds. BETTMANN ARCHIVE.

delightedly inquired of him whether he had seen a print of the Reynolds portrait. The student said that being newly married he had not really had time to acquire one, and Goldsmith chided him, saying that if the print had been of the student, he, Goldsmith, would not have let a moment pass without buying one. Then, forgetting that the pupil was now an adult, he wanted to buy him some apples or candy or some little present that would have pleased him as a boy.

Goldsmith attended meetings of the Royal Academy in splendid clothes. At the first of the annual dinners in 1771 the talk turned to a brilliant young poet, Thomas Chatterton, who had poisoned himself August 24, 1770, in a garret while near starvation. Chatterton had been born in 1752 at Bristol. The office of sexton to the Church of St. Mary Redcliffe in Bristol had been in the family for nearly two centuries. The boy became fascinated by the ancient and neglected documents in the muniment room of the church. He loved to lock himself in a room reading these and living in thought the life of the fifteenth century's heroes and heroines. He conceived an imaginary monk, Thomas Rowley, and wrote a romance, supposedly by him, in archaic English—bits of verse and prose—so good that antiquarians thought the work was genuine, and had lain unknown for centuries in a neglected chest in the church.

In December, 1768, Chatterton, then sixteen, wrote to Dodsley offering him "copies of several ancient poems and an interlude, perhaps the oldest dramatic piece in existence, written by one Rowley, a priest in Bristol, who lived in the reigns of Henry VI and Edward IV." Dodsley made no reply. Chatterton wrote to Horace Walpole, sending other manuscripts. Walpole, deceived at first, was told the manuscripts were fakes and rejected them coldly after first expressing warm interest. Chatterton had such a command of English that he could write in any style of any period. He was a superior poet in his own right. His mistake was to attempt to pass off his work as being that of a man who had lived two centuries earlier. He came to London, hoping to find a market for his writing, but though he wrote copiously, he was paid in shillings, praise, and promises. After a few months in London, having had nothing to eat for several days, he spent his last few pennies on some arsenic, took the poison in his room and died. He was not quite eighteen years of age.

Everybody who knew him recognized his genius, but they all abhorred the fakery. Goldsmith, however, always the dreamer, believed the Rowley manuscripts were genuine. At the Academy dinner he talked about the treasure of ancient poems discovered at Bristol by Chatterton.

Walpole, who was there, later told the story of what took place. "Goldsmith," he wrote, "expressed enthusiastic belief in them [the Rowley manuscripts and poems] for which he was laughed at by Dr. Johnson, who was present. I soon found this to be the *trouvaille* of my friend Chatterton, and I told Dr. Goldsmith that the novelty was known to me, who might, if I had been pleased, have had the honor of ushering the great discovery into the learned world. You may imagine, sir, we did not agree in the measure of our faith; but though his credulity diverted me, my mirth was soon dashed; for on [my] asking about Chatterton, he [Goldsmith] told me he had been in London and had destroyed himself. The persons of honor and veracity who were present will attest with what surprise and concern I thus first heard of his death."

A little more kindness and understanding on Walpole's part, and a little more generosity on the part of the booksellers might have saved the life of a man whom everybody recognized as a misdirected genius. The only one in London who had been kind to him was the landlady of the garret, who allowed him to fall behind in his rent and even tried to get him to eat some food she had brought for him. But he would not eat.

Goldsmith stuck by Chatterton. He even got into an argument with Dr. Thomas Percy, the eminent author of *Reliques of Ancient Poetry* who was an undoubted expert on the subject, over the authenticity of the Rowley papers. That quarrel was so hot that the two were estranged for a while though

Percy had been one of the first to recognize Goldsmith's worth. Goldsmith was fighting for a fantasy which he needed to believe in—that in a neglected Bristol church were unknown ancient poems and stories of outstanding merit. Percy had no use for fantasies and dealt only in fact. They made their quarrel up later when tempers had cooled.

Goldsmith, perhaps in 1771, gave up his Edgeware cottage and took rooms with a farmer near the sixth milestone on the Edgeware Road. Why he gave up the cottage is not known, but the farmer had children and, Goldsmith liking children, that may have been one reason. Another may have been that, living in someone else's house, he was less likely to be interrupted by callers. Overloaded with work, he needed a great deal of time to himself now, and he sent all the reference books he needed for writing his *Animated Nature* down from London to Farmer Selby's house. There were so many that two post chaises were needed to transport them.

His friends, accustomed to Goldsmith's credulity, believed that it would be impossible for him to write a book about animals, for he knew practically nothing about them, with the exception of the animals of the English and Irish countryside and those he had seen in his wanderings through Europe. When Boswell scoffed at the idea of such a book by such an author, Johnson said, "Goldsmith will give us a very fine book upon the subject; but if he can distinguish a cow from a horse, that I believe may be the extent of his knowledge of natural history." But Goldsmith's book, he predicted, would have all the fascination of a Persian tale.

Johnson was right. To the little that he knew about animals, particularly birds, Goldsmith added all that he had heard. It never occurred to him to doubt the truth of anything he was told. He believed everything like a child, and he put everything down in a charming, warm, loving manner so that of all the books of natural history ever published, Goldsmith's may claim the distinction that, whatever the errors, it is certainly the most readable.

Goldsmith put more labor, more thought, more rewriting

into this work (it will be remembered that it was actually eight volumes) than into anything else he ever wrote. His sources were varied and solid for their times. They ranged all the way from Pliny (in whose writings he had first got the idea for the work) and Aristotle to George Louis Leclerc, Count of Buffon, who had but recently completed a natural history in sixteen volumes. His errors, then, were to a great extent those of others. But he was not a scientist really, and he leaned always toward believing a charming or dramatic story. It was hard for him to let go of little tales and fancies. That failing in itself contains some virtue, for while Buffon's tremendous work is hardly read today by anyone not interested in the field, Goldsmith's is as readable as ever—and it contains a great deal of instruction and solid worth as well.

Buffon himself was guilty of mistakes of the same sort—errors of prejudice if that is the right expression. He held, for instance, that the antlers of horned animals in Europe were greater than those in America and General John Sullivan of Washington's Army was so incensed that he sent Buffon, at great expense, the head and antlers of an elk to prove him wrong. Apart from his copious readings, Goldsmith undertook a lot of firsthand research. He went often to the Royal Menagerie, which was kept in the Tower of London, and was particularly fond of lions. When he first saw an elephant he was amazed at its size. He tried to measure the length of a tiger through the bars of the Royal Menagerie and nearly got clawed, and at the Queen's Menagerie he insisted on walking up to a zebra and was almost kicked to death.

He said of zebras that with proper breeding they would evolve into an animal bigger than and as useful as a horse, and far more beautiful.

Country fairs, at Edgeware and elsewhere, were another source of "information." He noted a raven that could sing a song called "Black Joe" with "distinctness and humor," thus "proving" the "intelligence" and "acting ability" of ravens. He found a parrot that could recite the ninth commandment, "Thou shalt not bear false witness against thy neighbor," with a good, clear articulate voice. (The parrot was hung by its angry owner near the porch of a man who had gossiped about him.) He talked with giants and with dwarfs at village shows, marveled at a hare with an ear for music—it would stand on its hind paws, dance to music, and even beat out the time on a drum—and announced that he had seen a sheep that ate meat and a horse that had a passion for oysters. The horses of Patagonia, he asserted, though standing only fourteen hands (four feet, eight inches) at the shoulder, could readily carry a warrior nine feet tall; a pike had been known to kill a mule by seizing it by the nose and dragging it into the water (he may have been thinking of crocodiles); nightingales were known to repeat word for word conversations they had overheard; and in China, where they were eaten, the dogs of a town would often gather together and attack the dogcatcher. "This I should hardly believe but that I have seen more than one instance of it among ourselves," Goldsmith wrote. "I have seen a poor fellow who made a practice of stealing and killing dogs for their skins pursued in full cry for three or four streets by all the bolder breed of dogs, while the weaker flew from his presence . . . such is the fact."

And so on—a child relating marvelous tales of the animal world. Yet there was more to it all than that. Goldsmith was vain and touchy at times among his fellow creatures, but he was humble and affectionate among animals.

In writing of the transformation of a grub into a butterfly, he pointed to it as "a strong proof that while this little animal is raised to its greatest height, we are as yet in this world only candidates for perfection."

He had a special love for birds, calling them the "beautiful and loquacious race of animals that embellish our forest, amuse our walks, and exclude solitude from our most shady retirement. From these man has nothing to fear; their pleasures, their desires, and even their animosities may serve to enliven the general picture of nature and give harmony to meditation."

Those who insisted that birds were without sexual morality

he advised, "We must not take our idea of the connubial fidelity of birds from observing the poultry in our yards, whose freedom is abridged and whose manners are totally corrupted by slavery. We must look for it in our fields and our forests, where nature continues in unadulterated simplicity."

As for the goose, whose very name connotes foolishness, Goldsmith, writing with a feather from a goose's wing, said, "I feel my obligations to this animal every word I write"—and suddenly the humble goose is the link between thought and literature.

On and on the work went, line by line, paragraph by paragraph, page by page, with no one to help him but himself. Every animal in the world had to be described not merely in its appearance and its methods of breeding and its places of habitat, but in its personality as well, and he did not even dismiss sea serpents who he said had been known to seize a bullock and crack its bones with a report as loud as cannon shot. The huge work was to include also a description of the earth, its origins, mountains, seas, volcanoes, and composition, so that when completed it would embrace what is now known as geology, botany (for all vegetable life was to be described), anthropology (a description of the races of Man), marine biology, and zoology.

He bought more and more books, new and rare, and talked with tinkers and gypsies and cattle drovers and shepherds and milkmaids and zoo keepers and animal trainers and aviarists and perhaps even to animals themselves, for the whole work reads as if he had had many conversations with the subjects of his writing. He wrote a delicious description of the African night, saying that as the sun went down there could be heard, above the barking of the hyenas and jackals, the hissing of multitudes of serpents, in a chorus as powerful as the dawn chanting of birds. Of the death march of the lemmings, he described how on reaching a lake each lemming gets a piece of bark, climbs aboard, squatting on its haunches, and launches "fanning the air with its tail. . . . In this orderly manner they set forward. But the slightest additional gust of wind oversets the little sailor and his vessel together. The whole navy, that but a few moments before rode proudly and securely along, is now overturned, and a shipwreck of two or three thousand sail ensues."

In the section devoted to Man he made some astute and some ridiculous statements. Apart from maintaining, as already mentioned, that both the upper jaw and the lower jaw moved in eating—the upper jaw much the less, however—he said that men were taller in the morning than they were in the evening. This, he said, was well known to Army recruiting officers, and the reason was that on one's awaking, the bones have between them a sort of lubricating oil which extends the whole skeleton. By night, the oil has been used up and everybody is shorter.

But it is breathtaking to find him speculating on the possibility of taking a cutting from a human being and growing another complete individual from it—cloning, in fact. And on the subject of failing eyesight in old age, he said, "The cornea . . . may become too rigid to adapt itself and take a proper convexity for seeing minute objects; and its very flatness will be sufficient to fit it for distant vision"—which is approximately the situation as we recognize it now.

He had some thoughts on the education of children which are matched among some today, writing, "I have ever found it a vain task to try to make a child's learning its amusement; nor do I see what good end it would answer were it actually attained. The child, as was said, ought to have its share of play, and it will be benefitted thereby; and for every reason also it ought to have its share of labour. The mind, by early labour, will be thus accustomed to fatigues and subordination; and whatever be the person's future employment in life, he will support the drudgeries of office with content. . . . In this manner, a child by playing with its equals abroad and labouring with them at school, will acquire more health and knowledge than by being bred up under the wing of any speculative system-maker. . . ."

Whatever he heard or whatever he read or whatever he saw, or remembered from his boyhood and his travels, he made a note of and pinned on the walls of his room so that the room was soon papered with these notes, and some of them were written on the boards themselves. Buying books (for to lend Goldsmith a book was to lose it) cost him a lot of money and long before he had finished his *Animated Nature* (which was not published until after his death) he had spent the whole advance—though certainly not all on books. The eight hundred pounds, in short, was gone and with four or five more volumes to write, and while still working on the English history, he looked around for another quick and easy way to make money.

His thoughts turned to a novel. *The Vicar of Wakefield* had been a success though it had got off to a slowish start. Its sales were increasing, and he proposed to Francis Newbery, nephew of John, that he write another book of the same sort. Newbery agreed and gave him an advance of at least two hundred pounds. Goldsmith started work and had soon finished the manuscript. Unfortunately, he had taken the plot of *The Good Natur'd Man* as the basis for the novel, and Newbery said he wasn't interested in publishing what was basically a rewrite. Goldsmith read several chapters to Mary Horneck, but that didn't help to find a publisher. He told Newbery that he just couldn't write another novel for him but he would find some way of returning the advance. As it was, when Goldsmith was dead, a botched-up version of the novel was printed in France under the title *Histoire de François Wills, ou le triomphe de la bienfaisance, par l'auteur du Ministre de Wakefield*. (The Story of Francis Wills, or the triumph of *Goodwill,by the author of the Vicar of Wakefield*.)

The amount of work he was doing at this time was stupendous. The life of Bolingbroke, the life of Parnell, the new novel, the history of England, and the eight-volume natural history all occupied him, and he was working on a new play.

He went for country walks in all kinds of weather, thinking over his various projects, and once arrived back at Farmer

Selby's house minus his shoes, which he had lost in the mud somewhere and had been too deep in thought to bother about.

Eventually his health broke down.

He began to have difficulty urinating, and he ran a high temperature. In his day the condition was called stranguary, and the cure, at least for the temperature, was the famous Dr. James' Fever Powders. Goldsmith took them, was relieved, went on working, fell sick again with the same condition, and decided to return to London for treatment.

He underwent an operation on his bladder which relieved him, but he decided to stay in London, taking his masses of reference books with him, though he retained his room at the farmer's house, for he was fond of the family and often joined them in the kitchen for a drink of ale, a chat, or games with the children, who adored him for his skill in card tricks.

The Selbys called him "The Gentleman" and were used to his suddenly appearing in their kitchen to stand for a moment in deep thought and then going back to his writing desk. Mrs. Selby herself brought him the bowl of fresh boiled milk which was his invariable supper.

In London, Goldsmith went often to Reynolds, who allowed his friends to watch him paint and to The Club, where he appeared one evening in a wine-colored coat of which he was so proud that he strutted about so that none could fail to notice it and comment on it. He made some remark or other about being dressed as a gentleman and Garrick said, "Come, come, talk no more of that. You are perhaps the worst—" He did not finish the sentence, Goldsmith interrupting him, for he thought himself insulted. "No," said Garrick. "You will always look like a gentleman, but I am talking about being well or ill dressed."

"Well," replied Goldsmith huffily, "let me tell you, when my tailor brought home my bloom-colored coat [wine-colored] he said, 'Sir, I have a favor to beg of you. When anybody asks you who made your clothes be pleased to mention William Filby at the Harrow in Water Lane.' "

"Why, sir," said Johnson, "that was because he knew the

strange color would attract crowds to gaze at it, and thus might hear of him, and see how well he could make a coat even of so absurd a color."

Goldsmith was often mocked in the streets about his appearance by chairmen and porters. Little groups of people would follow him around making remarks on his clothes, to which he managed to pay no attention. But sometimes his self-control failed. Once a man set the crowd laughing by saying that Goldsmith with his long sword looked like an insect impaled on a pin.

"Beware the thief," cried Goldsmith, turning and pointing to his tormentor. "The man's a notorious pickpocket. Watch out for him."

The man moved toward Goldsmith, who drew his sword. "Come on, fellow," he cried. "Let me see if your liver is as bold as your mouth."

The man hesitated, and then went off with the crowd jeering at him and applauding the little poet.

Goldsmith was sensitive not only about his clothing and appearance but also his character. He was aware of his personal pride, and often ashamed of it.

One afternoon, he was on his way to Sir Joshua's house in Leicester Square, where he had an invitation for dinner. Burke was to dine there too and found Goldsmith standing near a crowd of people who were staring and calling out to some foreign women in the windows of a hotel.

"Watch Goldsmith," said Burke to a friend who was with him, a certain Colonel O'Moore of Cloghan Castle in Ireland. "Watch him and then see what happens when we meet at Sir Joshua's."

When they arrived, Goldsmith went up to Burke to greet him and Burke was very cold. Goldsmith wondered whether he had somehow offended Burke and begged him to say if this was so. Burke said he didn't want to speak of the matter.

Goldsmith pressed him for an explanation, and Burke said that he was ashamed to keep up any intimacy with someone who could be guilty of such monstrous indiscretions as Goldsmith had just exhibited in the square.

"What monstrous indiscretions?" pleaded Goldsmith, his eyes wide with surprise.

"Why," said Burke, "did you not exclaim, as you were looking up at those women, what stupid beasts the crowd must be for staring with such admiration at those painted Jezebels, while a man of your talents was passed unnoticed?"

"Surely, surely," said Goldsmith, "I never said anything like that."

"Look," said Burke. "If you didn't say so, how would I have known that you did?"

"It's true," said Goldsmith, completely humbled. "I am very sorry—it was very foolish; I do recollect that something of the kind passed through my mind, but I did not think I had uttered it."

In short, he confessed to something he had never said but to a thought that had flashed through his mind. Maybe the same thought had flashed through his mind in Paris when the crowd was staring at and calling out to the Horneck sisters.

Burke was among those who, knowing Goldsmith's credulity, liked to play jokes on him. Once he introduced Goldsmith to a woman who claimed to be a poetess, Irish, and a widow. She was, she said, bringing out a book of her verse and soliciting subscriptions. Burke had made up a number of very poor verses for her, which she recited. Goldsmith praised them politely and gave her a couple of guineas to help with the publication of her book. He wasn't in the slightest degree angry when he learned the truth, for he knew how readily he could be duped. So long as people laughed he didn't mind.

In his desire to raise a laugh himself, he sometimes made a mess of things and appeared a fool. Once when he was dining at Reynolds' house, a dish of peas was put on the table. The peas were yellow.

"They should be sent to Hammersmith," said one of the guests, sending his peas back.

"Why Hammersmith?" he was asked.

"Because that's the way to Turnham Green," was the reply.

Goldsmith begged to be allowed to repeat the joke, and accordingly at another dinner, when yellow peas were served, Goldsmith quickly picked up his plate, gave it back to the servant and said loudly, "Send these to Hammersmith."

"Why Hammersmith?"

"Because that's the way to make 'em green. I mean Turnham Green."

Nobody laughed. He'd muffed the whole thing.

CHAPTER

WHILE HE WAS LIVING AT FARMER SELBY'S HOUSE IN EDGE-ware, in an airy room at the top of two flights of stairs, with a view over the woodlands toward Hendon, Goldsmith began working on his new play. He reflected on the time when, as a young man, he had mistaken the house of a squire in Ardagh for an inn and had bought himself a fine dinner and taken lodging for the night.

There was something here he could work up into a play, he thought, and the more he pondered on the adventure the more it appealed to him.

As noted earlier, mistaken identity was the basis of all comedy and indeed of almost all plays at the time, and all he had to do was flesh out the idea with characters and as much misunderstanding as could be contrived. But the misunderstanding must come out of the characters themselves—out of their nature—rather than be forced upon them by outside circumstances.

So he started on the play—a gamble, for there was no guarantee at all of its being produced, and Garrick could not be looked to for help. Garrick still produced the older style tragicomedy, in which the characters were very largely puppets; or worse still, he produced mutilated versions of Shakespearean plays saved from disaster only by Garrick's genius as an actor.

Goldsmith's *History of England* was completed and pub-

View of the Theatre Royal, Drury Lane. BETTMANN ARCHIVE.

lished in August, 1771. There was a great deal of fuss over it in the newspapers and he was accused of betraying the liberties of the people. The abuse hurt him and he wrote to Bennet Langton saying, "God knows I had no thought for or against liberty in my head; my whole aim being to make up a book of a decent size, that, as Squire Richard says, would do no harm to nobody."

He had his *Animated Nature* halfway finished and said he was fed up with this kind of work. So for three months he worked on his play and, when he had it finished, looked about for a producer.

The play was called *She Stoops to Conquer.* He showed it to Johnson and Johnson thought it good. There was no sense even sending it to Garrick, so he sent it to George Colman, still manager of the Covent Garden theater.

Colman kept the play for a year, saying neither yes nor no to it.

Goldsmith's self-confidence, under this tension, began to ooze away. He even related the plot of his play to a stranger and asked his advice on it. The stranger said that the whole premise—a man mistaking a private dwelling for an inn—was unbelievable. When the stranger had finished his criticism Goldsmith was gloomily silent and then took him by the hand and said, "I am much obliged to you, my dear friend, for the candor of your opinion; but it is all I can do; for alas I find that my genius, if ever I had any, has of late totally deserted me."

In addition to funds to pay his debts, he desperately needed at this time some kind of boost for his ego, and he went to the most childish lengths to try to restore his self-confidence. If one man remarked that his shoes were shiny and black, Goldsmith would immediately say that his own shoes looked better. Once at The Club someone was praising a speech made by Burke in the House of Commons and Goldsmith had to say immediately that making a speech was merely a knack, and he could make as good a speech as Burke's in Latin, Greek, or English. The company took him up on the challenge, but allowed him to pick English. He mounted a chair, started, blurted out a few sentences, and then was utterly at a loss for words.

"I find that this won't do," he concluded lamely, "therefore I'll write my speech."

"No, Doctor," said someone, "we don't question your talent for writing. It was speaking you engaged for."

"Well," said Goldsmith, climbing down from the chair, "I'm out of luck now, but you may depend on it, as I said before, that oratory is a mere knack, which any man of education may practice with success in a very little time." There was nothing but the vanity of a spoiled child in all this, a shallow envy which arose out of a lack of any real confidence in the value of his own work.

As the months dragged by, and Colman still had his play

and was doing nothing about producing it, Goldsmith's depression deepened. In January of 1773 he finally broke down and wrote Colman a letter entreating him to be relieved of suspense.

"Whatever objections you have made or shall make to my play I will endeavor to remove and not argue about them," he pleaded. This was utterly the reverse of his attitude when Garrick had proposed alterations in *The Good Natur'd Man*; and Goldsmith had rejected his suggestions in angry contempt. Now he had no pride about the work at all. "I have, as you know, a large sum of money to make up shortly; by [your] accepting my play I can readily satisfy my creditors that way; at any rate, I must look about to some certainty to be prepared. For God's sake take the play and let us make the best of it, and let me have the same measure at least which you have given as bad plays as mine."

Colman was curiously cold-hearted to Goldsmith. He returned the play with some hurtful criticism written on the manuscript. But he wasn't rejecting the play outright. He would stage the play—presumably with all his criticisms answered—sometime or other. Broken, Goldsmith took the play humbly to Garrick.

At this point Johnson intervened. He didn't like to see Goldsmith toyed with as if he were some unknown writer fresh up from the country. Something was due Oliver Goldsmith, and Johnson told Colman in no uncertain terms to put the play on right away. After all, who was Colman compared with Goldsmith? Colman, who still did not believe in the piece, shrivelled before Johnson's wrath. Johnson was not the kind of man of whom to make an enemy. He agreed to put the play in rehearsal but still held that the plot, involving a lover mistaking his future father-in-law's house for an inn, was unconvincing.

So the play was retrieved from Garrick and rehearsals started. But the cast had taken its cue from Colman and disliked the piece from the start. Actor after actor resigned, and substitutes had to be found on a moment's notice. So many quit that someone advised Goldsmith to postpone the opening but he was desperate now.

"Let it go on," he said. "I'd rather my play was damned by bad players than saved by good acting."

To boost the thing up, Johnson, who had very little use for theater, attended the rehearsals and so did Reynolds and his sister (who thought herself a painter and painted exactly in her brother's style but always produced bad portraits). Mary and her sister and mother turned up too, and so did Joseph Cradock, a gentleman from Leicester who had become a friend of Goldsmith. They took their seats determined to laugh, but they did not have to force their laughter, for the play was very funny. The plot didn't matter. The laughter came very naturally out of the characters.

Colman was still sour. The play lacked an epilogue, an essential piece of theater in those days. Arthur Murphy, Johnson's playwright friend, wrote one, but one of the cast objected to it. Goldsmith wrote two which were rejected by the cast and by Colman. Cradock wrote one which was also rejected, and eventually an epilogue of Goldsmith's was accepted by the cast and by Colman and that hurdle had been jumped.

Then there was the title. *Mistakes of a Night* was the first title but it was rejected as undignified. *Old House a New Inn* was thrown out as awkward. Reynolds proposed *Belle's Stratagem*. Goldsmith finally came up with a line from Cowper and the play was called *She Stoops to Conquer* or *The Mistakes of a Night*. When Walpole heard of the title he commented, "Stoops indeed: So she does, that is the muse; she is draggled up to the knees and has trudged, I believe, from Southwark Fair."

Meanwhile, the view that the play was bound to be a failure, spread in part by the disgruntled actresses who did not want to appear on a stage with their petticoats muddied as was called for in the script, was all over London. The Duke of Gloucester sent his servant to the theater to reserve a box and was told at the box office that the thing was going to be a flop. Goldsmith was so depressed that he hadn't even the heart to look about for a publisher for the play but at last approached Francis Newbery. He said quite honestly—for it was a business fault of his that he was incapable of deceit—that the play was likely to fail, but Newbery decided to publish it and so recoup the advance given Goldsmith for the novel he had rejected. Opening night was March 15, 1773.

Johnson had ordered himself a seat in a front box and, knowing that there would be a lot of enemies of Goldsmith hissing and booing, he rallied all his and Goldsmith's friends, arranging that they would all dine together at St. James' Coffee House beforehand. Johnson always dressed in brown, but for this occasion he put on a suit of another color. George Stevens, one of the company who were to support the play, reminded Johnson that the town was in mourning over the death of the King of Sardinia, and so a colored suit would be highly inappropriate. Johnson quickly changed to black. They had their dinner, Johnson determined that everybody including poor Goldsmith should be in high spirits, and headed for the theater. Johnson's front box seat proved a distraction for he was so famous everybody tended to stare at him rather than at the actors. Also he spoke so loudly that his conversation drowned out what was being said on the stage, for he was never a man to speak in whispers.

Goldsmith didn't go to the theater. He got cold feet. During dinner, he hardly spoke a word and he was so nervous he could scarcely get a mouthful of food down without choking. He sneaked off, and a friend found him walking alone in the Mall of St. James's Park, at eight in the evening, long after the curtain had gone up.

"Why aren't you at the theater?" his friend asked.

"I couldn't endure it," said Goldsmith.

"But you may be needed. Supposing an alteration is required—something to be added or something to be taken out. Who is to do it?"

So Goldsmith called a coach, rattled over to Covent Garden, and entered the theater by a side door, feeling like a man about to be condemned in a courtroom. As soon as he was inside he heard someone hiss at the improbability of Mrs. Hardcastle, actually in her own garden, thinking she was forty miles off on Crackskull Common.

"What's that?" he said, trembling.

"Bah," said Colman, who was standing nearby, "don't be afraid of a squib when we have been sitting these two hours on a barrel of gunpowder," implying that from the opening curtain people had been booing and hissing and roaring down the play.

Goldsmith was horrified. But Colman had lied and lied cruelly. From the rise of the curtain the play was a smash hit. Nobody had to wait for Johnson and his friends to laugh at it and applaud before laughing themselves. The theater from the start echoed with roar after roar of laughter as the farce unfolded. It was the hit of the season and the one hiss Goldsmith heard seems to have been the only one heard all night.

"I know of no comedy for many years that has so much exhilarated an audience, that has answered so much the great end of comedy, making an audience merry," said Johnson, and the whole of London agreed. In three nights, playing to an overpacked house, the play made between four and five hundred pounds. It ran for twelve nights—which was to the end of the season—and the tenth night was a command performance on the order of the King. The play was put on again in the summer at the Haymarket (a small theater which was devoted to puppet shows and juggling rather than to plays) and, when winter returned, it was staged again at Covent Garden. Again the King demanded a royal performance. Even Walpole paid it a reluctant and circumscribed tribute. The newspapers were ecstatic and turned their wrath on Colman, who had been so loathe to stage the play. They roasted him so badly, he was mocked so often in company and in the streets, that eventually he fled to Bath and wrote Goldsmith begging him to take him off the rack of the newspapers.

Goldsmith did his best, but he never forgave Colman his cruel remark over that solitary hiss.

Goldsmith got four or five hundred pounds for the play after paying off his debt to Newbery. Colman, who had had to be bludgeoned into producing it, counted his profits in the thousands.

CHAPTER XVIII

THE MONEY GOLDSMITH RECEIVED FOR *She Stoops to Conquer* gave him a little time now to relax. He had been working very hard and had almost finished *Animated Nature*. But he had had a whole year of worry about the production of the play and was emotionally exhausted.

He went then often to London and dined with, among others, General James Edward Oglethorpe, soldier, philanthropist, and founder of the colony of Georgia, whom he seems to have met in 1768. Oglethorpe was at this time in his seventies and his life's work had been done.

Although there was no quarrel between them, Goldsmith, nervous and run down, was beginning to resent Johnson's insistence upon winning every argument and making room for no point of view but his own. He remarked of Johnson that in argument he leveled a pistol at your head, and if it misfired, he knocked you down with the butt. It wasn't only Goldsmith who resented this but Topham Beauclerk and others as well.

Goldsmith in the past had often been willing to let things go. Now he started to stand up more for himself, and the friction was all the more evident in the presence of Boswell. Goldsmith hated to be made to feel small when Boswell was around, and Johnson ordinarily had an almost brutal insensitivity to his feelings. For his part Boswell was jealous of Goldsmith and probably feared that Goldsmith might write a life of Johnson, which was something Boswell had planned to do from the moment the two met.

At one Oglethorpe dinner, however, things went off pleasantly enough and Goldsmith, who loved to sing in company (he had put aside playing the flute) sang Tony Lumpkin's song of the "Three Jolly Pigeons" from *She Stoops to Conquer*. It had not been sung in the production because the actress involved was not able to sing, so this was a premier performance and everybody enjoyed it.

A few days later they were both at dinner with General Pasquale Paoli, who freed Corsica from the rule of Genoa only to lose it to the French, after which he went to England in exile. Paoli was Boswell's special friend, for Boswell had visited him in Corsica and written a book about him. At this dinner there was another argument between Goldsmith and Johnson. An Italian, Signore Martinelli, had written a history of England and the point was raised whether he should continue the history down to the present day. Goldsmith said he should. Johnson said he should not because it would give great offense to a lot of people. "He would have to tell of almost all the living great what they do not wish to be told," he said.

Goldsmith said that maybe he would have to be a little cautious, but after all, a foreigner, being impartial, would be a better judge of the rights and wrongs of a situation.

Johnson bristled and said that a foreigner could be a victim of error in his judgment as readily as anyone else.

Goldsmith would not let the subject drop. "Sir," he said, "he [Martinelli] wants only to sell his history and tell the truth: one an honest, the other a laudable motive."

"It is laudable in a man to wish to live by his labors," retorted Johnson, "but he should write so as he may live by them, and not so as he may be knocked on the head."

The argument went on, Johnson getting more and more irritated.

"There are people who tell a hundred political lies every day," said Goldsmith. "And they are not hurt by it. Surely then, one may tell truth with safety."

"Why, sir," said Johnson, "a man had rather have a hundred lies told of him than one truth which he does not wish to be told."

Goldsmith said he'd tell the truth and shame the devil.

"I wish to shame the devil as much as you," said Johnson, "but I should choose to be out of reach of his claws."

"His claws can do you no harm when you have the shield of truth," replied Goldsmith, and then that argument ended not with agreement but with friction.

The talk turned to a book about Greece by a now forgotten author, Harris of Salisbury, father of the first Lord Malmesbury. Johnson didn't think much of it and Goldsmith said that Harris might not be much of a Grecian (Greek scholar) but he was something much better—a worthy and humane man. Johnson in a bad mood said that whether he was worthy and humane had no more to do with his being a good Grecian than if he could play excellently on the violin. It was an uncalled for reply—Johnson could have just agreed that Harris was a kindly man and let it go, but it was his failing that he did not like to be crossed, and the doctrine of the divine right of kings which he upheld became at times the divine right of Johnson.

Someone, to ease the tension, wondered whether the King would attend Goldsmith's play and Goldsmith said, "I wish he would." Then he had a surge of childish pride and quickly added, "Not that it would do me the least good."

Johnson burst out laughing. "Let us say it would do him good," he said. "No sir, this affectation will not pass; it is mightily idle. In such a state as ours, who would not wish to please the chief magistrate?"

"I do wish to please him," said Goldsmith, repentant, and quoted a line of Dryden, "And every poet is the monarch's friend," adding that the line should be reversed.

There were other arguments between the two about whether a man who committed suicide did so out of fear or courage, the vanity of Garrick, about Garrick interposing some lines to flatter the Queen in a play by Beaumont and Fletcher, and about the building of nests by birds. Mostly Goldsmith would give way and say something that would placate Johnson.

But on one occasion Goldsmith lost his patience and they quarrelled. They were dining at the home of a bookseller, Dilly, who was a Dissenter—that is, a Protestant but not a member of the Church of England. Among the guests were a Dr. Mayo and a Dr. Toplady, also Dissenters, and the talk turned to persecution of one group of Christians by another. Johnson, pressed, admitted that perhaps the only way to establish a religious truth was by persecution on the one hand and endurance on the other. This brought up the subject of martyrdom and Johnson said that a martyr must have a conviction that he has a "delegation from Heaven" for the sacrifice of his life.

Goldsmith said that for himself he would first consider whether there was a greater chance of good or of evil resulting from his martyrdom. "Were I to go to Turkey," he said, "I might wish to convert the grand signior to the Christian faith; but when I considered that I should probably be put to death without effectuating my purpose to any degree, I should keep myself quiet."

It was an argument on which something could be sensibly said on both sides, but Johnson would not have it that way. He had to be right. Toplady entered the discussion and Goldsmith found Johnson would pay no attention to him and he could not get a word in. He had been dismissed as if he were a child, not worth listening to. Everytime he wanted to say something, Johnson's booming voice cut him off. He got so angry he picked up his hat as if to go and then flung it on the floor. Then Toplady was about to say something and Johnson interrupted him by clearing his throat. This was too much for Goldsmith.

"Sir," he said, "the gentleman has heard you patiently for an hour; pray allow us to now hear him."

"Sir," roared Johnson, "I was not interrupting the gentleman. I was only giving him a signal of my attention. Sir, you are impertinent." Goldsmith said nothing for a while. Then he picked up his hat and left for The Club.

There he remained with Garrick, Burke, and others, brooding. Johnson came by later and said to Langton, "I'll make Goldsmith forgive me." He then called out loudly to him, "Dr. Goldsmith! Something passed today where you and I dined; I ask your pardon."

"It must be much from you, sir, that I take ill," replied Goldsmith generously and the incident was closed. But not quite over. A few days later at the Thrales', Johnson brought up the question of who would be his biographer (he never doubted that he would have one).

"Goldsmith without a doubt," said Mrs. Thrale, "and he will do it best among us."

"The dog would write it best to be sure," said Johnson, half laughing, half resentful. "But his particular malice towards me and general disregard of truth would make the book useless to all and injurious to my character."

That was a misjudgment, for Goldsmith was incapable of being unfair to anyone in his writing. He was too open a man and devoid of malice.

These quarrels were, then, partly the result of Goldsmith's rundown condition and partly conflicts of personality. They did not really lessen the affection between the two men. Goldsmith needed to be listened to and respected, whether he spoke sensibly or not. He felt that he had always been made a fool of. Johnson had a habit of listening only to contradict. He did so wittily, intelligently, with deep thought. And often boorishly.

With Reynolds, Goldsmith was much more at ease. He dined often at the artist's house, watched him paint, and went for walks with him about town or in Vauxhall gardens under the lush elms. Goldsmith was always dressed outlandishly in colors that shouted or clashed—in the plumage of a parrot. His sword was four inches too long for a man of his size. His cocked hat had too much brocade and the buckles of his shoes were too showy. But Reynolds never made any comment and, with quiet interest, listened to him prattle on about birds, pictures, poetry, and what Johnson had said to him and what he had said to Johnson.

They presented an odd contrast—the quiet, mild, business-like, English Reynolds and the excitable, envious, candid, generous, emotionally insecure, and overdressed Irishman. They attracted attention when they walked down the Strand together or through the parks and gardens of London. Goldsmith loved that and Reynolds was amused.

There was, for all his earnings, still the problem of money.

Goldsmith produced a two-volume Grecian history to follow up his English history, though he was still finishing up *Animated Nature*. He got two hundred and fifty pounds for the Grecian history from Griffin but part of that went to pay some of the debt that he owed the bookseller. If only he could find some way of making money without having to do so much writing. The eternal problem.

Perhaps after talking to Reynolds, he hit on the idea of a dictionary of the arts and sciences. Garrick would provide a section on acting, and Reynolds one on painting. Garrick was kind enough to get his friend, Dr. Charles Burney, eminent musicologist, to promise a contribution on music. Goldsmith would write a section too—perhaps on history, for much of his fame depended on his ability to make history readable. Goldsmith wrote a prospectus for his dictionary and took it around to bookseller after bookseller.

None would undertake to finance it.

They all knew of the advances he had received and of the work he had undertaken to do which was still unwritten.

The whole thing came to nothing though in his enthusiasm he wrote an introduction to the dictionary, working without a break all through one night. He showed it to Joseph Cradock. "Here are some of my best prose writings," he said. "I have been hard at work ever since midnight, and I desire you to examine them." Cradock thought them excellent.

But when the booksellers weren't interested, Goldsmith lost the manuscript. He was careless with his work in any case, and sometimes on an impulse he would just walk off and leave it. Once he asked Dr. Percy and Cradock to call on him at his chambers in the Temple. When they arrived Goldsmith was gone to Windsor, but he left them a note begging them to correct some proofs of his *Animated Nature* which lay on his writing table and with which he had become completely bored.

His rooms were in complete disorder. Expensive books he had bought to do the work lay scattered all about, some lying opened on the floor, some tossed in corners, some piled on tables and chairs. He was never careful with books.

Once John Hawkins, who was doing some research into the history of music, asked Goldsmith to write down some things he had come across about music in his own reading. Goldsmith promised he would do so, but when Hawkins came round next day for the notes, he hadn't written a word.

"Oh never mind," said Goldsmith, "here is what you need." He pulled a book off a shelf, leafed through it, and tore out six pages. "It's all there," he said. "Read it at your leisure."

CHAPTER XIX

GOLDSMITH IN JOHNSON'S WORDS HAD "RAISED MONEY AND squandered it by every artifice of acquisition and folly of expense." His friends had no doubt at all that he would continue to do so. Booksellers were beginning to be very wary of giving him advances against the brilliant ideas for books which popped into his mind whenever he needed fifty or sixty pounds. It was decided to try to get a government pension for him. The government was becoming a little more broadminded in granting pensions to writers. A writer no longer had to be politically useful to be granted a pension. Indeed, in proposing the pension for Johnson, one government official had said that it was the determination of the ministry not to restrict pensions to political considerations, but extend them to other writers provided they had "distinction in the literary world, and the prospect of approaching distress."

Goldsmith certainly had distinction in the literary world, and a very real prospect of approaching distress—but entirely of his own making. The pension was turned down. Either Goldsmith was not considered a big enough figure, or the ministry still remembered that he had refused to lend his talents for political purposes a few years before.

This occurred in 1773 when Dr. James Beattie had come to London from Scotland, been received by the King, and given a pension of two hundred pounds a year for his *Essay on Truth* published three years earlier.

The universal praise of Beattie brought about the only real falling out between Goldsmith and Reynolds.

Reynolds was caught up in the wild enthusiasm for the book and went with Beattie to Oxford, where Beattie was given an honorary doctorship of civil law. On their return to London, Reynolds painted a portrait of Beattie in his Oxford robes, holding a copy of *Essay on Truth* under his arm with, in the background, the Angel of Truth chasing away the demons of Infidelity, Sophistry, and Falsehood.

The three figures of evil bore a marked facial resemblance to the historian and philosopher, David Hume; to Voltaire (whom Goldsmith adored); and to Edward Gibbon, all critics of the church.

When Goldsmith saw the portrait he could not restrain his contempt.

"It very ill becomes a man of your eminence and character," he said, "to debase so high a genius as Voltaire before so mean a writer as Beattie. Beattie and his book will be forgotten in ten years, while Voltaire's fame will last forever. Take care it does not perpetuate this picture, to the shame of such a man as you."

But Sir Joshua went on with the painting and probably lived to regret the work. He was too large a man to let Goldsmith's criticism make any difference to their friendship.

The debts pressed. It is possible that at this time they weighed so heavily that Goldsmith was arrested on the order of one of his creditors and was about to be sent to the sponging house. The evidence lies in a very hastily written letter, without address or date, sent by Goldsmith to Garrick. In it Goldsmith asked for a loan of sixty pounds, and spoke of altering *The Good Natur'd Man* to suit Garrick who had mentioned the possibility of reviving the play. After the scrawled signature are the words, "I beg an answer."

Garrick wrote on the letter "Goldsmith's palaver" but sent the sixty pounds. Goldsmith thanked him and spoke of writing a new play for Garrick in a season or two. And on that letter as well, Garrick scribbled "Goldsmith's palaver."

A heavy depression settled on Goldsmith. He realized he would never be free of his debts and for the first time in his life he began to despair. More and more he fell into solemn moods even when surrounded by his friends at some party. At times he would make a cheerful remark and then a moment later become silent and leave the room to go home.

Reynolds noted the change in him and so did Cradock. Johnson, who for all the friction between the two might have helped him, was away on a tour of the Scottish highlands and the Hebrides with Boswell.

Cradock called on him. (He lived in Leicestershire but was in town while his wife went to a dentist.) He found him depressed and discovered that the only way to cheer him up was to tell him of something Johnson had said of him that was friendly or admiring. On one visit Cradock, who knew about the money problems, suggested that a special edition of *The Traveller* and *The Deserted Village* could be brought out if it was agreeable to the publishers who held the copyrights.

"Do what you please with them," said Goldsmith despondently. But he didn't encourage the scheme. His enthusiasm was gone and the idea collapsed. Even the trades people whom he patronized knew of his money difficulties and sympathized with him. There were two sisters, milliners, named Gunn, who took care of his clothes and to whom he owed money. They said they would work for him free, for they knew that somehow or another he would manage to pay them.

Reynolds offered to help but Goldsmith wouldn't hear of it—he never borrowed money from his friends to pay his debts. If he had called them all together and told them of his troubles, they probably would have raised enough to relieve him. But he would never think of doing such a thing. Cradock asked him out to dinner toward the end of his stay in London and Goldsmith accepted the invitation on condition that he was not asked to eat anything. He took only a little wine and some biscuits and, though he tried to be cheerful, he could not hide his gloom.

But now and again he would have brighter periods and take a hand in cards with his friends. One evening, playing whist at the home of Sir William Chambers, one of the most noted architects of the time, who had designed a villa for Reynolds on Richmond Hill, and with the rubber at stake, Goldsmith suddenly threw down his cards, hurried out of the room, was gone a few moments, and then returned. The play was resumed.

"Why did you leave so suddenly?" Sir William asked.

"While I was looking over my hand," said Goldsmith, "I heard a woman singing in the street below."

"So?" said Sir William. "We all heard her."

"What you did not hear was the desperation in her voice," said Goldsmith. "You do not know of that. I gave her a little money."

One of the players at this game was Giuseppe Marc Antonio Baretti, who had written an Italian dictionary and grammar which Johnson had praised highly. He was a pompous, quick-tempered man, and Goldsmith disliked him. Some years before, Baretti had been insulted in the street, got into a fight, pulled a knife, and killed a man. He was charged with murder and brought before the magistrate Sir John Fielding, who was blind and reportedly able to recognize three thousand thieves by their voices. Though Goldsmith could not stand the Italian, he went immediately to his defense, offered him his last shilling, and insisted on going with him in the coach to Newgate.

But neither Baretti nor any of the others at that whist table left to give a little money to the woman singing below. They did not know poverty as Goldsmith had known it.

Later in that year, 1773, Johnson returned from his tour of the Hebrides and the meetings of The Club were resumed. Goldsmith's spirits revived. While he was away from The Club (and quite often when he was present) the members made jokes about him. Though they all loved him, he was the favorite topic for witticisms, and at one meeting someone suggested that they should all write epitaphs about him. The only one of the epitaphs which has been preserved was Garrick's and of that only two lines are known. They are:

Here lies Nolly Goldsmith, for shortness called Noll
Who wrote like an angel but talked like poor Poll.

The epitaph was read to Goldsmith and everybody laughed heartily at it. Others then read their efforts while Goldsmith squirmed, but nobody seemed to notice how hurt he was by this public guying except the playwright Richard Cumberland, who had recently been admitted to The Club. Even Sir Joshua didn't seem to understand how deeply Goldsmith was suffering and did a sketch of him, like a marble bust, on one of the epitaphs.

Cumberland hesitated to write anything but he was pressed to produce something; he went to a side table and wrote a couple of lines. The company demanded that he read them. Goldsmith begged him not to. Cumberland was about to tear up the paper when Johnson snatched it from his hand and read the lines out in a loud voice. Unlike the others, they were complimentary, and Goldsmith was grateful.

That is Cumberland's story and it approximates Garrick's account of the incident. Cumberland said he could not remember exactly what his lines were but they contained the sentence: "All mourn the poet, I lament the man."

Among those who wrote epitaphs about Goldsmith besides Garrick were Dean Barnard of Derry, who was later Bishop of Killaloe; Richard Burke (brother of Edmund); and Caleb Whiteford, a journalist whose reputation died with him but who was considered a great wit in his day. His particular epitaph was so caustic that others present, including Topham Beauclerk, who certainly had an evil tongue, denounced it.

Goldsmith was invited to retaliate to all these epitaphs. Some say he was asked to write something about Garrick there and then, but could not do so. Whatever the truth, at subsequent meetings of The Club, he produced his replies which he called *Retaliation* and which took him several weeks to compose. They were certainly not all given at one meeting.

There was no bitterness against anyone, or any caricature in them, but only an apt portrait of each man, with his virtues and weaknesses beautifully drawn. In fact, the best portrait we have of Goldsmith's famous contemporaries comes not out of Boswell or other writers but from the epitaphs Goldsmith wrote. In the opening of the poem, he likened each to a particular dish, as follows:

Our Dean shall be venison, just fresh from the plains
Our Burke shall be tongue, with a garnish of brains . . .

Our Garrick is salad, for in him we see
Oil, vinegar, sugar and saltness agree. . . .
To make out the dinner, full certain I am
That Ridge is anchovy and Reynolds is lamb;
That Hickey's a capon, and by the same rule
Magnanimous Goldsmith a gooseberry fool.

(John Ridge was an Irish barrister and Joseph Hickey legal adviser to Reynolds.)

Then follow the epitaphs, probably one or two at succeeding meetings of The Club.

On the Dean he wrote:

Here lies the good Dean, re-united to earth
Who mixed reason with pleasure and wisdom with mirth;
If he had any faults, he has left us in doubt;
At least, in six weeks, I could not find 'em out;
Yet some have declared, and it can't be denied 'em
That the sly boots was cursedly cunning to hide 'em.

Then follows his picture of the statesman, Edmund Burke:

Here lies our good Edmund, whose genius was such
We scarcely can praise it, or blame it too much;
Who, born for the Universe, narrowed his mind
And to party gave up what was meant for mankind.
Though fraught with all learning, yet straining his throat
To persuade Tommy Townshend to lend him a vote;
Who, too deep for his hearers, still went on refining
And thought of convincing, while they thought of dining;

Though equal to all things, for all things unfit,
Too nice for a statesman, too proud for a wit.
For a patriot too cool, for a drudge disobedient;
And too fond of the right to pursue the expedient.
In short, 'twas his fate, unemployed, or in place, sir,
To eat mutton cold and cut blocks with a razor.

He wrote of two or three others of no great note, and produced a masterpiece in describing Garrick.

Here lies David Garrick, describe me, who can
An abridgement of all that was pleasant in man;
As an actor, confessed without rival to shine;
As a wit, if not first, in the very first line:
Yet with talents like these, and an excellent heart,
The man had his failings, a dupe to his art.
Like an ill-judging beauty, his colours he spread
And beplastered with rouge his own natural red.
On the stage he was natural, simple affecting;
'Twas only that when he was off he was acting.
With no reason on earth to go out of his way,
He turned and he varied full ten times a day.
Though secure of our hearts, yet confoundedly sick
If they were not his own by finessing and trick:
He cast off his friends, as a huntsman his pack,
For he knew when he pleased he could whistle them back.
Of praise a mere glutton, he swallowed what came,
And the puff of a dunce he mistook it for fame;
'Till his relish grown callous almost to disease,
Who peppered the highest was surest to please.
But let us be candid, and speak out our mind
If dunces applauded, he'd pay them in kind. . . .

Retaliation concludes with an unfinished epitaph on Reynolds:

Here Reynolds is laid, and to tell you my mind,
He has not left a better or wiser behind:
His pencil is striking, resistless and grand;

His manners were gentle, complying and bland;
Still born to improve us in every part,
His pencil our faces, his manners our heart:
To coxcombs averse, yet most civilly steering,
When they judged without skill he was still hard of hearing,
When they talked of their Raphaels, Correggios and stuff,
He shifted his trumpet and only took snuff. . . .

Copies of the epitaphs were made and circulated privately. Garrick alone was sufficiently annoyed to retaliate to Goldsmith's retaliation. He read his reply to some friends—but apparently not to The Club. It contained some revealing lines about Goldsmith and some telling insights into his character as well, and so it is worth reprinting. It went:

Here, Hermes, says Jove, who with nectar was mellow
Go fetch me some clay—I will make an odd fellow:
Right and wrong shall be jumbled, much gold and some dross
Without cause be he pleased, without cause be he cross;
Be sure as I work to throw in contradictions,
A great love of truth, yet a mind turned to fictions;
Now mix these ingredients, which warmed in the baking,
Turned to learning and gaming, religion and raking.
With the love of a wench, let his writings be chaste;
Tip his tongue with strange matter, his pen with fine taste;
That the rake and the poet o'er all may prevail
Set fire to the head and set fire to the tail;
For the joy of each sex on the world I'll bestow it,
The scholar, rake, Christian, dupe, gamester, and poet,
Though a mixture so odd he shall merit great fame
And among brother mortals be Goldsmith his name;
When on earth this strange meteor no more shall appear,
You, Hermes, shall fetch him—to make us sport here.

It is not known whether Goldsmith was aware of this poem, but he would scarcely have been offended by it, for he never tried to hide or deny the truth about himself.

But while the epitaph game was being played, Goldsmith

had still his work to attend to, and left London to go to the farmhouse at Edgeware and get on with it. He decided, in fact, to sell the lease on his apartment in the Temple, spend his time in the countryside, and come to London only two months out of every year. He had discovered that in the country, his mind was more at ease and he wrote better.

Sometime in the winter of 1773–74, Goldsmith at last finished his monumental eight-volume *Animated Nature*. Griffin had originally owned the copyright, but hard pressed for money he had sold it to another publisher, Nourse. Now that the work was done, Griffin wanted to buy back a portion or share of the copyright and asked Goldsmith to use his influence with Nourse to achieve this.

Goldsmith wrote to Nourse on Griffin's behalf and also thanked him for an overpayment for the books which Nourse had made—that is, an amount beyond the stipulated price, paid because he was so heavily in debt.

While he was writing the work Goldsmith had groaned almost everytime he had to sit down at his desk and pick up his pen.

But now that it was done, he proposed to Nourse that the volumes be extended to include the vegetable kingdom and the world of fossils as well. Fossils were the great scientific curiosity of the time. Even Thomas Jefferson collected them and was so keen on his hobby that he was known as "Mastodon Tom."

Since very little was known about them, Goldsmith would have ample room to use his fancy and tell charming anecdotes about fossils and fossil collectors. But nothing came of the idea. Goldsmith, meanwhile, having finished his Grecian history, prepared a new edition of his *Polite Learning*, for which he received five guineas from Dodsley. He was also working again on *A Survey of Experimental Philosophy,* which appears to have been unsatisfactory when he turned the manuscript in several years before. Rehashing old work, his zest for writing was gone.

But despite his own worries, he never lost his sympathy for other writers, and wrote to Nourse on behalf of a Dr. Andrews who had finished a book on Denmark. Goldsmith had read the book, found it good, and recommended it to Nourse, who accepted it and published it in the spring of 1775.

Then the "stranguary" returned and he began to have difficulty urinating again. He blamed it on the long hours he spent sitting at his writing table, and thought more exercise would help.

It didn't.

He wasn't very worried about the condition. He'd had it before and he'd cured it before, but he left the Edgeware farmhouse in the middle of March, 1774, to get medical help in London.

Sure enough, after he had been a week or so in London, the condition was gone. It was probably a symptom of something more serious, for he was immediately attacked with what was called a "low nervous fever."

The fever wasn't severe enough to prevent him from seeing his friends. The Hornecks were in town and he was able to spend an hour or two with Mary. But the fever got worse after a while, so that on Friday, March 25, he had to go to bed in the middle of the day. He was annoyed because that evening he wanted to go to The Club, to which Charles Fox had recently been elected. He was an admirer of Fox. He became more ill as the afternoon progressed and at eleven at night had a splitting headache, his pulse was ninety, and there was a great deal of saliva in his mouth.

He sent his servant, John Eyles, out to fetch a friend of his—an apothecary-surgeon (who later got a medical degree) named William Hawes, whom Goldsmith had supported in his efforts to found a humane society.

Hawes came around immediately and Goldsmith told him that he needed some of his favorite remedy—Dr. James' Fever Powders.

Hawes didn't agree that the powders would help. Goldsmith was plainly in a weakened condition and Hawes thought they would weaken him further. He told Goldsmith that it would be dangerous for him to take the medicine but Goldsmith would not be convinced. After all, he was a doctor; Hawes, though a friend, only an apothecary-surgeon.

Hawes argued with him for half an hour, but to no purpose. "All right," said Hawes, "if you prescribe the powders for yourself, it is against my judgment, but you shall have them. However, let me bring in Dr. Fordyce, who has attended you before, so we have the benefit of another opinion."

Goldsmith didn't want another opinion. He was distracted and in a petulant mood. He said that Fordyce was probably a guest at The Club where he would be himself if he wasn't sick. Eventually, Hawes sent for Fordyce and went back to his shop to make up some medicine for Goldsmith. Fordyce arrived and was of Hawes' opinion—that the fever powders should not be taken. Hawes sent a boy over with some medicine and a bottle of leeches to bleed Goldsmith.

Goldsmith applied the leeches, ignored the medicine, and told the boy to go back to Hawes and bring the fever powders.

When they arrived, he took more than one dose and then complained that they were not the correct powders but some substitute. He became angry with Hawes, said Hawes was trying to deceive him; he would pay the man off the next day and have nothing more to do with him.

Goldsmith was worse the next day, and sent Eyles to Newbery's to get a fresh packet of genuine fever powders. He felt anxious and lonely and asked his laundress to come and sit with him until Eyles returned. He was still angry with Hawes and when the new powders arrived he took two doses.

Hawes came round to see him that Saturday morning but Goldsmith was dozing. He returned again that night and found Goldsmith exhausted, his pulse fast and small, his eyes glazed.

"I wish," said Goldsmith in a very low voice, "that I had taken your good advice last night."

Hawes asked him a few questions about his symptoms but Goldsmith was too weak and dispirited to reply.

On Monday, after Goldsmith had spent a night without sleep, Fordyce called in a Dr. Turton. The case was, however, beyond them. Sometimes Goldsmith was a little better; at other times he was much worse. At times he was cheerful and at times he could hardly whisper a word. His pulse was irregular and the fever persisted. He could not eat, but his mind was quite clear.

The activating element in Dr. James' Fever Powders was antimony. Antimony is an emetic and also a powerful cardiac depressant, reducing the strength and the frequency of the heartbeat. In large doses it lowers temperature, but it also interferes with breathing and respiration. Whatever else was the matter, plainly Goldsmith was suffering from antimony poisoning. The antidote, which consists of taking strong coffee or tea or a teaspoonful of tannic acid in half a glass of water followed by raw eggs or milk, was unknown. Goldsmith, determined to play doctor, had poisoned himself.

He lay dying for a week, unable to sleep. Dr. Turton thought that if he could get some sleep, he would be greatly improved and, thinking that something other than his sickness was troubling him, said, "Your pulse is in greater disorder than it should be from the degree of fever which you have. Is your mind at ease?"

"It is not," said Goldsmith.

They were the last words he spoke.

Shortly afterwards he was able to sleep. His breathing became easier and his temperature dropped. That was at midnight of Sunday, April 3. At four in the morning his body made a tremendous effort to eject the poison. He was seized by a fit of vomiting and convulsions which lasted for forty minutes. His heart, weakened by the antimony, could not withstand the fit and at a quarter to five he dropped back on his mattress, dead.

He was forty-five years and five months old.

CHAPTER

As a student at Edinburgh, Goldsmith had written to his Uncle Contarine, "A quack, unable to distinguish the particularities of each disease, prescribes at a venture: if he find such a disorder may be called by the general name of fever, for instance, he has a set of remedies which he applies to cure it, nor does he desist until his medicines are run out or his patient has lost his life."

This was precisely what had happened to him and, dismissing a competent man, he had practiced medicine on himself as a quack and paid with his life.

None of his friends were with him while he was dying or even sent to inquire about him. He had not seemed seriously ill and the report of his death fell on them like a thunderbolt. Burke, when told, burst into tears. Sir Joshua Reynolds threw aside his palette and could not paint.

Johnson fell into a deep melancholy. He never spoke of Goldsmith's death afterwards without grief, as if he had died only the day before. Johnson wrote the news to Boswell, who had remained in Scotland, and said, "He died of a fever, made I am afraid more violent by uneasiness of mind. His debts began to be heavy and all his resources exhausted. Sir Joshua is of the opinion that he owed not less than two thousand pounds. Was ever a poet so trusted before?"

When the news spread through the neighborhood, the staircase leading up to Goldsmith's apartment was filled with ragged mourners—homeless men and women, beggars of

Oliver Goldsmith. After a statue by John Henry Foley, in Trinity College, Dublin. BETTMANN ARCHIVE.

every kind, whom he had befriended. They were among the first to arrive and the last to leave after the coffin was removed from his apartment for burial.

At first a public funeral was proposed, the pallbearers to include Reynolds, Burke, Beauclerk, and Garrick. But the idea was dropped—perhaps because of the extent of Goldsmith's debts—and he was buried privately in the Temple churchyard. Before the coffin was closed, Mary Horneck begged a lock of his hair which she kept until she died, nearly seventy years later.

The funeral did not take place for five days, during which time he lay in state in his apartment, visited by scores of people, among them, as noted, many of the outcasts of London. At the funeral, Hugh Kelly, whose *False Delicacy* had completely overshadowed Goldsmith's *Good Natur'd Man*, and who had quarrelled with Goldsmith later, broke down in tears and remained weeping at the grave after the others had left.

No memorial was put over the grave, and its exact location has now been lost. Reynolds, however, proposed that a memorial be erected in the Poets' Corner of Westminster Abbey and picked out a spot beside the monument to Gay and the Duke of Argyll. Joseph Nollekins, who was the most famous portrait sculptor in London and who had done a bust of George III, was commissioned to do a medallion head of Goldsmith for the memorial under which his epitaph would be carved.

Johnson was asked to compose the epitaph. When it was done he sent it to Reynolds with a note which said, "I send you the poor dear Doctor's epitaph. Read it first yourself; and if you think it right, show it to The Club."

Reynolds invited the principal members of The Club who had been close friends of Goldsmith to his house for dinner to consider Johnson's inscription. There were a lot of objections to it which were put in writing and signed by everyone.

Burke worded the objections, and after complimenting Johnson on his masterly style and elegant composition said that the character of Goldsmith as a writer, particularly as a poet, had not been sufficiently stressed.

Johnson wasn't annoyed. He said he'd make any alterations they desired.

But Johnson had written the inscription in Latin and the members of The Club thought it should be in English "as we think that the memory of so eminent an English writer ought to be perpetuated in the language to which his works are likely to be so lasting an ornament, which we also know to have been the opinion of the late Doctor himself."

Everybody signed this except Langton, who was too much of a classicist to object to a Latin epitaph.

On this point Johnson wouldn't budge. He said flatly that he would never disgrace the walls of Westminster Abbey with an English inscription, a strange view since Westminster Abbey is one of the oldest English abbeys and could hardly be disgraced by the English language.

But they deferred to Johnson. So the inscription was carved in Latin with the result that perhaps not one in a hundred who visit it today understands what it says. In effect, Goldsmith, whose clear, simple, vivid, and charming English could be understood by everybody, is divided in death from his admirers by a Latin fence erected by Johnson.

Johnson's inscription read:

OLIVER GOLDSMITH

Poetae, Physici, Historici
qui nullum fere scribendi genus
non tetigit,
nullum quod tetigit non ornavit:
sive risus essent movendi,
sive lacrymae,
affectuum potens, at lenis dominator;
ingenio sublimis, vividus, versatilis;
oratione grandis, nitidus, venustus:

hoc monumento memoriam coluit
Sodalium amor,
Amicorum fides
Lectorum veneratio.
Natus Hibernia, Forneiae, Lonfordiensis
in loco cui nomen Pallas
Nov. *XXIX MDCCXXXI*
Eblanae literis institutus,
Objit Londini
Apr. *IV MDCCLXXIV*

In John Forster's *Life of Goldsmith*, this is translated as follows:

Of OLIVER GOLDSMITH

Poet, Naturalist, Historian
who left scarcely any kind of writing
untouched
and touched nothing that he did not adorn:
Whether smiles were to be stirred
or tears,
commanding our emotions, yet a gentle master:
In genius lofty, lively, versatile;
In style weighty, clear, engaging—
The memory in this monument is cherished
by the love of Companions,
the faithfulness of Friends,
the reverence of Readers.
He was born in Ireland;
at a place called Pallas
[in the parish] of Forney [and county] of Longford,
on the 29th November, 1731
Trained in letters at Dublin.
Died in London
4th April, 1774.

As noted at the beginning of this book, Johnson had the date of birth wrong.

There were two other memorials erected to Goldsmith—a tablet in the Temple Church and a full-length statue of him by John Henry Foley, the Irish sculptor, which now stands inside the gates of Trinity College, Dublin. The statue shows him reading a book which is held before him in his left hand, while in his right hand he has a pen.

Goldsmith would have liked it.

The figure is well dressed, excellently proportioned, dignified, and almost handsome.

A SELECT BIBLIOGRAPHY

Bate, Walter Jackson. *The Achievement of Samuel Johnson.* New York: Oxford University Press, 1955

———. *Samuel Johnson.* New York: Harcourt Brace Jovanovich, 1977

Bedderstan, Catherine C. *The History and Sources of Percy's Memoirs.* Cambridge: University Press, 1926

Black, William. *Oliver Goldsmith.* New York: Harper and Brothers, 1902

Bloom, Edward A. *Samuel Johnson and Grub Street.* Providence: Brown University Press, 1957

Boswell, James. *The Life of Samuel Johnson, LLD* (with an introduction by Herbert Askwith). New York: Random House, Modern Library Edition, no date

———. *Boswell's London Journal.* Edited by Frederick A. Pottle. New York: McGraw Hill, 1950

———. *Boswell on the Grand Tour.* Edited by Frank Brady and Frederick A. Pottle. New York: McGraw Hill, 1955

———. *Boswell in Search of a Wife.* Edited by Frank Brady and Frederick A. Pottle. New York: McGraw Hill, 1956

Boynton, Percy H. *London in English Literature.* Chicago: The University of Chicago Press, 1913

Brown, Ivor John Carnegie. *Dr. Johnson and His World.* London: Lutterworth Press, 1965

Cleeve, Rowley. *Sir Joshua Reynolds, PRA.* London: G. Bell and Sons, 1902

Clifford, James L. *Young Sam Johnson*. New York: McGraw-Hill, 1955

Craig, Maurice. *Dublin 1660–1860*. Dublin: Allen Figgis Ltd., 1969

Craig, William Henry. *Dr. Johnson and the Fair Sex*. London: Low, 1895

Dennis, John. *Dr. Johnson*. London: G. Bell and Sons, 1905

Dobson, Austin. *Eighteenth Century Studies*. London: J. M. Dent and Co. (c1914)

———. *Eighteenth Century Vignettes*. London: Oxford University Press, 1923

———. *Life of Oliver Goldsmith*. London: W. Scott, 1888

Farrington, Joseph. *Memoirs of the Life of Sir Joshua Reynolds*. London: T. Cadell and W. Davis, 1819

Forster, John. *The Life and Times of Oliver Goldsmith*. New York and London: Harper and Bros. Four volumes. Library Edition, 1871

Fussell, Paul. *Samuel Johnson and the Life of Writing*. New York: Harcourt Brace Jovanovich, 1971

Goldsmith, Oliver. *The Citizen of the World*. Two volumes. Edited by Austin Dobson. London: J. M. Dent and Co. Philadelphia: J. B. Lippincott Co., 1893

———. *The Bee*. London: Milford (Oxford Edition), 1914

———. *The Vicar of Wakefield*. London: J. M. Dent and Co. Philadelphia: J. B. Lippincott Co., 1893

———. *The Plays of Oliver Goldsmith,* edited by Austin Dobson. London: J. M. Dent and Co. Philadelphia: J. B. Lippincott Co., 1899

———. *An History of Earth and Animated Nature*. Four volumes. Philadelphia: J. B. Lippincott Co., 1863

———. *Collected Poems,* edited by Austin Dobson. London: Henry Frowde (Oxford Edition), 1911

Grant, Lt. Col. F. *Life of Samuel Johnson*. London: W. Scott, 1887

Gwynn, Stephen. *Oliver Goldsmith.* New York: Holt and Co., 1935

Hale, Susan. *Men and Manners of the 18th Century.* Philadelphia: Jacobs (c1898)

Halliday, Frank Ernest. *Dr. Johnson and His World.* London: Thames and Hudson, 1968

Hallis, Christopher. *Dr. Johnson.* London: Victor Gollancz, 1928

Hawes, William. *Account of the Late Dr. Goldsmith's Illness.* London: printed for W. Brown and H. Gardner, 1774

Hibbert, Christopher. *The Personal History of Samuel Johnson.* London: Longman, 1971

Hodgart, Matthew J. C. *Samuel Johnson and His Times.* London: Batsford, 1962

Hopkins, Mary Alden. *Dr. Johnson's Lichfield.* New York: Hastings House, 1952

Hudson, Derek. *Sir Joshua Reynolds.* London: G. Bles., 1955

Irving, Washington. *Life of Oliver Goldsmith.* New York: A. L. Fowle, 1900

Jenks, Tudor. *In the Days of Oliver Goldsmith.* New York: A. S. Barnes, 1907

Johnston, Edith Mary. *Ireland in the Eighteenth Century.* Dublin: Gill and Macmillan Ltd., 1974

Marshall, Dorothy. *Dr. Johnson's London.* New York: Wiley, 1968

Massingham, Hugh and Pauline. *The London Anthology.* London: Spring Books (No date of publication)

Masson, Rosaline. *In Praise of Edinburgh.* London: Constable and Co., 1912

Maxwell, Sir Robert. *Edinburgh; a Historical Study.* London: Williams and Norgate, 1916

Miller, C. *Anecdotes of the Literary Club.* New York: Exposition Press, 1948

Molloy, Joseph Fitzgerald. *Sir Joshua and His Circle.* London: Hutchinson and Co., 1906

Moore, Frank Frankfurt. *Life of Oliver Goldsmith.* New York: E. P. Dutton and Co., 1911

Mowat, R. B. *England in the 18th Century.* London: G. G. Harrap and Co., 1938

Paul, K. *Sir Joshua Reynolds.* London: Trench Trubner and Co., 1941

Pearson, Hesketh. *Johnson and Boswell.* London: Heinemann, 1958

Prior, James. *Life of Oliver Goldsmith.* MB, London: J. Murray, 1837

Pulling, F. S. *Sir Joshua Reynolds.* London: Low Marston and Co., 1929

Raleigh, Sir Walter Alexander. *Six Essays on Johnson.* Oxford: Clarendon Press, 1927

Roberts, Sydney Castle. *Dr. Johnson.* London: Duckworth, 1935

Sells, A. Lytton. *Oliver Goldsmith, His Life and Works.* London: Allen and Unwin, 1974

Sherwin, Oscar. *The Life and Times of Oliver Goldsmith.* New York: Twayne Publications, 1962

Slater, Gilbert. *The English Peasantry and the Enclosures of the Common Fields.* New York: A. M. Kelley, 1968

Sweaton, Oliphant. *Edinburgh and Its Story.* London: J. M. Dent and Co., New York: The Macmillan Co., 1904

Thrale, Mrs. Lynch. *Anecdotes of the Late Samuel Johnson.* Cambridge: The University Press, 1925

Tuberville, Arthur Stanley. *Johnson's England.* Oxford: Clarendon Press, 1933

Wain, John. *Samuel Johnson.* London: Macmillan (c1974)

Wardle, Ralph M. *Oliver Goldsmith.* Lawrence: University of Kansas Press, 1957

Waterhouse, Ellis. *Reynolds.* New York: Phaidon, 1973

Wheeler, C. B. *Essays on Oliver Goldsmith by Scott, Macaulay and Thackeray.* Oxford: Clarendon Press, 1929

INDEX